Food in the Great War

Bully Beef and Biscuits

John Hartley

Pen & Sword
MILITARY

First published in Great Britain in 2015 by
PEN & SWORD MILITARY
an imprint of
Pen and Sword Books Ltd
47 Church Street
Barnsley
South Yorkshire S70 2AS

ISBN 978 1 47382 745 5

Printed and bound in England
by CPI Group (UK) Ltd, Croydon, CR0 4YY

Typeset in Times New Roman by Chic Graphics

Pen & Sword Books Ltd incorporates the imprints of
Pen & Sword Archaeology, Atlas, Aviation, Battleground, Discovery,
Family History, History, Maritime, Military, Naval, Politics, Railways,
Select, Social History, Transport, True Crime, Claymore Press,
Frontline Books, Leo Cooper, Praetorian Press, Remember When,
Seaforth Publishing and Wharncliffe.

For a complete list of Pen and Sword titles please contact
Pen and Sword Books Limited
47 Church Street, Barnsley, South Yorkshire, S70 2AS, England
E-mail: enquiries@pen-and-sword.co.uk
Website: www.pen-and-sword.co.uk

Contents

Introduction

It was, perhaps, inevitable that I would write this book. In recent years, my interest in both the Great War and food has developed. I confess to having become something of a foody and something of a war "anorak". Reading through soldiers' memoirs and letters home while I was researching for my two previous books, I realised how often men would refer to food. For some, there was correspondence with loved ones about food parcels – telling Mum how nice her cake had been, or asking his wife if she would send some sweets next time. And it became clear just how important these parcels were, not just for filling the belly, but as a vital link with "normal life" at home. Others would write about the monotony of meals in the trenches – the bully beef and biscuits which give the book its title. Other men would record the dangers of going to collect rations under shellfire, although this was usually in later memoirs – there was no need to unnecessarily worry relatives in letters. The importance of food in the daily lives of the soldiers cannot be overestimated. It really was the case that the "army marches on its stomach" although, during the Great War, it was more about spending time in trenches than in marching.

In 1914, Britain had a small professional army of about 250,000 men. Roughly half of them were stationed at home whilst the remainder were scattered on garrison duty throughout the Empire. Provisioning was on a small scale and easily managed. But, within weeks of war being declared, reservists had been called up, the Territorial Force mobilised and thousands upon thousands more men had enlisted into newly formed battalions. Supplying them with food, ammunition, clothing and the other essential equipment necessary to go to war would be a major challenge.

The supply chain was long and complex. Meat might originate in South America and be shipped first to ports in Britain or France, before being transported to the Western Front where it would pass through several hands of soldiers of the Army Service Corps. Eventually it would find its way to a man in a trench, looking out across No Man's Land, wondering if he would be able to eat his stew in peace before the shelling started again.

I am also interested in the home front and how the war affected the daily lives of people. In this, I've tended to describe life in Stockport where I now live. Then it was an industrial town, surrounded by more rural areas and, in that respect, it was entirely representative of many communities up and down Britain. Everywhere would be affected by rising food prices and food shortages. Everyone would be affected by having loved ones killed, wounded or posted as missing. Throughout the country, the role of women in society would change forever and that would be part of making our country what it is today.

In writing the book, I've included extracts from many personal accounts and I'm grateful to the staff of the Imperial War Museum and the Liddle Collection at the University of Leeds for their help. I'm also grateful to the copyright holders who have allowed me to use their ancestors' words to tell my story. In a number of cases, efforts have been made to contact the copyright holder but without success. My thanks also to the estate of wartime cartoonists, Bruce Bairnsfather, for allowing me to include several of his works, showing there was a wry, lighter side to war. As always, the members of the Great War Forum have provided information and have answered even the most obscure questions. And it would be remiss of me if I did not thank Nigel Cave at Pen & Sword Books. Without his support, this book would not have seen the light of day.

Please treat the book as a seven course meal which will take you from a starter course of the early days of the war in August 1914, through to dessert where men had their celebrations of Christmas, promotions or just safely coming through another tour of duty in the trenches. And, perhaps on the way, you'll cook yourself one of the recipes of the time that end each chapter.

John Hartley
Spring 2014

CHAPTER 1

1914

On 4 August 1914, Britain declared war on Germany. It was the culmination of just over a month of diplomatic manoeuvring, which had seen first one European country mobilise its armed forces, then another, until all of the major powers had become involved. The trigger had been the assassination of the heir to the Austro-Hungarian Empire – Archduke Franz Ferdinand – and his wife in Sarajevo on 28 June. The murder had been carried out by a group of Bosnian Serb nationalists. At first it seemed as though the conflict might remain a local matter between Austria and Serbia but, when the former mobilised, Russia declared it would also mobilise to assist Serbia. Over the next couple of days, Germany and France also brought their armies to readiness. On 2 August, Germany invaded France and announced its intention to march through neutral Belgium to attack France on that front. The next day, Belgium appealed to Britain for assistance. Britain and France had been guarantors of its neutrality since the 1839 Treaty of London. Britain's involvement in the conflict had become inevitable.

In comparison with the other major powers, Britain's professional army was small, numbering only some 250,000 men. There were another 150,000 in the reserves. These were men who had served in the army and had been discharged but were subject to recall in times of crisis. Typically, they would serve for seven years and then be discharged to the Reserve for another five years. Most of these men served, or had served, as infantry, organised into 73 regiments, each usually organised into two battalions of around 1000 men each and most having a close association with the counties of England, where they would undertake much of their recruitment. It was usual that, at any given time, one battalion would be serving overseas on Empire duty, while the other was at home. So, for example, at the outbreak of war, the 2nd Battalion, Cheshire Regiment was stationed at Jubbulpore, India. They had been there since 1911 and it would be several weeks before they could leave, arriving back in Britain on Christmas Eve. They left for France on 16 January. The Regiment's 1st Battalion was in Londonderry where there was considerable civil unrest over the possibility that Home Rule might be imposed on Ulster.

The regular army was supported by regimental county battalions of the Territorial Force comprised of part-time volunteer troops known, somewhat disparagingly, as the "Saturday Afternoon Soldiers". The Cheshire Regiment had four such battalions – the 4th with headquarters at Birkenhead, the 5th at Chester, the 6th at Stockport and the 7th at Macclesfield. These men were not obliged to serve overseas but could be mobilised for full-time duties, at home, if the need arose.

And the need had now arisen. In Derry, well established plans for mobilisation were put in place and, across the country, notices appeared in the newspapers summoning reservists to report to their respective barracks. They already had travel warrants, issued to them when they had undertaken their "refresher training" earlier in the year. Over the next three days, 556 men arrived to join the 1st Battalion. In North Cheshire, Territorial soldiers of the 6th Battalion, Cheshire Regiment, reported to their drill halls in Stockport, Glossop, Hyde and Stalybridge and, during the evening of the 4th, were inspected. Similar scenes were repeated across the country.

In spite of the detailed plans, there were many difficulties in the immediate aftermath of mobilisation, not least that as well as feeding the regular battalions, the army had to find food for the many thousands of Territorials who were now needing three meals a day.

The official rations allowance for a soldier in 1914 was 4193 calories a day. It is a lot of food, reflecting the heavy work they would undertake and generally comprising:

Bread	16oz
Meat	16oz
Bacon	4oz
Vegetables	9oz
Sugar	3oz
Cheese	2oz
Butter/margarine	6oz
Jam	3oz

Many of the Stockport men worked in the town's cotton mills and hat making factories. They were not well paid, lived in poor conditions and were often not in the best of health. They would quickly find that their diet improved considerably now that they were full-time soldiers. In civilian life, meat might be eaten only a couple of times in a week and now it would be a daily occurrence, although there would be a monotony of stews. The Territorials left the town on 8 August, joining the other battalions of their division at Shrewsbury.

In the days prior, there had been much discontent in the town about food prices. A large protest meeting had been held in Reddish complaining that grocers in the district had increased their prices on goods already in stock and on the shelves before the outbreak of war. However, Mr Charlesworth, the Secretary of the Grocers and Provision Dealers' Association had responded in the local newspaper, the Stockport Advertiser, that the rises were due to panic buying and the grocers wished to point out to the public *that there is more danger of enhanced prices through abnormal buying than from any scarcity of supplies and recommended customers to continue to buy from traders who they normally buy from. All retail trade should be for cash.*

Nationally, the President of the Board of Trade, Walter Runciman, announced that Britain had sufficient stocks of home grown wheat to last four months. It had been many years since the country was last self-sufficient in food and, in particular, imported wheat accounted for over 75% of the total used. Runciman had only been in office since 5 August, his predecessor resigning in protest at the war. He quickly gained popularity by acting swiftly to try to control the price of some foodstuffs. A meeting was held with representatives of the grocers' federation concluding with an agreement to limit prices. As yet, there was no legislation in place to compel retailers to conform but the wide publicity the agreement was given meant that most did not step out of line. Prices were set for the following week and did reduce those which had generally prevailed across the country in previous days. The prices set were:

Sugar	3¾d per pound
Butter	1s 6d per pound
Margarine	10d per pound
Bacon	1s 3d per pound

*   *   *   *

It had long been considered that, if Britain was to go to war with Germany, the fighting would be in France. The plan for mobilising the army had been established in 1911 and it involved moving six infantry divisions and the cavalry division across the Channel. There would, of course, also be the artillery and the various support units, such as the transport companies of the Army Service Corps which would move supplies of food, equipment and ammunition needed by the fighting men. It envisaged that the British Expeditionary Force (BEF) would be in France by the ninth day after mobilisation and would concentrate around Maubeuge in the north of the country, near to the border with Belgium.

The first units to disembark on the 9th and 10th of August were the important support troops – the signal companies of the Royal Engineers and units of the Army Service Corps, who set up base depots near to the Channel ports. Eighteen-year-old Fred Osborne, from West Haddon in Northamptonshire, had joined the army the year before. He had been working as a baker's assistant and, on becoming a full-time soldier, had continued with his craft. He was now serving with 4th Field Bakery, Army Service Corps. The Field Bakery arrived in France on 13 August and immediately got to work baking bread for the rapidly increasing numbers of men needing to be fed. They would be expected to bake daily rations for over 20,000 men.

Private Fred Osborne, 4th Field Bakery. Photo: Antony Osborne.

However, the number of troops arriving in France was in excess of the capacity of the various Field Bakery units which had disembarked and the war diary of the Deputy Assistant Director of Supplies (DADS)[1] records that, on 15 August, *"The French will be supplying 80,000 rations of bread."* The DADS was also in negotiation with French officials to acquire some flour supplies from them. The same day, he received news from the War Office that the refrigerated meat carrying ship, SS *Highland Brigade*, had left Liverpool for Le Havre. Built in 1901 for the Nelson Line, the ship had previously spent its time carrying meat from Argentina. The company had a large fleet of refrigerated ships and, during the course of the war, would lose several to enemy action. Over the course of the war, *Highland Brigade* made many voyages to South America until she was sunk, without warning, by an enemy torpedo fired from the German U-

SS *Highland Brigade.*

boat, UC-71, on 7 April 1918 while she was sailing from London to Buenos Aires.

Cyril Helm[2] qualified as a doctor in about 1912 and joined the Royal Army Medical Corps soon after. The 25-year-old was now a Second Lieutenant, attached to the 2nd Battalion, Kings Own Yorkshire Light Infantry, as its medical officer. The Battalion had been based at Portobello Barracks, Dublin and landed at Le Havre on the 16th.

We entrained next morning and left at 8pm, arriving at Landrecies at midday on the 18th. Our food on the train consisted chiefly of sardines and French bread but we thoroughly enjoyed it. All were as cheery as possible, regarding the future with absolute equanimity, in fact, looking on the whole thing as the realisation of the dream of every soldier.....We marched to Maroilles that afternoon where we spent two happy days. The men were given a splendid time in the farms in which they were billeted. People gave them as much butter & milk as they wanted, also fruit and eggs. In fact, too much as I as Medical Officer found out to my cost.

Cyril Helm, Royal Army Medical Corps

On 18 August, the Base Supply Depot notified the DADS that twenty cases of OXO cubes were en route from England aboard the SS Clock and that it wished to order a further hundred cases. Although OXO had been in production since the middle of the nineteenth century, this had been as a liquid product until 1910 when the now familiar cube was developed. The ease with which the cube could be transported meant it was soon included in army rations. The restorative power of a hot drink was noted in 1916 by a Canadian medical officer, Captain Richard Herald, attached to the 72nd Battalion, Canadian Expeditionary Force:

My dressing station was in the cellar of a ruined chateau and made a first rate place to handle the wounded. I established a soup kitchen and had hot pea soup, Oxo and coffee, steaming hot night and day and this, I insisted, was given to all who came in, wounded, carriers, runners and those exhausted. I don't think that I ever got so much pleasure from anything as I did from this, and watching the marvellous change that it works in the tired and worn out men. It bucked them right up and back they went to the firing line feeling like new men.

The other day two runners came in, caked with mud, wet, chilled and weary. They were two boys from Winnipeg, 19 years old, bright and smiling in spite of their condition and such good soldiers. They answered my questions so nicely and were ready to leave when I asked them to have some hot soup and promptly proceeded to fill up their bellies. You should have seen the thanks and gratitude in their eyes.

The men of the 1st Battalion, Cheshire Regiment left Londonderry on 14 August, boarding a ship at Belfast later in the day and arrived at the port of Le Havre during the afternoon of the 16th. The next day, they moved by train to join with other troops near the town of Le Cateau. On the 21st, the men marched fifteen miles north east to Gommignies. It was a hard march but, as they went through the villages, they received a very warm welcome from the French, who gave them gifts of food and drink. Crossing into Belgium the next day, they took up positions to the west of the town of Mons and, on the 23rd, occupied trenches which had been quickly dug by

Belgian miners. Other units of the British Expeditionary Force engaged the advancing Germans throughout the morning but were forced to withdraw in the late afternoon to a line near the positions held by the Cheshires. During the morning of the 24th, the Cheshires received their orders to withdraw, a movement they would carry out covered by the 1st Manchesters. They now took up a position near the village of Dour and, later in the morning, moved to near Audregnies, where they and the 1st Norfolks formed a rearguard, covering the withdrawal of the rest of the division.

They came under heavy artillery and machine gun fire at about 1pm. As the German infantry attacked, orders were issued for the rearguards to also withdraw but, in spite of three messengers being sent to the Cheshires, none arrived and they continued to hold their positions alone. The Official History of the War records:

> As the Germans came closer, the main body of the Cheshires fell back to the Audregnies road, where they were fired on by two machine guns placed in a dip in the ground, a couple of hundred yards away. These were promptly silenced by the machine guns of the Cheshires, and a little party of men charged forward with the bayonet to dislodge the enemy from this point of vantage. The Germans turned at the sight of them, and during this short respite the opportunity was taken to draw off a small part of the battalion across country to Audregnies Wood, which they reached under heavy fire, thence making their way to Athis. But the Germans, seeing how few were their assailants, returned to the attack, and there was nothing left for the remainder of the Cheshires, mere handful though they were, but to fight to the last. They still had ammunition and could keep up rapid fire, and, by this time separated into at least three groups, they continued to defend themselves desperately until nearly 7 P.M. Then at last, surrounded and overwhelmed on all sides, they laid down their arms. Of the main body on the Audregnies road, only forty remained unwounded. Their captors were the 72nd Regiment, belonging to the German IV. Corps.

Although it had not been intended, the stand made by the Cheshires had held up the German advance for several hours, allowing an ordered withdrawal of the remainder of 5th Division. Fifty-six of their number were dead and many more wounded or taken prisoner but some had managed to escape. The Cheshires had started the action almost 1000 strong but when the roll was called the next day, only 206 were present. They were tired, thirsty and hungry. And it was going to get worse.

The Cheshires, along with the rest of the BEF, started a retreat that would last until 5 September and would see the Army march over 200 miles. They would have to fight a major battle and regular rearguard actions as the German threat remained constant. There would be little sleep, irregular supplies of food and restrictions on the supply of water. The Germans harried the retreating British from the start and, by nightfall on the 25th, the exhausted troops of II Corps were near the small town of Le Cateau. Its commander, Lieutenant General Horace Smith-Dorrien, realised that his troops were scattered and that, if the retreat continued in the same way, they would gradually be overwhelmed by the Germans. He ordered that the Corps would make a stand the next day and engage the enemy. He intended it to be a "stopping blow" that would enable the British troops to slip away before the Germans had time to reorganise.

The hastily conceived plan worked and large numbers of casualties were inflicted on the advancing Germans, mainly by very accurate fire from the British artillery. It took the Germans a full day to reorganise and it allowed the British forces to withdraw in something approaching good order, although over 7000 were dead, wounded or taken prisoner. The 1st Cheshires had been held in reserve all day and, in the late afternoon, they formed a rearguard allowing the other battalions of their brigade to continue the retreat.

We had a very long march but the weather being perfect, made it bearable. The custom on the march, was to halt for ten minutes every hour. Our blessed ten minutes during the day time was always occupied by eating the apples which were given us by the peasants or picked up at the side of the road. About midday we passed through Noyon, a very pretty town, then on to cross the Oise, at Pontoise; the river here being very broad, extremely rapid and very difficult for navigation. About this point the sides of the road were strewn with addles and boxes of ammunition. We heard later, that some Divisional Ammunition Column had heard that the Uhlans were upon them, panicked, thrown out all their loads and galloped off as fast as they could. About two miles the other side of Pontoise we halted until about 7 that evening. By jove! We made the most of

A roadside bread dump. Photo: National Library of Scotland.

it. My Battalion was allotted a nice farm in the middle of some trees. The Mess cart was brought up and the Mess Sergeant soon got us a good meal of eggs, fresh butter, bread, milk etc. This we ate round a table in the middle of the farmyard.

I was the Mess President and it was my duty to see that we got as good a meal as possible. After eating, I saw what sick there were, mostly men with sore feet. Then I lay down for a few hours sleep.

One of the most marvellous things at this time was the way the Regimental ration cart used to roll up every night with our grub and sometimes mail. Frequently it had to go for miles and miles before it found our position, several times running the gauntlet of Uhlan patrols.

(Lt Cyril Helm, Medical Officer, 2nd Battalion, King's Own Yorkshire Light Infantry)

Helm was fortunate to get regular food. For many of the men, they would only be able to pick up supplies of tinned corned beef and army biscuits from caches that the Army Service Corps dumped along the line of retreat as its Motor and Horse Transport Companies also retreated.

Sometimes the kitchens would come up with you but chiefly it was the old biscuits and a tin of bully beef, or at that time I was with

Corporal McCabe and Corporal Allen and we had never drank but we could get a drop of rum at times, you see. Well, neither of us [sic] drank the rum. So he used to go one end of the company and I used to follow down the other end. Cpl Allen used to go and change it for any jam, outside of plum and apple. It wouldn't matter if it was marmalade or blackcurrant or anything at all. As long as it wasn't the usual plum and apple.
(Corporal John Hammond,[3] 1st Battalion, Queen's Royal West Surrey Regiment)

Corporal Arthur Chambers[4] was serving with 5th Field Company, Royal Engineers and kept a diary during this time.

Wednesday, 26 August 1914 – Am feeling the strain somewhat. Have had no food since Sunday, except a small bit of bully beef and biscuit. Our mouths are sore from eating the salt meat and hard biscuit. We have really kept going on apples of which there are plenty. We find our CO [Commanding Officer] about 11am and march till dark and billet in a field. A sapper gets seven days field punishment for firing a round of ammunition. He is tied to a cartwheel for two hours. Get first mail from home, also some food.

During an engagement near the Belgian town of Ypres, on 11 November 1914, Chambers took command of a party, when the officer was killed,

and led them to drive the enemy out of a wood, under heavy machine gun fire. For this act of bravery, he was awarded the Distinguished Conduct Medal.

The men of the 1st Battalion, King's (Liverpool) Regiment had been marching for much of the night of the 27/28 August. Commanding its 10 Platoon, C Company, was 22-year-old Second Lieutenant William Meredith.[5] His diary entry for the 28th records,

> *Soon after passing a place called Les Mezieres we halted for breakfast. We only got biscuits and jam and cold water as we had no time for cooking. They reached Rouy at about 8.30 in the evening where they would get some welcome sleep for a few hours overnight. An old lady saw our plight and insisted on filling each of our caps with the most delicious greengages. We were grateful and I am ashamed to say, we were both silent until we finished every one. We then picked a nice lot of blackberries which grew round the ruins of the village.*

Meredith was the son of a wealthy surgeon and came from Massingham, Norfolk, where his father employed seven live-in servants. He was wounded in January 1915 and is believed to have then been posted to the reserve battalion in Ireland for the remainder of the war. He died of pneumonia on 7 December 1918, no doubt falling victim to the worldwide influenza pandemic of that year.

The 1st Battalion, Lincolnshire Regiment, fared less well than Meredith and his comrades. Rations had not reached them and a party was sent to the appropriately named town of Ham to see what food could be found. It was to be disappointing, with the party returning with only a single tin of army biscuits and a dozen small tins of bully beef. The Regimental History notes,

> *These were distributed amongst the troops, each receiving a tiny morsel. But it was better than nothing and seemed to give them fresh energy when a further retirement was ordered about midday on Noyon.*

They arrived at Noyon in the early evening and,

> *Having found the battalion cooks and their wagons, little time was lost in making tea, which all ranks had not tasted for five days. By*

the time it was ready to be served darkness had fallen. The men with their canteen tins formed up and filed past their respective Company Quartermaster-Sergeants, who ladled out the precious liquid. Alas, in the darkness salt instead of sugar had been put into the tea.

By the end of the month, the German pursuit weakened as their supply lines became stretched. In 1930, Bernard Denore's recollection of the retreat was one of sixty published in *Everyman at War*. He served as a corporal with the 1ˢᵗ Battalion, Royal Berkshire Regiment, and had been a regular soldier since joining up in 1909. During the retreat, two of his comrades, who could take no more of the strain, shot themselves in the foot.

My feet were sore, water was scarce: in fact, it was issued in half-pints, as we were not allowed to touch the native water. The regulations were kept in force in that respect - so much so that two men were put under arrest and sentenced to field punishment for stealing bread from an empty house. Then, again, it wasn't straight marching. For every few hours we had to deploy, and beat off an attack, and every time somebody I knew was killed or wounded. And after we had beaten off the attacking force, on we went again - retiring.

Denore records that, during the afternoon of 1 September,

We fought for about three hours - near Villers-Cotterets I think it was, but I was getting very mixed about things, even mixed about the days of the week. Fifteen men in my company were killed, one in a rather peculiar fashion. He was bending down, handing me a piece of sausage, and a bullet ricocheted off a man's boot and went straight into his mouth and out of the top of his head.

Denore was later wounded in action and was discharged from the army on 26 May 1915.

The 2ⁿᵈ Battalion, King's Own Yorkshire Light Infantry, took many casualties whilst acting as one of the rearguard units at Le Cateau. As with the other units, the retreat had been a hard march south.

The next day, 3rd September, we crossed the Marne at Isles Les Villenoy, some five miles to the west of Meaux. The bridge by which we crossed it was blown up with a tremendous explosion shortly after we got across. In the afternoon as we were halted for several hours, I went to scour the country for some eggs and butter. After a long search I managed to get a dozen, which we had for tea. One thing, however, I did find was an acetylene lamp for the operating tent of a Field Ambulance. A complete store wagon, for some reason or other, had been abandoned and most of the medical stores had, by the time I got there, been looted. The lamp remained so I took it, presenting it to the mess. We used to start it going early evening whether we were in the open or under cover. With the lamp burning and a fire blazing, an evening meal in the middle of a field could be quite a cheery thing. That evening, I went on to look for a billet for the officers, and by Jove, I found one! It was some billet, as they say, and the finest one I have ever been in. I suddenly came on it near the village of Magny Saint Luz; it was a huge big chateau standing back in a big park and belonged to an old lady who was then at Meaux. I went in to prospect and found an old caretaker who was only too delighted to give me the run of the house. She opened up all the rooms and handed out sheets by the dozen from the linen

cupboard and actually showed me two priceless bathrooms. I really think I deserved a large vote of thanks for that find.

We spent the night there and all the next day until evening. Most of the day we spent wandering round the flower garden and also, I am ashamed to add, in the kitchen garden. For the first time in my life I gorged myself to depletion on the most perfect peaches I have ever seen; they were in the pink of condition and growing there by the score. If we did not take them the Germans would the next day so what did it matter. I should like to go back to that chateau some time after the war, when the peaches are ripe.
(Lieutenant Cyril Helm, Medical Officer, 2nd Battalion, King's Own Yorkshire Light Infantry)

On 4 September, French General Joseph Joffre, effectively the Allied commander in chief, ordered that the retreat would halt and that, the next day, the British and French would turn and attack. The History of the Cheshire Regiment records the final day of the retreat.

Pile arms and fall out. We remain here a few hours. The scene was a little orchard on the outskirts of Tournant just on the 18th kilo stone from Paris. A little band of dirty, bearded soldiers, mostly capless and without puttees, had wheeled into the orchard, a captain in command. Not even their best friends would have recognised this little band of tatterdemalions as the 1st Battalion, a short fortnight ago one of the smartest and best turned out battalions in the whole army. Since then, however, their lot had been such as had seldom been endured by soldiers before. Two hundred and five miles on foot, little food, two battles and several running fights make up a summer programme not calculated to improve either Tommy's appearance or his outlook on life.

During the forthcoming attack, later officially called the Battle of the Marne, the British forces would play a supporting role to the French. It was hard fought on both sides and, at first, it looked as though the Germans might be successful. The arrival of some 10,000 French reserve troops, many of them transported by Paris taxi cabs, helped to tip the balance. It would now be the German Army which had to withdraw. It fell back forty miles between 9 and 13 September.

As the 2nd Battalion, Kings Own Yorkshire Light Infantry moved forward again, its medical officer, Cyril Helm recounted,

When we did get under way we were passing through continuous orchards for several hours. Girls and women were picking the most delicious ripe peaches and apples as hard as they could, filling baskets with them and allowing us to take as many as we could carry. Personally my haversack was soon full to overflowing and my pockets as well..... We were to advance in extended order and go on until the Germans were compelled to retire. The M.O., in an attack like this, is in a difficult position and there are two courses open to him: (1) to stay in the rear and form an Aid Post, sending the stretcher bearers forward to bring back any wounded; (2) to keep up with the troops and attend to cases as they occurred.

As we were to advance some distance I decided to go with the men and I certainly got plenty of excitement out of it that morning..... In the village I found a convent with a Red Cross flag flying and the good sisters said they were all prepared to take in some wounded. (I was very relieved at being able to leave some of my friends in such good hands.) They also produced some very nice little peaches, which were very welcome as it was a scorching hot day and we had had nothing to eat or drink for many hours...... As we went on up the hill we saw a good many Germans dead by the side of the road; a fair number of prisoners also, many of whom were wounded. At the top, the thickest part of the scrap had evidently taken place. We halted here and had a great time helping ourselves to the contents of the wagons which were scattered about the place, with the usual dead horses. These were German wagons filled with provisions looted from the French. There was one full of tinned meats, asparagus, petits pois, coffee and sugar etc. It had been hit by a shell as the two horses were lying dead there and very much knocked about. I whistled up our Mess Cart and filled it to overflowing. For many a day we appreciated the petits pois and asparagus.

The casualties of the previous days would have received treatment from their own unit's medical officer before being evacuated to a field hospital (Casualty Clearing Station) some miles behind the front line. They would then be further evacuated to hospitals in Britain or to one of the military hospitals being established near the main ports in France. The staff and equipment for No. 2 General Hospital arrived at Le Havre on 17 August, establishing themselves on the outskirts of the town. No. 9 General Hospital arrived on the 22nd and proceeded to Rouen, where it set up on the city's racecourse. Commanding the latter was Lieutenant Colonel Bertal Scott.[6] He had served as a doctor with the Royal Army Medical Corps since 1887 and had been wounded in action in Sierra Leone in 1899 but continued to treat his injured comrades, before seeking aid for himself. He quickly found that army food supplies were insufficient for the hospital's needs as the number of patients grew, particularly for those foodstuffs thought beneficial in aiding recovery. Contact was made with the Deputy Assistant Director of Supplies who gave approval for the hospital to make local purchases of fresh vegetables, eggs and butter. Approval was also given for No. 2 General Hospital to buy bread locally.

The diary of a French soldier gives some insight into the experiences of Britain's ally at this early stage of the war. As a young man, Jacques Roujean had undertaken his compulsory military service. He was called up on 11 August 1914 and assigned to the 27th Company, 352nd Regiment. On the 25th, the Regiment advanced to engage the Germans in Lorraine.

> We are greeted with a storm of bullets. I hear the orders to form a skirmish line and to set our rifles at the 800 yards range. Very soon we are being fired at from the front and from both sides. The lieutenant runs the entire length of the skirmish line. He brings the men forward in tens, according to regulations. I watch him and feel certain that he will be shot. No, he continues his course right in the thick of the bullets. If only we could see the enemy! But he is safe in his trenches or hidden in the wood and is able to fire at us as he pleases. Lying flat on the ground, for the first time we hear the bullets whistle past.[7]

Later in the day, the 352nd Regiment was forced to retreat. Although reported to have been killed, Roujean had come through the day unscathed. He had, however, lost his glasses, on which he heavily depended and was evacuated away from the battlefield. By the beginning of September, he had returned to the Regiment's depot and had been billeted with a family called Giradot. On the 9th, orders arrived for the men to move forward and rejoin the 352nd.

French alpine troops in the Vosges mountains in eastern France. Photo: Gwyneth M Roberts.

> *Final preparations: all the tins of preserves we had piled up in Giradot's loft are divided out amongst the men of the squadron; these tins - foies gras, tongue, knuckle of ham, corned beef – are called Rimailhos, because of their calibre. At seven in the morning, we leave Humes. The entire depot is present and the people of the district bring us flowers with which we adorn our rifles. A short address by the commander of the depot. Shouts of "Vive la France" en route as we thunder out the Marseillaise.*

On 20 September, Roujon and his comrades were preparing to go into action to recapture the village of Fontenoy but news came that it had been taken by other troops. The 352nd went into nearby billets for three days.

> *We are quartered in a wretched-looking farm, reeking with manure and filth of every kind. We rise at a quarter to three. It is quite cold. We hurry to the kitchen, where Varlet and Charensac, the cooks of our section, are preparing coffee and cooking beefsteaks. They have not slept at all; in fact, they only received supplies about ten at night, for revictualment carts can approach the line only in the dark. The fire flames up in the vast country chimney, lighting up the whole room. The farmer and his wife, grumbling and blink'-eyed, are seated in a corner. The coffee is very hot; already we feel better. It is followed by a quart of broth. Then Varlet portions out to each man a small piece of calcined meat; the beefsteak for the noon meal.*

*   *   *   *

Back in Britain, the army recruiting offices had seen brisk business in the days immediately following the declaration of war. In Stockport, a few experienced men joined the local Territorial Battalion, the 6th Cheshires, now at Shrewsbury, bringing it up to full strength. North of the River Mersey, the 6th Battalion, Manchester Regiment had traditionally recruited its Territorial soldiers from amongst the middle class men working in the city centre, mainly in professional occupations in commercial, legal or financial businesses. They assembled at their drill hall near Manchester University. Ovens had been set up and the men were receiving a midday meal, usually of roast beef and potatoes and, for tea in the early evening, bread, jam and cheese. Towards the end of August, they would also take on new recruits to bring them up to strength.

Most of the new recruits were joining new 'service battalions' which had been formed for the duration of the war only. The Manchester Regiment recruited three complete battalions in August at its depot at Ashton under Lyne. However, by the end of the month, it was clear recruitment was slowing down. Sir Henry Rawlinson, then commanding 4th Division, hit on the solution, writing to a friend suggesting that many men working in the City of London would be willing to enlist if *"they were assured they would serve with their friends"*. It was an instant success with what was to become the 10th Battalion, Royal Fusiliers being formed in three days. In the north west, Edward Stanley, the Earl of Derby, took up the idea. In his youth, he had served in the army, later becoming a Member of Parliament, before succeeding to the family title. He now proposed recruitment of a similar battalion of the King's (Liverpool) Regiment, saying *This should be a battalion of pals, a battalion in which friends from the same office will fight shoulder to shoulder for the honour of Britain and the credit of Liverpool.* Within days, Pals Battalions, as they quickly became known, were being recruited in towns and cities across the country.

In Manchester, recruitment opened on 31 August and, by 3 September, around 2000 had joined up, forming the first two of the City's battalions. They were all men who worked in 'white collar' jobs – clerks and warehousemen – for the city centre's major employers. Within a few days they moved to a hastily erected tented camp at Heaton Park, on the northern outskirts of the city, to commence their training. The speed of recruitment had overwhelmed everyone and it would not be until the end of October that the *Manchester Evening Chronicle* was able to report that *A proper Army system of supplying rations and cooking is also being introduced at the park.* Until then, the battalions had to make whatever local arrangements they could make. Within a few days of arrival, initial supply problems had been resolved and the *Chronicle* was able to report that cooking equipment was now working properly and that one battalion was having its meals in the Park's tearooms while the other was in the 'hot water' garden. Daily food consumption for the 2000 men was impressive:

Potatoes – 1 ton
Bread – 2500 pounds
Beef – 400 pounds
Mutton – 400 pounds
Boiled hams – 30
Butter (Irish) – 2 hundredweight
Oatmeal – 200 pounds
Jam & Marmalade – 700 pounds
Mixed pickle – 100 jars
Milk – 60 quarts
together with a large quantity of tea, cheese and cake.

The *Manchester Guardian* later reported a week's meals. For breakfast each day, there was bread and butter with tea one morning and coffee the next. There would also be something "extra" each day. On Sunday, it would be bacon and tomato; Monday – bacon; Tuesday – Quaker Oats, treacle and jam; Wednesday – sausages; Thursday – liver and bacon; Friday – sausages; Saturday – bacon.

The midday dinner was substantial if somewhat repetitive:

Sunday – meat pies, roast meat, potatoes and pudding
Monday – tomato stew, carrots, turnips, potatoes and fruit
Tuesday – roast meat, meat pies, beans, potatoes and fruit
Wednesday – cowheel stew, potatoes and pudding
Thursday – meat pies, roast meat, potatoes, peas and fruit
Friday – tomato stew, potatoes, carrots, turnips and fruit
Saturday – roast meat, meat pies, potatoes, beans and fruit

For tea in the early evening, they had bread and butter and an 'extra' – tinned pears, jam, currant cakes, boiled ham, stewed prunes or figs.

The 6th Manchesters were also being well provisioned. They, and others of the Regiment's Territorial battalions, had moved to Hollingworth Lake, near Rochdale. Food was good and plentiful and the *Manchester Evening*

News reported that a man's daily ration included 1¼ lbs of fresh meat, 1¼ lbs of bread, 4 ounces of bacon, 3 of cheese and 2 of peas, beans or dried potato. There was also an allowance of jam, tea and sugar. They left camp on 9 September and moved, by train, to Southampton where they joined other units of the East Lancashire Division. The following night, they left port bound for Alexandria in Egypt. Amongst them were three brothers from the Stockport area who had all joined up only a few days before. Sidney 'Cider' Heydon was the eldest, followed by Arthur and Frank (known as 'Nip'). Sidney wrote home describing the voyage, which was rough when the ship crossed the Bay of Biscay.

> *Woke up this morning and found it very rough....Nearly everyone on board is ill. Both Arthur and Nip have been ill all day and I have been sick, although I have not missed a meal and am feeling fit.*

The History of 42nd (East Lancashire) Division commented that

> *It was noticed that even the worst sufferers from seasickness never lost hope as, although whole messes did not eat a meal during those three days, the daily indent for one bottle of beer per man was always drawn.*

Conditions for the Heydon brothers and their comrades had improved a couple of days later.

> *We should have had two hours drill every day, but we are only starting today. We get up at 6 o'clock, have breakfast at 7.15, dinner and tea and bed at 9. As for food, we do a lot better than at camp. For breakfast we have porridge or hashed beef and potato, bread and butter and jam and tea. Dinner, soup, roast beef and potatoes or stewed beef, rice and currant pudding. For tea, we have bread and butter, jam, tea or cold beef, pickles, so we do very well for food.*

The Manchesters arrived in Alexandria towards the end of the month, taking up a role as part of the city's garrison. Their colleagues from the 7th Battalion had been posted to Khartoum. Among them was 22 year old Jack Morten, from Stockport. Writing home, on 24 November, he described the food:

We are settled down, especially in the food line. Here is a rough outline of the daily menu:

Breakfast – one morning liver & onions, the next porridge, the next tinned salmon or herrings. We have these on alternate mornings (not all on one, we are not at Belle Vue, Port Erin).

Dinner – soup and stewed steak with peas or other vegetables which I cannot name, as when it is served up it resembles grass; I imagine it's a vegetable only grown in Khartum [sic]. Then the next day, by way of a change, we have the same kind of meat served up in the form of a steak pie, but we kid ourselves that it's different until our teeth get into it, and occasionally we have macaroni pudding.

Tea – bread and stewed tea only, so I always have a stock of jam or syrup in and on Sunday, by way of a special treat, two of us whack at a small tin of sardines or stewed fruit, but I would sacrifice jam or stewed fruit for a good plate full of nicely cut bread and butter. Butter can be bought here but, from reports of chaps who have tried it, I am quite satisfied to go without it.

Then, with regards to pay, we are getting our thirty-seven piastres regularly on a Friday and every month we get Khedive's pay so I have just managed to exist frugally. On reading this, you might think that I've been extravagant, but when you take into consideration that in most cases, especially in eatables, that what you buy at home for a penny, out here costs you a piastre, you will come to the conclusion that thirty-seven piastres is a great deal more on paper than in reality. Fresh eggs can be bought reasonably off the natives (½ piastre each or 1¼ d) and for the last fortnight I've had about six a day, as I beat them up and have them raw in my tea, which makes a jolly good substitute for milk. I am investing five piastres in a small spirit stove so most likely when you receive this I shall be having fried, poached, boiled and all kinds of egg dishes.

With regard to the above menu, usually dinner is the worst on account of the meat being so tough, but in that case I make up for it in jam. I pity some of the poor chaps with rotten teeth. More than one has broken them when struggling with a piece of steak. But, today, they've started a new system: we had pie and when opened we discovered that the meat was minced and it was a decided improvement.[8]

The early weeks of war saw a serious impact on many British industries. In Stockport, the cotton mills had been particularly hard hit as overseas orders all but dried up. Men were quickly laid off and, by the end of August, it was estimated that most of the Borough's spinners were no longer in work. There were similar lay-offs in the town's other major industry of hat making. For men who had enlisted, there would be some income for their families, but, for many, there was no alternative but to rely on charity. Schools were quick to assist and, by early September, several had set up canteens to provide breakfasts for the children.

Towards the end of October, the *Stockport Advertiser* reported that 2000 children were now receiving free school meals.

> *Whatever privation the parents may have to endure, we must see to it that the children are not allowed to suffer from lack of food.*

There were, of course, those who would take financial advantage of the situation and, also in October, several farmers from the Stockport area were prosecuted for watering down milk, tests showing that there had been up to 7% added water. Three of the farmers were each fined ten shillings – around £40 at modern values. It was hardly a significant deterrent and prosecutions would continue to be a regular feature of the magistrates court proceedings throughout the war.

Towards the end of the year, the War Office supported an appeal for new laid eggs to be donated to military hospitals, both at home and overseas, as reported by the *Stockport Express* on 10 December.

> *The wounded soldiers and sailors in our hospitals are sorely in need of new laid eggs and to meet the demand which amounts to no less than 200,000 eggs weekly, a National Egg Collection has been introduced by an influential committee with the approval and support of the War Office. Receiving depots are now being formed all over the country......It is pointed out that if only every person*

who keeps fowls in Great Britain and Ireland would promise a few eggs each week, this pressing need of our wounded can easily be supplied.

With Queen Alexandra acting as the collection scheme's patron, it proved to be a great success, not just in the outcome of eventually collecting a million eggs per week, but also in the way it involved the community. Schools would hold 'egg days', when each pupil would bring in an egg to donate to the scheme. In March 1915, the Army's Director of Medical Services was reported in *The Times* that the eggs were the *greatest possible boon to the sick and wounded*".

By August 1915, the scheme had 50,000 collectors, including members of the Boy Scouts, the Church Lads' Brigade and the Salvation Army. There were 1200 collecting points which would send the eggs on to a central packing depot, which had been provided in London by Harrods Ltd.

Henry McClelland joined the army in 1905 and was serving with the 4th Battalion, Royal Fusiliers when war was declared. He had a difficult childhood and had previously lived at the Union Cottage Homes, in the North Cheshire village of Styal. The Homes were run as an offshoot of the workhouse in south Manchester. He landed in France on 13 August but by early December was in a prisoner of war camp in Germany. The Fusiliers saw some of the heaviest fighting at the Battle of Mons, with two of McClelland's comrades winning the first Victoria Crosses of the war. It was probable that this was when he was captured. He wrote of the food at the camp in a letter home to his sister, published in the local newspaper.

We used to laugh at the black pudding man in Stockport Market. He would be a most popular man here. I would be amongst the first to welcome him. The German authorities give us that black sausage and I assure you it really is most excellent. I have forgotten what butter and sugar taste like. The dry brown bread is most welcome each day and there is not a crumb wasted.

*   *   *   *

Meanwhile, back in France, as the size of the army grew, so did its bureaucracy. Edward Courtney had been commissioned as a Second Lieutenant in December 1887, spending most of his career with the Army Service Corps. Now holding the rank of Lieutenant Colonel, he had gone to France as an Assistant Director of Supplies (ADOS), in charge of the Central Requisition Office. Part of his job was to investigate and settle claims for compensation, as he recorded in the unit's war diary.[9]

> *Investigated a claim personally at a place named Pont Remy, in the arrondisment of Abbeville. According to the claimant's letter, it was a very bad case of house breaking and consuming large quantities of wine. The claim was, it appears, lodged with the Mayor within 12 hours of the departure of the troops, and the local authorities, after investigation, reduced it from 68 to 34 Francs, hence an appeal from the claimant.*
>
> *There were certainly signs of the side door having been broken open and a large pipe, used for the purpose apparently, was found close by. It appears that the man's wife was waiting upon some British officers in the Station Hotel opposite at the time of the alleged burglary, but, strange to say, she did not report the incident*

Looks like it's stew again, mate.

to them. The Mayor of the town was afterwards interviewed and he assured me that the person making the claim was notorious for powers of exaggeration in most things and consequently, he, the Mayor, in all his dealings with him generally, made a corresponding allowance.

I have dealt at length with this subject just to show the class of claim that is being received and the difficulties that arise in safeguarding the interest of the British Government and, at the same time, satisfying the inhabitants who make out they are the victims of all sorts of unlawful acts committed by British soldiers. The Mayor, at the close of my interview, informed me that the British troops behaved in an admirable manner during their brief stay in the village; the inhabitants turned out to welcome them on arrival, and were most enthusiastic in wishing them 'God Speed' on their departure.

Courtney's diary entry for 15 November suggests he was also involved in the negotiation for the purchase of food supplies from the French and a scale of prices had been agreed:

Sheep	2 francs 25 cents per kilo (dead weight)
Cattle	1 franc 70 cents (dead weight)
Vegetables	15 – 20 francs per 100 kilos
Bread	1 franc 20 cents per 3 kilos
Tea	6 franc 50 cents per kilo
Sugar	80 cents per kilo
Jam	1 franc 10 cents per jar

The Royal Naval Division was formed at the beginning of the war and comprised Royal Marines, together with naval reservists for whom no ship could be found at the time and who had received basic retraining so that they could serve as infantry. In late September, it arrived at Dunkirk with orders to move north to assist with the defence of Antwerp.

The Division deployed in the city between 4 – 6 October but the defence would soon be over. The Reverend H C Foster was chaplain to one of the brigades of reservists and wrote an account[10] of this time. The 2nd Naval Brigade arrived in the city on the 6th, marching to positions on the outskirts. Foster and the other officers were billeted for meals.

I found myself in a house where the only occupants appeared to be three old ladies, who could not speak a word of English. I made them understand, however, that I was ravenously hungry; the table was quickly set, and I was provided with a delicious omelette and some fried ham, with a bottle of light beer to wash it down.

Afterwards, he managed a couple of hours sleep before the men were moved forward towards the front line, arriving at the village of Vieux-Dieu, some five miles away.

We were told that we were to be quartered for the night in an old chateau, standing in its own grounds and surrounded by trees. There was abundant evidence that its occupants had been wealthy people, and that they had fled away in haste. There was a quantity of valuable furniture, and we found everything just as its late owner had left it.

We ascertained that one of the servants belonging to the house was still at her home in the village, and after a good deal of persuasion we succeeded in getting her to come and cook some supper for us. Those of us who are still alive will not readily forget the scene in that old room of the chateau. There we sat round the table, a light being supplied by a candle stuck securely in the neck of an empty bottle, eating like the gourmands who haunt Simpson's in the Strand and other famous eating-houses. Plates and forks were scarce, but, pocket-knives came in exceedingly handy. The windows had been plastered up with brown paper so as not to let out a single streak of light. There sat such well-known personages as Lieut.-Colonel George Cornwallis West, Arthur Asquith, Denis Browne and Rupert Brooke, eating pieces of veal with their fingers and drinking coffee out of tumblers and milk jugs.

They went into the front line at dawn on 7 October, coming under attack shortly afterwards.

When Thursday, October 8, dawned, both officers and men looked exhausted and fagged out. Stores were getting somewhat low, and for breakfast we had each a tin mug of coffee, one biscuit, a piece of bread, and a small bit of cheese.

The Naval Brigade withdrew from Antwerp during the evening of the 8th. Some of them managed to escape south and were able to return to Britain but others marched north, crossing the Dutch border and were interned for the remainder of the war.

Some weeks later, a requisition for payment arrived on Edward Courtney's desk at Abbeville. It came from the biscuit manufacturers, Huntley & Palmer Ltd, for *chocolate, potted and tinned meats and biscuits, to the value of 3667 Francs, supplied to the order of Colonel, the Rt. Hon. J Seely, DSO, by a Mr Billoons-Dierick, Antwerp.* Seely was on the Headquarters staff of the Royal Naval Division. Prior to the conflict, he had served as a Member of Parliament and was the Secretary of State for War from 1912 until forced to resign in the spring of 1914.

Courtney's war diary entry continues,

> *It transpired that the requisition was made in order to provide food in a portable form for the men of the Royal Marines and Royal Navy in General Paris' force at Antwerp. It was impossible for the force to take transport with them on evacuating the city, because of the necessity of having to cross the Scheldt by boat. Further, it was impossible to obtain food of any kind on the left bank of the river, owing to the enormous number of refugees from Antwerp and the neighbourhood, who had fled the city. The number of men in General Paris' force was about 7000 and entirely a naval force administered from the Admiralty. The claim was sent to the Secretary of State for War for transmission to the Admiralty for settlement.*

*   *   *   *

Although the United States of America would remain neutral until 1917, its government kept a close eye on the conflict, including how the war was affecting the home fronts of the various nations. Its Department of Labor was particularly interested in the increase in the price of food.[11] Taking some of its information from the documents published by the British Board of Trade, it concluded that, by the end of 1914, prices had risen by 15 – 17% above the pre-war situation in July. The greatest increases had generally affected sugar and eggs, the former being nearly 70 per cent dearer by the end of the year and the latter over 60 per cent. In November, American consuls in Britain were asked to report to their government the price of foodstuffs in the cities where they were working. The exercise showed wide variations across the country, with the price of eggs increasing by 80 per cent in the Worcestershire town of Redditch but only by 20 per cent in Nottingham. There were other dramatic increases in other foods. For example, the people of Glasgow and Troon had seen lentils and split peas double in price. Fish had also seen large price increases, no doubt due to a reduction in the tonnage being landed. It had added 50 per cent to the price of haddock for shoppers in Sheffield. In Burslem, cod was 60 per cent higher than July prices. However, some areas appeared barely affected. In Bristol, fruit, vegetables and tea had been unaffected by increases. The American consul who examined prices in Huddersfield reported that, whilst wholesale prices for sugar, flour

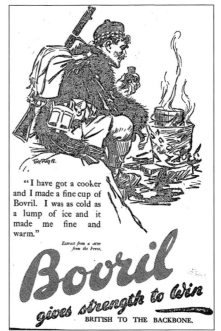

"I have got a cooker and I made a fine cup of Bovril. I was as cold as a lump of ice and it made me fine and warm."

Extract from a letter from the Front.

Bovril

gives strength to win

BRITISH TO THE BACKBONE.

and canned goods had increased, retailers had, to date, not completely passed this on to their customers. As such, the general cost of living remained pretty much as it was pre-war. A similar fortunate situation existed in Liverpool, where sugar was the only product showing large increases.

As Christmas approached, British traders were getting ready for a busy festive season much as they had done in previous years, despite the price increases. The *Stockport Advertiser* was able to report that Ellis', a confectioner's shop on Underbank, had *an attractive display of Christmas fare. A speciality is Christmas cakes, puddings which are very tempting and seasonal. There is a large stock of large and small fruit and meat pies, fruit loaves and biscuits, with a choice assortment of chocolates.* The newspaper was also very supportive of one butcher's shop –*The Christmas dinner will be a sure success if the meat is supplied by Mr J E Smith, family butcher, of Bramhall Lane. At this shop, only the best English beef and mutton are supplied and the animals are killed on the premises.*

As well as buying for their own Christmas meals, many purchases were made to send to relatives serving in the forces. Parcels were always welcomed by troops, not only as reminders of home but also as treats to break what was often the monotony of army food. Eighteen-year-old

Ridley Sheldon[12] was a vicar's son from North Manchester. He joined the 6th Manchesters on 1 September and was now preparing to enjoy his first Christmas away from home in Alexandria, Egypt. A letter from home arrived telling him that a parcel of presents was on its way to him. It mentioned that there would be nine mince pies and this caused him something of a problem as it was the custom to share things out with close comrades and, at this time, Sheldon was sharing a tent with eleven others. It arrived just before Christmas Day:

There were draughts and dominoes, and chess and ring board, in the way of games; then besides, there were cakes and sweets and chocolates, in the shape of eatables. Yes! There were nine mince pies. Nine mince pies to be divided amongst twelve men; just think of it! Whatever was I to do? For I did not want to cause any disappointment; still it was a very knotty problem to solve – how to make the nine pies go round for the twelve men, without either breaking or spoiling them. But, at last, after a great deal of thought and consideration, we got over the difficulty and this is the way in which we managed it. We decided to take pieces of paper and make a mark in the form of a cross on three of the pieces. When this had been done, they were all placed into a hat and, well shaken up, we each drew in our turn on the distinct understanding that whoever got a paper with a cross on it would have to forego the pleasure of feasting on a mince pie.....but those unfortunate enough to miss the pie had it made up to them by an extra supply of cake.

Sheldon thought himself lucky that he had not drawn a cross. He enjoyed Christmas Day which started with a good breakfast, much better than usual, he thought.

We were regaled with porridge, some fine bacon and eggs, bread butter and tea.

The mess huts had been decorated with palm branches, flowers, lanterns and chains of coloured paper. After a church parade, the sergeants served dinner to the men at 1pm.

We had roast beef, carrots, cabbage, cauliflower and potatoes, followed by plum pudding and sauce, nuts and oranges. I had a mineral water to drink but for those who were not Total Abstainers, there was a pint of beer each and also tobacco for those who smoked. But tea was somewhat disappointing, for we only got bread, jam and cake with the tea….I thought they might have given us something else besides. After all, I missed the turkey and the other good things which I knew they were having at home and, certainly, the day seemed very strange indeed. I well remember that I had not even the opportunity of going on church parade; for unfortunately, I was on Quartermaster's fatigue and my time was spent in peeling onions, potatoes and carrots and preparing cabbage to be cooked. Well, I suppose someone had to do it and it fell to my lot. (Private Ridley Sheldon)

Ninian Duncan was also celebrating Christmas in Egypt. He was born in Rothesay and emigrated to Australia, some time before the war, where he lived near Sydney. He was a baker by trade but, when he enlisted on 28 August 1914, was assigned to the 3rd Battery, Australian Field Artillery as a gunner.[13] The troops arrived at Alexandria on 7 December and were now stationed at Mena Camp, close to the Pyramids outside Cairo. The Liddle Collection, at the University of Leeds, holds a menu card for the Battery's festive dinner:

Potage Auspare Parts
Roast beef a la Pyramids
Turk-he-Trot
Pommes de terre a l'allegmaine
Cauliflower sauce
Christmas pudding, brandy sauce
Fruit conserve, shrapnel custard

* * * *

Stockport's Territorial soldiers, the 6th Cheshires, left the town on 8 August and spent several weeks in training in Britain, before arriving in France on 10 November. Unlike their middle class comrades in the 6th Manchesters, Stockport's factory workers would have been used to not being able to afford to eat meat every day. Surveys of the time suggest that the unskilled working class might only consume one pound of meat per week, with much of the diet being made up of bread and potatoes. As a result, many of them would find army food to be pretty good.

Keeping warm while the Maconochie cooks. Photo: National Library of Scotland.

One Cheshire wrote home[14] about the meals they were enjoying. *Maconochie rations enough for two men, but we have one a piece and would have given francs for another, bacon, "possy", bread and cheese.* As will be seen later, the tinned stew made by the Maconochie Company was generally not enjoyed by the troops when they had to eat it. Another Stockport man had been to visit the Cheshires: *You should have seen the scramble. I thought Maconochie was great but the good old potato pie wants some beating. Just fancy, potato pie being served to the Cheshires. Why, the casualties would never be known in the rush.* For Private Willie Metcalfe, writing to his father, it was the issue of butter that was a treat. *The food is just the same as in England, except they give us butter, which is quite a luxury. I have just received your parcel of cigs for which I thank you very much.*

The Cheshires had their first taste of trench life on 11 December, when half the Battalion was attached to the 1st Manchesters and the 1st Duke of Cornwall's Light Infantry. The conditions were very poor, with the trenches being deep in mud and water. The next day, they suffered their first fatality, when Walter Williamson, from Hyde, was shot by a sniper. They spent 48 hours with the regular army troops and then the other two companies of the Battalion took over their positions. However, before the changeover, there was a lucky escape for two men from Hyde, as reported in the Battalion history. And a cooking pot was the cause of it. They had argued about *whose duty it was to take back a dixie, and so they got on the top to fight it out. They were both promptly hit by the enemy—one a graze on the forehead and the other a graze on the cheek.*

The Battalion was relieved from the tour of duty on the 16th, moving into billets at the village of Neuve Eglise. There were parcels from home to welcome them. The *Stockport Advertiser* published a corporal's letter home. *Some plum pudding just came in a parcel from one of the men's home. He is sharing it out amongst fifteen men – you should hear them shout! It only weighs a pound but it is a taste of good old English Christmas pudding.*

Private William Tapp, 1st Battalion, Royal Warwickshire Regiment also received a Christmas parcel from home, as noted in his diary entry for 22 December.[15] The following suggests he was then one of the officers' servants (the term 'batman' was not commonly used at the time).

We ate at our old billet – a private house. I and three more servants have all received parcels from home and we are making this our

Cooking the Christmas geese. Photo: Illustrated War News, 30 December 1914.

> *Xmas Day, we had bacon, one egg and chipped potatoes for breakfast; eggs are a luxury now they are 3½d each and hard work to get any at all. Dinner, roast beef, Brussels sprouts, which we had seen on the way down, also plum duff and mincepie and a couple of jugs of beer, cigarettes; for tea we are going to have a milk loaf which has come from England, butter, cake, sweets, etc. I hope everyone in England has as good food for their Xmas Day.*

The Cheshires returned to front line duty on the 18th, occupying trenches near the road between the Belgian village of Wulverghem and town of Messines. Temporarily, they were attached to the three regular army battalions that formed the rest of 15 Brigade – the 1st Dorsets, 1st Bedfordshires and the 1st Norfolks. Their experiences of the coming days would, therefore, be slightly different, depending on where in the trench system they were, but they were about to celebrate Christmas as part of one of the most remarkable events of the War.

From the early morning of Christmas Eve there were signs that the mood had changed on both sides of No Man's Land. On the German side, decorated Christmas trees started to appear on top of the trench parapets. Elsewhere, in the quieter sectors, troops called out and unofficial agreements were reached not to shoot at each other until the festivities were over. However, in the Wulverghem sector, near Ypres, it was pretty much 'business as usual' and the day saw the deaths of two of the Stockport Territorials – John Carruthers and Henry Roberts. It would be different the next day.

Private John Carruthers, 6th Cheshires, killed in action on Christmas Eve.

John Carruthers' inscription on the Thiepval Memorial to the Missing. His body was never identified. Photo: Author.

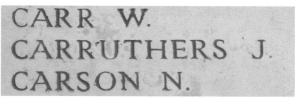

The day opened with the usual stand-to before dawn. Soon after daylight arrived someone in our lines began to play "Christians, awake!" on a mouth organ, and the thoughts of the men in the trenches immediately turned to the folks at home, who they knew were living under better conditions than they were. It was, says one who was there, nothing but mud, mud, mud, a parapet and two strands of wire between us and the Boche, who was 200 yards away. After "Christians, awake!" the Boche responded with the popular melody "Come over here!" and lo! we saw the Boche coming out of his trenches and we wondered whether it was an attack. The Germans were waving their arms, and immediately our men went out to meet them in No Man's Land, where we fraternised. We ate their Saukeraut, and they our chocolate, cakes, etc. We had killed a pig just behind our lines. There were quite a lot of creatures rambling about the lines, including an old sow with a litter and lots of cattle and poultry. We cooked the pig in No Man's Land, sharing it with the Boche. We also buried several dead Frenchmen who were lying out there. So ended our first Christmas in the line. The Boche, and we also, thought the war would soon be over. On the 2nd September, 1918, in our attack from Locre, we re-took the trenches in which we spent Christmas Day, 1914.

(The War History of the 6th Battalion, Cheshire Regiment)

George Blease was a relative rarity in the army. It is a popular myth that there were many underage soldiers but, in fact, there were relatively few. Born in 1898, George was old enough to join the Stockport Territorials but was not old enough for overseas service until he was 19. A blind eye must have been turned to his real age as he was now in the trenches at Wulverghem and wrote home just after Christmas:

On Christmas Day, when dawn broke, it was very foggy, so we were able to have a short run on top of the trenches to keep us warm. Anyhow the fog lifted and our men as well as the Germans were exposed to fire but none fired. Then the Germans started to wave umbrellas and rifles, we answering. They sang and we sang. Then, getting bolder, we advanced towards their trenches. When one met, we found they were fairly old fellows. We exchanged greetings, they giving us sausage, cigars, cigs, sweets, parkin. We all mixed up together and men played mouth organs and tin whistles and danced

*and, my word, the Germans can't half sing. The time came when
we had to part. Shaking hands and saluting, they and we went back
to the trenches.*

Company Sergeant Major Bob Morton later recalled Christmas Day.[16] He
was the senior non-commissioned officer in A Company which had been
attached to the 1st Dorsets. Suspicious of the Germans' intent, he had
ordered his men not to leave their trenches but had been ignored, so he
ended up joining the others in No Man's Land. In return for the gifts of
sausage and cigars, the Germans were very interested in exchanging them
for British jack-knives. They were members of the 134th Infantry Regiment
from Saxony. The Germans then produced a football and scores of men,
from both sides, took part in a general kickabout. Morton and an officer
went off to try and shoot some chickens that were around the nearby
'Stinking Farm' with their service revolvers but without success. The farm
was known as such because of the smells from a number of dead cattle
and rotting turnips surrounding it. A hare then appeared in No Man's Land
and was chased by men from both sides, but it also escaped. But then the
pig referred to in the Battalion history appeared with her piglets. It was
shot, cut up, cooked and shared out between Cheshires and Saxons alike.

   Ernie Williams, one of the Cheshire men out in No Man's Land, talked
about his experiences in a TV interview in 1983. He confirmed that the
popular story of a formal football match being played in No Man's Land
was, indeed, a myth.

*The ball appeared from somewhere. I don't know where, but it came
from their side. They made up some goals and one fellow went in
goal and then it was just a general kickabout. I should think there
were about a couple of hundred taking part. I had a go at the ball.*

*The area around Stinking Farm. The Cheshires held trenches near the line of
trees, with the German positions towards to the hill leading to the town of
Messines. Photo: Author.*

I was pretty good then, at nineteen. Everybody seemed to be enjoying themselves. There was no sort of ill-will between us. There was no referee and no score, no tally at all. It was simply a melee – nothing like the soccer you see on television.

Sergeant James Boardman spent Christmas just behind the front line and did not take part in the truce.

At this place there were very few trenches. The defences were simply sandbags built up into a parapet...... We were losing a lot of men, who were going sick with bad feet, due to the cold and the water-logged state of the trenches. I spent my Christmas Day in the Priest's House at Wulverghem. We had a young pig between eight of us, and also plum pudding and plenty of rum. About this time we had a great deal of trouble in getting rations to the front line as the nights were so moonlit, in fact, it was nearly as light as day.[17]

The truce only affected troops in a comparatively small section of the front line and, elsewhere, the war continued as normal. Christmas Day saw forty-one British soldiers killed in action. Although there was little fraternisation after Christmas Day, the days leading up to the New Year were generally quiet and, in several sectors, the truce held firm.

By now, the nature of the war had changed. The days of armies moving forward or falling back great distances were over and would not return until 1918. The Western Front now saw lines of trenches which stretched from Nieuwpoort, on the Belgian coast, to Pfetterhouse, near the Swiss border – a distance of around 445 miles. At the end of 1914, British forces occupied 25 miles of the line, increasing to 123 miles in 1918. Despite the popular view, it was never going to be "over by Christmas".

*   *   *   *

Irish Stew
(British Army Field Service Pocket Book, 1914)

Ingredients: Meat, potatoes, onions, pepper, salt. Peel, wash and slice the potatoes; peel, clean and cut up the onions; cut up the meat into small pieces, place a little water in the kettle and a layer of potatoes at the bottom, then a layer of meat and onions; season with salt and pepper; then add another layer of potatoes and so on to the top, potatoes forming the top layer. Barely cover the whole with water and stew gently for about two hours.

Winter Soup
(Simple Cookery for the People, 10th edition, circa 1916)

Ingredients: 1 teacupful lentils, ½ teacupful oatmeal, 1 teacupful mashed potato, 1 breakfastcupful, in all, of chopped onion, carrot, turnip, salt and pepper, 3½ pints water. Average cost, 4d

Soak the lentils overnight, drain, put into a saucepan with the water, cook one hour, add the vegetables, salt and pepper, cook half an hour longer, sprinkle in the oatmeal and add the mashed potato. Stir frequently, simmer gently until the lentils are quite soft and serve. When coarse oatmeal is used, the soup must simmer half an hour after adding it.

NOTE: This soup may be mashed through a sieve or colander before serving and a little milk added to enrich it.

Gingerette Pudding
(Thrift for Troubled Times, 1915)

Quarter of a pound of suet
Quarter of a pound of treacle
Half a pound of flour
One ounce sugar
Rind and juice of one lemon
One teaspoonful of ginger
One teaspoonful of carbonate of soda
Half a gill of milk

METHOD: Chop the suet, add to the flour, sugar, carbonate of soda, lemon rind and ginger. Make a well in the middle, add the treacle and milk and mix until the mixture drops easily from the spoon. A little more milk should be added if necessary. Put into a greased basin, cover with greased paper and steam for three hours.

CHAPTER 2

Bully Beef and Biscuits

For the men in the trenches, food over the next four years would be generally plentiful, although many would complain of its monotony. On a daily basis, parties from each infantry company would make their way to the rear areas and collect supplies. The food would be in one of two forms. It may have been prepared by the battalion cooks or it may be in the form of canned products, which the men would heat up for themselves in the trenches.

Frederick Cane was a Company Quartermaster Sergeant [CQMS], serving with the 16th Battalion, London Regiment – a Territorial unit known as the Queen's Westminster Rifles. A married man, with two children, he worked as a commercial traveller. Cane joined the Territorials in 1908 and had arrived in France, with the Battalion, on 1 November 1914. For a few days after the Battalion went into the front line, south of Armentières, he kept a diary, which is now held by the Imperial War Museum:

About four miles away at our little base, our RQMS [Regimental Quartermaster Sergeant] lives and, early every afternoon, he rides with our transport wagons to our Regimental HQ (about a mile and a half from here), where he hands over to each CQMS one day's rations for each company. From the trenches , every evening, we send eight men per company to me, the CQMS, and they bring the food in hand carts to Burnt Hut Farm, where the party is again met by twelve men from each company, giving a total of twenty men per company. Then the fun commences as the food has to be humped into the trenches and handed over to the four Company sergeants

who distribute to each man. Boxes of biscuits, cases of tinned meat, parcels of jam, cheese, sacks of bread, parcels of tea and sugar and, sometimes, also bacon. And, best of all, the mail bags of parcels and letters.

As Cane mentions, 'humping' the rations to the front line was a difficult job and one not without its own dangers from random bullets and unseen shell holes, filled with water and deep mud, into which a man might easily slip, possibly drowning. Percy Jones[18] was another man serving with the Queen's Westminster Rifles, one night making his way back to Burnt Hut Farm to receive rations from his CQMS:

One night, Corley, of section 12, went with me to bring in rations and we got fixed up with a large box of tinned meat and vegetables. It was pouring with rain and at every step one sank knee deep into the mud. The wretched box was perfectly smooth and soon became so greasy with mud and slime that it slid from our hands every few yards. We tried the communication trench but the weight, 56lbs, caused us to sink so deep in the mud that we nearly stuck tight. We therefore decided to strike across country and chance running into the firing line. Progress was slow, very slow. In fact, for every four paces the muddy box slipped from our equally muddy fingers or else we had to halt to pull one or another out of the slush.

After struggling for about twenty minutes, the unhappy Corley plunged headlong into a shell hole full of water and came out

Bruce Bairnsfather's 'Old Bill'.

hopelessly demoralised, swearing he would leave the box where it was. I managed to get him to have another try and we finally tumbled into the firing line, only to find ourselves in "F" Company, about 200 yards from our own section.

This was too much and, with a wild yell, Corley fell on the box and battered it to pieces with an entrenching tool, after which we took out the tins and carried them in three journeys piecemeal up to our trenches.

In September 1915, Private Anthony Brennan[19] was a member of the ration carrying party of the 2nd Battalion, Royal Irish Regiment, which was then serving near the Somme village of Auchonvillers – known to the troops as 'Ocean Villas'. He had enlisted on 13 April and had only arrived in France on 26 July.

At night the ration party would set out for Auchonvillers, a ruined village about a mile to our rear. Our transport wagons came up here every night after dark and it was a busy time at the crossroads when the Quartermaster Sergeants started the job of dishing up the rations for each platoon. To get to the village from our trenches, one had to cross about three or four hundred yards of open space. Once or twice, we did have the unpleasant feeling of the close "swish" of a bullet but I don't remember that anybody was ever hit. Later when the weather broke and this much traversed pathway became muddy and slippery, it was a way of tribulation for many over-burdened ration carriers and many the heartfelt curse went up to Heaven from the lips of an exasperated Tommy as he measured his length on the slushy earth. Given a large four-cornered box of biscuits, a couple of sandbags loaded with anything from tins of Bully to bricks for the Captain's dug-out and slung around one's neck a rifle and two bandoliers of ammo and the things that could happen to one's person and one's temper on that three hundred yards of slippery uneven footpath on a dark night was enough to try the patience of even the most meekest of Tommies.

Brennan was a specialist machine gunner, one of the two-man teams which fired the light Lewis machine guns. On 4 August 1917, he and three other machine gunners took up positions in what, until 31 July, had been the British front line. There had been a major attack and the front line had

Ration party carrying hot food to the trenches, near Arras, 1917. Photo: Australian War Memorial.

moved forward. Sometime during the day, a shell exploded amongst them, injuring three and mortally wounding Lance Corporal Walter O'Brien, who died at a field hospital on the 9th. Brennan was badly wounded in his legs and feet, and spent a year in hospital before being discharged from the army on 26 September 1918. Army records indicate that he was 22 when he was discharged but, in fact, he was only 20, having joined up underage at 17. Presumably he had added on a couple of years to his real age at the recruitment office.

> *We were able to send up hot food at frequent intervals by day and by night, cooked in the Brewery Yard [at Suzanne] and carried up to the trenches in dixies by the platoon ration carriers, three men whose sole duty was to get hot food up to their mates in the trenches and this they did however deep the mud or heavy the firing. We had made wooden yokes which supported a Dixie or camp kettle and were carried each by two men, resting on the shoulders. The remaining man carried dry rations, bread or bully beef. These*

ration carriers were the bravest men in the Battalion. They were
consistently shelled but never failed to feed their platoons, Wallace
and Bell carried rations for my own platoon.[20]
(Second Lieutenant T Nash, 16th Battalion, Manchester Regiment,
describing conditions in early 1916)

Since arriving in France in November 1914, the Stockport Territorials of
the 6th Cheshires had lost a number of comrades killed or wounded in
action but they had lost many more reporting sick because of frostbite or
trench foot. The latter was a serious condition caused by standing in the
waterlogged trenches for long periods of time. If left untreated, gangrene
would develop and amputations were not uncommon. In the second half
of December, over 120 men from the Battalion were hospitalised, mainly
suffering with frostbite. Albert Fernley enlisted just after war was declared
and had been training with the Cheshires' reserve battalion at
Northampton. He was posted overseas, along with nearly 250 other new
recruits, who would join their Stockport comrades as reinforcements on
26 January 1915. Writing home, on 11 February, he described his first
experiences of life in the trenches, in a letter published in the *Stockport
Express*:

> *Every night, I was picked to go out to go to the village, about a mile*
> *away; it had been so shelled by the Germans that there was not one*
> *whole house in the place. I went for rations for the companies in*
> *the firing line. We had to return through the slush and water but*
> *had got used to it by now......For breakfast on the sixth day, we had*
> *bacon and cheese; for dinner, warm potatoes and beans and a*
> *pudding made with biscuits and jam; for tea, toast bread and butter.*
> *This was the best of all the seven.*

A few days after that, the Cheshires were having an even better dinner in
the trenches:

> *We had a stroke of luck on February 16. A group of cattle strayed*
> *near our trenches, so we shot a young steer. We cut a leg off and, in*
> *less than two hours, men and officers alike were having a feed fit*
> *for a king – fried steak – with the Germans 200 yards from us.*
> (Private William Brewster, 6th Battalion, Cheshire Regiment.
> *Stockport Advertiser*, 5 March 1915)

Ration party near Zonnebeke, Belgium, September 1917. Photo: Australian War Memorial, E00813.

This tour of duty in the trenches would be the last that the Cheshires would undertake for many months, as the Battalion was withdrawn into the reserve to undertake duties on the lines of communication. It would not be without an act of bravery noted in the war diary. At this time, the trench system was still being extended behind the front line trench. It meant that, from time to time, men had to move over the ground, exposing themselves to possible enemy fire. On 27 February, Company Sergeant Major Thomas Long was shot whilst on the open ground behind the trenches. Privates George Wood and Thomas Mather got out of their trench and ran to his aid. In doing so, Mather was also shot and killed outright but Wood managed to get his CSM into the protection of the trench. As far as is known, both Long and Wood survived the war.

Before enlisting into the army at the beginning of September 1914, Edward Higson had worked as a clerk for a shipping firm in Manchester. Along with many others from similar occupations, he joined the first of the newly formed Pals battalions of the local Regiment – later officially known as the 16th (Service) Battalion, Manchester Regiment. Along with the other Pals, he arrived in France on 8 November 1915. In 1917, he was commissioned as a Second Lieutenant and was transferred to the 10th Battalion, Cheshire Regiment. However, in early December 1915, he was another man taking his turn on ration party duty near the village of Hébuterne, where the Battalion was getting its first taste of life in the front line, under instruction from experienced Territorial units of the Gloucestershire and Worcestershire Regiments. Higson later recounted[21]

About 8 o'clock the CSM [Company Sergeant Major] came up asking for volunteers for a ration carrying party for the front line. There was a great rush to get into the party (oh, what rookies we were) and I deemed it quite an honour that I was included in the eight picked to go. We had first of all to put on huge rubber gum boots. Then we were paraded at the Company cooker and each given a petrol tin full of hot tea. As soon as the guide came up, we started.

He led us down a communication trench for a few hundred yards and got out on top to save time. It was only 1000 yards across country, or rather mud, to our destination but it took us 2 ¾ hours to get there. We tried to follow the guide round shell holes and over trenches, but somehow the shell holes seemed to attract our person and in we went, overhead in mud and water. The rest of the party would stop and help and on we went again, having to stop every few yards when a German Verey light went up, ducking and falling flat when the machine guns swept No Man's Land and our trench area. Every so often, one of the party would disappear in a trench he had not seen or trip over one of the numerous obstacles. But one got there and, much to our surprise, received a great deal of grousing because the tea was cold.

*   *   *   *

As noted by Higson, each of the four companies of a battalion had a mobile field kitchen or cooker, staffed by two cooks. The eight men were under the supervision of a sergeant cook. The field cookers were pulled by two horses and driven by the two cooks. There were two parts. The front limber, on which the men sat, also stored utensils, ingredients and other equipment. Attached to that was the actual cooker, which was, generally, wood fuelled and which had frying and four boiling sections, which could also be used to make tea, as well as the inevitable stews. Many of them

Mabbott field cooker.

Drawn by Private Joseph Prill, a cook with 3rd Battalion, Rifle Brigade. He was killed in action on 13 February 1917.

Belgian army cooker – donated by the people of Manchester.

Canadian field kitchen. Photo: Library & Achives Canada.

Lune Valley Cooker.

were manufactured by Joseph Sankey & Sons Ltd from the company's factories at Bilston, near Wolverhampton and at Telford. The Lune Valley Engineering Company, Lancaster, was another manufacturer, which supplied two travelling cookers to the 8th Battalion, Sherwood Foresters, the funds to purchase them being raised by the 'ladies of Nottinghamshire'. As with the other designs, the 'Lune Valley' cooker was able to provide meals for a company of 250 men. There were two 20 gallon boilers, a stove top for frying and two ovens which were also equipped with baking dishes. They were put to good use, with the Battalion's history noting that, in late 1916, they were near the Somme village of Foncquevillers – known to the Tommies as 'Funky Villas'.

> *Fortunately the trenches were no great distance from the village, where Company cooks had their cookers, whilst the Battalion was in the line, so that hot meals were sent up regularly, and included a hot supper issued generally about midnight, the meals being mostly carried up by the Support Company.*

There were also a small number of motorised field kitchens but they were dependent on good roads being available to operate efficiently. *The Times*, in its edition of 2 April 1915, noted that one had been financed by public contributions:

The War Office has accepted from the ladies hunting with the Pytchley Hounds, the gift of a motor field kitchen, which will shortly be sent to France and attached to the division which includes the 2nd Battalion, Northamptonshire Regiment and the Northamptonshire Yeomanry. The funds for the kitchen, amounting to about £600 were collected by Lady Frederick, of Lamport Hall and Mrs H S Horne, of East Haddon, wife of Major-General Horne.

There were perks in becoming a cook. Firstly, you would be sent away on a course for a few weeks, avoiding any dangers of the front line. And, when you returned, you took up a position at the transport lines, several hundred yards behind the front line danger. Of course, you would also get first pick of any foodstuffs.

Before the war, William Taplin[22] worked as a clerk in a building firm and, in his spare time, was a Territorial soldier serving with the London Regiment. When he went overseas, in April 1916, he was attached to its 28th Battalion, known as the Artists Rifles:

I was a company cook for a year or so. I volunteered for the job because I thought there might be some advantage for me. And there was.

For one thing, I was sent on a cookery course at an Army Cookery School in a village hall well behind the lines for a month. We were taught how to cook meat, vegetables and the sort of

Photo: Diane Shakespeare.

Cooks of the 8th Lincolns, photographed before they left Britain on 10 September 1915. Private Ralph Unthank, aged 20, holds the bucket. He was killed in action sixteen days later at the Battle of Loos.

puddings that could be made from the rations we got and were possible for a company, usually sixty to eighty men, on the cooking apparatus we had. For example, if we were lucky enough to get currants, we could make plum duff, boiling it in cloths in the dixies, long ones as being easier to serve a lot of men. We were also taught how to cut up quarters of beef, whole carcasses of sheep and sides of bacon, because that's how the rations came.

The cooking apparatus with the Battalion was a "field kitchen". This consisted of a large, very strong, iron box on two large wheels. It was drawn by two draught horses. The top was pierced by four large oblong holes and there was a fire in the lower part with a firebox at the back.

There were two frying trays shaped like dixies, but only three inches deep. When we were lucky enough to get a side of bacon, we cut the rashers and fried them. We put about an inch of fat in the tray, brought it to the boil and dropped the rashers in, side by side, from one end to the other and, by the time the pan was full, started at the end to take the rashers out with a long fork.

Once a wooden crate came with our rations and, on opening it, we found it full of rabbits, frozen absolutely stiff, complete with furry skins and the innards still there. It was a most difficult and unpleasant job to prepare them for cooking.

Once, I and the other cook, went to the Quartermaster's store to draw rations and, on arriving back at our pitch, found a hole in the ground where our dixies should have been. A shell had dropped on them and blown the lot to bits.

We made tea in dixies, hanging a teabag made of muttoncloth, in which we put two to three ladles of tea into the water when it boiled. We also made porridge for breakfast and boiled rice for "pudding", both of which needed continuous stirring to prevent it getting lumpy.

If we were in rest camp, behind the line, we would roast any joints in an Aldershot Oven. The oven was made by making a heap of clay, beating it quite solid, then making a sort of tunnel in it, in which are lit a fire of wood. This we fed with wooden sticks for about three hours until the clay was very hot. Then we drew the fire, put joints of meat on trays and sealed the door with clay. After a couple of hours, the meat would be cooked. It needed a certain

*amount of experience to judge both when the oven was hot enough
and when the meat was done.*

*In addition to the meat, porridge, rice and dried fruit, our
rations included bread, vegetables, margarine, jam (Tickler's plum
and apple became a byword) and iron rations. But the rations most
looked forward to were cigarettes. They were regularly supplied in
reasonable quantities. They were specially made and packed for
the troops. I remember Ruby Queen, which I avoided, Red Hussar,
which were tolerable and, the best, Woodbines.*

Taplin's catering training in France was a relatively recent introduction,
caused by the rapid expansion of the army to meet wartime conditions.
Prior to that, all the training of cooks had taken place at the Army School
of Cookery at Aldershot. Up until the spring of 1915, it could only
accommodate a maximum of ninety students at any one time, of which
ten were undertaking a more advanced course to learn to cook for officers'
messes. Prior to the war, the course would last for four months but the new
demands meant that the training had progressively shortened to fourteen
days or twenty one days for the men preparing to cook for officers. There
were plans to double the capacity of the School during the spring and other
measures were being considered. *The Times*, in its edition of 10 March
1915, reported:

*Meanwhile work goes on at high pressure and everything possible is
done to make a man in the course of 14 days into a reasonably
competent cook for Army purposes, in the barrack or in the field.
There is not much time to spare to take the students outside the strictly
useful routine of simple dishes not difficult of attainment with army
rations – soup, baked meat, meat pies, and puddings and savoury
stews of various descriptions – curry stew, plain stew, brown stew
and Irish stew – to which are added the frying of bacon and liver and
the making of solid sweets, such as plum pudding, rice pudding, jam
rolls, currant rolls, bread pudding and so forth. For barrack cooking
the men are instructed in the use of different kinds of ranges, from
the early Deane range to the latest Richmond, adapted for either coal
or gas. But more interesting are the classes in field cookery.*

*This, of course, is done in the open air and no equipment or
utensils are furnished except what would be at hand on active
service. The men are taught how efficient ovens to cook dinner for
a company can be made of nothing but mud. If some bricks are*

handy to form the base, or a sheet of tin to be curved into the domed top of an 'Aldershot oven', so much the better. But excellent cooking is done without such advantage. Empty biscuit tins and tea canisters, filled with earth, serve well in place of bricks and the oven walls; and dinners cooked in mess tins – appetizing meat puddings and the like – and onions and potatoes baked in open ovens full of ashes. It is the actual cooking under field-service conditions and, while instructors are at hand and cooking for several companies may be going on simultaneously side by side, the dinner for a company is cooked by two men only, just as two men only would have to do it in the field. Short though the course is, experience is already showing that, under the system in use, the men pass out from it by no means ill-equipped as Army cooks. Reports on some 800 cooks who have been furnished to the New Army have all been favourable, with only one single exception and, in that case, the man was proved to be more than ordinarily competent but to be merely a shirker.

By 1918, nearly 100,000 men had been trained as cooks. Most were trained in Britain but there were also eight cookery schools on the Western Front which trained 25,277 men. A further 6000 men received their training at schools in Egypt, Italy, Salonika and Mesopotamia.[23]

The cookhouse of the Australian 57th Battalion, near Messines, Belgium, November 1917. Photo: Australian War Memorial, E01268.

Australian cookhouse. Photo: Australian War Memorial

An Australian field kitchen somewhere on the Somme battlefield, 1918. Photo: Australian War Memorial, E02297.

As well as its primary role of emergency medicine, the Field Ambulance units of the Royal Army Medical Corps had responsibilities for the general public health of the troops in their sectors. As far as possible, they would help to maintain clean water, hygienic cooking facilities, de-lousing arrangements and the like. 3rd Highland Field Ambulance took its responsibilities a stage further in June 1918, when it started to run cookery classes. Its war diary[24] notes that the first course, of five men, would last for two weeks.

> *The aim has been to train the men as cooks so that they will be able to supply their units with well cooked food, varied in character, and attractively served up. Special attention has been given to the necessity for cleanliness in person and in clothing. The use of the stock pot as well as the general need for avoiding waste have been inculcated. The sanitation of the cookhouse has been carefully explained by a Medical Officer of the Ambulance.*

The newly trained cooks would quickly gain experience in the craft of stew making. In one form or another, it would be served to the men on an almost daily basis. Colonel Frederick Foster, commanding the 2/5th Battalion, Royal Warwickshire Regiment, kept a notebook[25] detailing all the food served to the men during September 1917. They spent most of their time in billets at Watou in Belgium and Warlus in France, before returning to the trenches near Gavrelle in the final week of the month. For breakfast, they had porridge, rissoles and bacon monotonously on almost every day, except for D Company which, on the 26th, breakfasted on fried steak. For dinner on the 15th, half the Battalion ate stew with hard army biscuits, while the other half had boiled beef and peas. On the 20th, a few days before going back to the front line, there was something of a variety served to the different companies with shepherd's pie, Irish stew, roast beef and a plain stew being served, respectively to A, B, C and D Companies. For tea on most days, the men were issued with rissoles again, or bread and jam, although the B Company cooks managed to find potted beef on most days.

Things were no different for the men of the Australian 57th Battalion in April 1918, as shown by the following schedule of meals prepared for C and D Companies, for the week commencing 22 April. At the time, the men were in the reserve trenches near the French village of Aubigny.

	Breakfast	*Dinner*	*Tea*
Monday	Rissoles & tea	Stew & tea	Bread, jam, cheese, tea
Tuesday	Fried bacon & tea	Stew, pudding & tea	Veal loaf, bread, jam, & tea
Wednesday	Meat & vegetable ration & tea	Boiled beef & tea	Rissoles, bread, jam & tea
Thursday	Boiled bacon & tea	Stew, biscuit, pudding & tea	Bread, jam, butter, cheese & tea
Friday	Boiled bacon & tea	Boiled beef, potatoes & tea	Bread, jam, cheese, & tea
Saturday	Boiled bacon & tea	Boiled beef, potatoes & tea	Bread, jam, butter & tea
Sunday	Boiled bacon & tea	Boiled beef, potatoes & tea	Bread, jam, cheese & tea.

Perhaps aided by the efforts of cookery courses, the food at 3rd Highland Field Ambulance was more varied than that served to the Australians. For dinner in the week commencing 29 June 1918, patients and medical staff ate:

Sunday	– Rissoles, potatoes, pickles, boiled rice
Monday	– Scotch broth, boiled meat, rice
Tuesday	– Maconochie stew, golden pudding, tea
Wednesday	– Fried steak, gravy, potatoes, tea
Thursday	– Rissoles, potatoes, pickles, cocoa
Friday	– Stew, onions, boiled cabbage, tea
Saturday	– Mince meat, onions, potatoes, tea

Although the perks of the job probably outweighed other factors, it could be a difficult, thankless task being a battalion cook.

We moved from La Gorgue on the 26th and it rained again as usual. We were all wet through when we stopped. I was up all that night making tea for the lads as they came out of the line. We moved again on the 27th and it was no fun cooking for your own men and making tea for 1000 men and officers and having to drive your own cookhouse about. We stopped two days and moved again at night

Canadian 4th Battalion field kitchen. Photo: Library & Archives Canada.

Photo: Library & Archives Canada.

Good cooking facilities for the 2nd Field Ambulance. Photo: Library & Archives Canada.

Australian 2nd Battalion, November 1917. Photo: Australian War Memorial, E01064.

and it rained in torrents. I am about half dead with cooking all day and then at night in the saddle six or seven hours at a stretch with two spirited horses.

(Private William Binks, 1/8th Battalion, West Yorkshire Regiment. Diary entry, June 1915)[26]

Private Shallett Raggett did not think much to the efforts of the cooks in the 22nd Battalion, Royal Fusiliers. He joined up early in the war and went overseas with the Battalion on 16 November 1915. He later wrote an account of his war service:[27]

I am not a cook - I never saw anyone in the army who was. But I fancy stew was made thus: one Dixie of hot water, one piece of fat meat, one piece of string. Tie the string round the piece of meat, securely and lower it into Dixie of hot water. Pull it out. Lower it in again and continue the motion for some minutes. Result – army stew. Then make tea in same Dixie. I have frequently removed "the fat" from the top of my tea before drinking. The daily rations were usually bread (if any) – loaf between four or five; jam (always plum and apple); cheese – plenty; cold meat – a very small portion and a little fat bacon. These were issued out every day and we made our own cooking arrangements. So much for the food. Joking apart, it was as good as could be expected and could have been much worse.

Raggett was later promoted to second lieutenant, and attached to the 1st Battalion, King's Own Royal Lancaster Regiment. In the closing weeks of the war, he undertook an act of bravery which would see him awarded the Military Cross. The medal's citation reads:

For conspicuous gallantry and devotion to duty during the attack against Drocourt-Queant Line on 2nd September 1918. All the officers of another company became casualties at the first objective, so he took command of it and led it to the second objective, where he proceeded to clear dugouts. The first he entered contained forty of the enemy, with machine guns. He shot the officer, who fired a revolver at him and made the rest prisoners. At the last objective, he was the only surviving officer

*of his own company. He took command, consolidated, put out
posts and gained touch with the flanks.*

Joseph Hobson was another man who was decorated for bravery and was
also disparaging about the cooks. He had been overseas since 7 October
1914 and, in the following February wrote home to his family in
Netherthong, West Yorkshire:

> *We are close up to the firing line and as I am writing these few lines,
> the guns are booming away, but we are quite used to that now. I
> must say we are living very well, plenty to eat. We had a jam roll
> for dinner the other day, and the only fault about it was the cook
> wrapped it in the towel that we wipe the patients feet with, but he
> said he washed it well before he cooked the pudding. Of course we
> could not answer for the truth of that, but anyway it went down
> alright; those little trifles don't amount to much out at the Front!*

He was serving with 22nd Field Ambulance and, only a few days before
his letter, there was official notification that he had been awarded the
Distinguished Conduct Medal. The citation, published in the London
Gazette, records that it was *for gallant conduct in the performance of his
duties, collecting the wounded whilst under fire.*

Sergeant William Rigden arrived in France with his unit in late
November 1916. He was serving with 196th Siege Battery, Royal Garrison
Artillery. Siege batteries fired some of the heaviest weapons in the British
Army and the 196th was equipped with four 6-inch howitzers. Situated
well behind the front line, the role of the batteries was to destroy enemy
artillery emplacements or to cause maximum damage to the German
infrastructure by attacking railway depots, strongpoints or munitions
dumps. Rigden later wrote a memoir, which is held by the Liddle
Collection, University of Leeds, in which he noted that in January 1917,

> *Edge, our cook, built a trench outside our hut and placed bars of
> iron across, under which he lit a fire and thus cooked our meals.
> Although a born grouse, he was an ideal cook and heaven only
> knows how he succeeded in getting a fire and frying our bacon on
> some wet morning when he had no cover. But he always turned up
> ready with a pot of tea and crisply fried bacon and bread, ready
> before we were. The morning after a rum issue, he was particularly*

Field kitchen area. Photo: National Library of Scotland.

French field kitchen in Alsace.

*amusing for he never failed to bring an early cup of tea in the hope
that there were some 'doings' (as the rum was called) and he might
get a drop. I have often lain in bed in the morning and seen old Edge
creep in and sniff at all the cups and drain the remains of them –
nor shall I ever forget his face when we put some paraffin in
overnight. With all his faults, we could always rely on a good meal.
He was a native of Leek, Staffordshire and was about 43 and an old
soldier in every sense of the word. An expert scrounger, he could be
depended on to do down any 'quarter bloke' for extra bacon, etc.*

John Clough Hargreaves joined the army in August 1916 and was assigned to the Royal Field Artillery. His service file is one of comparatively few which survived a fire in the 1940s and, whilst it seems several pages have been lost or damaged, those that remain suggest he did not serve overseas. In civilian life, he worked as a stone mason and appears to have had a related chest complaint which probably meant he was only fit for home service duties with a reserve battery of the artillery. He trained as a cook and kept a notebook[28] during this time, recording details of the recommended procedure when establishing a new line of trenches:

> *A trench for active service can be made in a zig zag way and a dugout can be made in the trench for preparing food. A clean water tank can be let in on the side and an oven and Dixie trench can be built in the trench and the two flues [illegible] into one chimney. Mess tin cooking can be done in the same trench and the best place to make these trenches, if possible, is near to a wood, so the chimney can be taken into the wood as far as two or three hundred yards either to the right or left, so the enemy cannot exactly see where you are. There is no need for any piping to make your flue below the ground – you can cut a small trench in the ground from the fireplace to the chimney and pieces of wood or iron, about two inches wide and eighteen inches long can be placed from one side of the trench to the other about one foot apart. Pieces of tin or iron can be placed over the top then buried in with the soil if you cannot get a pipe from the chimney. This is not only good for cooking but a great help to keep you warm.*

In late 1915 or early 1916, the Army set up a new School of Cookery in the grounds of Windlesham House Preparatory School, at Portslade near Brighton. The School comprised thirty eight huts and local history records suggest that some 14000 men trained there during the war. In 1917, Walter Corney, believed to have been from the Manchester district of Chorlton, was one of them. He also kept a notebook[29] in which he recorded how meals could be prepared just using mess tins:

> *Mess tins to be thoroughly cleaned inside and out and should be well greased on the outside, the following dinners can be cooked in a mess tin – plain stew, Irish stew, meat puddings, jam roll, etc. Different methods of making a mess tin kitchen with 5, 8 or 11 mess*

tins. Place tins on ground, two each side and one on top for five mess tins, or more if required. A very small fire is required for mess tin cooking. Another method is by making a trench with two bricks and placing tins on top and is generally used for cavalry mess tins. Another method is by getting tea or biscuit tins and make some holes all round the sides to act as a brazier. While the dinners are cooking, they should be turned alternatively so that all will be well cooked. Time for cooking in mess tins – 1 ½ hours.

He noted that rations for each man were:

Stews, meat pies, etc – 9oz
Baked and roast meats – 10oz
Rissoles and sausages – 3oz
Mutton chops – 5oz.

The notebook also contains the recipe for making brown stew for 100 men:

Meat – 60lbs
Flour – 3 lbs
Onions – 3 lbs
Mixed Veg – 7 lbs
Pepper – 1oz
Salt – 2oz

Remove the meat from the bones and cut up into small cubes. Peel & cut up the onions finely. Wash, peel and scrape the mixed vegetables and cut up small. Place the flour in a mixing bowl and drop in the meat, getting it well floured. Put a little stock or water in a deep baking tin, placing the meat, onions and mixed vegetables in it and mix well together; add pepper and salt to taste and barely cover with stock or water. Then place in a hot oven to cook. Time allowed for cooking from 2 to 2 ½ hours.

The ingredients for 100 rations of rissoles, often served at breakfast, were:

Meat – 60lbs
Fat – 1lb
Bread – as required

German field kitchen. Photo: Australian War Memorial, H13410.

German troops in the Vosges mountains. Photo: Gwyneth M Roberts

German field kitchen in the Vosges. Photo: Gwyneth M Roberts.

Onions – 3lbs
Mixed herbs – 1 pckt
Flour – 3lbs
Pepper – 1oz
Salt – 2oz

And for dessert, Corney's notes suggest apple pudding was going to be his favourite:

Make paste. Peel, core and cut up apples into slices. Line sides of a 'Dean's' or 'Warren's' cooker with a portion of the paste. Place in the apples, sugar, cloves and well cover the bottom of the cooker with water, cover with remainder of paste and place in a moderate oven to cook for 2 to 2 ½ hours.

On completing his training, Walter Corney served with a battalion of the Lancashire Fusiliers until he returned to civilian life after the war.

Although cooks were usually 'back room boys', two of them were involved in one of the more bizarre incidents of the war – taking the formal surrender of Jerusalem in December 1917.

The story goes that the two men, from a battalion of the London Regiment, went off to find water to brew drinks for their officers. Another version has them looking for eggs for breakfast. Unsuccessful, they walked on until they had reached the outskirts of the city, where they were welcomed by a group of citizens, holding a white flag, led by the Mayor. The 'keys to the city' were handed over to the cooks who saluted and went back to find their unit. According to one version of the story, they were too scared to say anything to the officers until their mates urged them to do so next day. Or, alternatively, and more likely, that they told two sergeants who they encountered on outpost duty. The men are widely recorded as being Privates Albert Church and Richard Andrews of the 2/20th Battalion, London Regiment.

Albert Church.

*　*　*　*

Whilst hot food, prepared by the cooks, could be the daily ration for men in the front line, it was more often supplied when the unit was on relief in the reserve areas. On other days, the men would have to do their own cooking, almost invariably using tinned products, such as the 'meat and vegetable ration'. This was a thin stew usually comprising beef, potatoes, beans, carrots and onions, or similar vegetables. Although the War Office entered into contracts with several suppliers, perhaps as many as thirty, the most well known was Maconochie Brothers Ltd. The company was founded by Archibald and James Maconochie towards the end of the nineteenth century. Their first factory is believed to have been at Lowestoft, where trade directories in the 1890s describe the company as a manufacturer of preserved provisions. By the turn of the century, the company held lucrative contracts to supply the Army with the tinned meat

Stew again. Photo: National Library of Scotland.

and vegetable ration during the Boer War and, at about the same time, was awarded a Royal Warrant to supply the King with 'preserved fish'. By the time of the Great War, Maconochie Brothers Ltd had greatly expanded, with its headquarters in Millwall, London and several preserving and canning factories in England and Scotland. The company also made the very popular 'Pan Yan' pickle which, along with other similar products, helped to counteract the bland and repetitive army food. In May 1915, Lieutenant James Sproule, Quartermaster of the 1st Battalion, Cheshire Regiment, wrote to the *Stockport Advertiser* to thank the town's Comforts Committee for recent donations.

> *The milk was a great luxury for the milkless tea, the cocoa proved an excellent extra drink but the best favoured article was the pickles, which the men were able to eat with the preserved meat ration (in tins) which are used by the troops when on trench duty.*

Moir, Wilson & Co was another company which started out canning fish but expanded its business to producing a good quality Army meat and vegetable ration. Private Frank Richards served as a regular soldier with the Royal Welsh Fusiliers before the war and was recalled to the colours in August 1914. He later wrote,[30]

A tin of Maconochie's consisted of meat, potatoes, beans and other vegetables and could be eaten cold, but we generally used to fry them up in the tin on a fire. I don't remember any man ever suffering from tin or lead poisioning through doing them in this way. The best firm that supplied them were Maconochie's and Moir Wilson's, and we could always depend on having a tasty dinner when we opened one of their tins. But another firm that supplied them at this time must have made enormous profits out of the British Government. Before ever we opened the first tins that were supplied by them we smelt a rat. The name of the firm made us suspicious. When we opened them my suspicions were well founded. There was nothing inside but a rotten piece of meat and some boiled rice. The head of that firm should have been put against the wall and shot for the way they sharked us troops.

The troops found whatever they could in the trenches to turn into cookers to heat up the Maconochie. Some would prefer to open the tin and heat the contents in their mess tins. Others would save some time and heat the unopened tin before opening it. Once the contents had been eaten, the tins could be put to use as a cooking pot, as described by the Manual of Military Cooking:

Make small holes in the bottom of the tin and place a few clean pebbles in it. Secure some wire from hay bales, etc, and cut into skewers about an inch shorter than the preserved meat tin. Cut the meat into pieces about the size of a walnut and place on the skewers, then insert these standing on end into the preserved meat

Bacon frying in a reserve trench. Photo: National Library of Scotland.

Photo: National Library of Scotland.

Cooking dinner near Thilloy. Photo: National Library of Scotland.

tin and close down the lid. Scoop a hole about 4 ins deep into the ground and stand tin in this on some more pebbles and place the loose earth around the bottom of tin. A small fire of peat, wood or rushes, etc may then be lit around the tin and the meat will quickly cook. Season to taste. The position of the skewers in the tin should be changed from time to time. Perforating the bottom of tin and planting the end in the ground on the pebbles is necessary to carry off the superfluous fat or it would fire and destroy the ration.

Larger cookers could be made by adapting biscuit tins or oil drums with holes drilled in their sides to turn them into braziers.

About dawn, we all start lighting our little "kitchen ranges" to make tea, etc. An old tin can with holes banged through, a tiny fire of wood and charcoal is lighted inside and our mess tins placed on top. After much blowing, fanning and much swearing, the water boils and tea is made. Food follows to taste.
(CQMS Frederick Cane, 16th Battalion, London Regiment)

There were difficulties with these improvised cookers. The basic material was not too easy to find. The braziers were not very portable – an important consideration for troops spending only around three days in the trenches on a tour of duty before being relieved back to the reserve area. And, perhaps of most concern, the wood or charcoal would make smoke which was an instant give-away to the enemy of where men were and where they could be targeted by snipers, machine gunners or trench raiders. What was needed was something portable and smoke free. It came in the form of the 'Tommy Cooker'. These were not generally issued to troops but many of them arranged for their families to buy one of the various designs that were on sale in Britain and send it to them. A popular one was the "Kampite Trench Cooker" made by Bryant & May Ltd, a company more usually known for its manufacture of matches. Its price was just 6½d. There was a small, foldable stand which opened out into a triangle. This would support the soldier's mess tin. One of the six blocks of solid fuel supplied would be placed underneath and ignited. The blocks were, generally, solidified alcohol. It was very portable and with the stand measuring only 8cm x 6m when folded, it would easily slip into a pocket.

The directions for use of the Kampite were :

> *Place a block on the ground, or on a piece of metal or other non-flammable material. Open stand to form a triangle. Put stand in position, light the wick at both ends and place kettle or saucepan on stand. A block burns for fifteen minutes. "Kampite" fuel does not liquefy or evaporate and can be used almost anywhere. A single block can be carried in the pocket with perfect safety.*

In the spring of 1918, the men of the 8th Sherwood Foresters were issued with Tommy Cookers so that,

> *the men might do a little cooking for themselves in the trenches, as it was impossible to take hot meals up to them by day......they were able to make hot drinks, and warm their savoury 'Maconochies', 'Meat and Vegetables', 'Pork and Beans' and other delicacies, whilst during the night hot porridge and tea were made at Battalion Headquarters, and sent round in food containers.[31]*

The Primus Stove was much more efficient than the Tommy Cooker. It was also much more expensive and it was marketed towards officers, although groups of soldiers might well club together to buy one. The Army

"Well Alfred 'ow are the cakes?"

The Historical Touch
" Well, Alfred, 'ow are the cakes ? "

& Navy Stores, on London's Regent Street, sold a pocket version for 12/6d, advertising it in the newspapers in September 1915, along with other items of 'officers' field kit'. The popularity of them had pushed the price up to 16/6d by the following April.

Winter Quarters on the Somme
In the trenches themselves the difficulty of keeping warm is well-nigh insuperable. For fires are not allowed. It was found that whenever a waft of smoke rose from a trench fire the Germans promptly sent over mortar or shells or hand-grenades – feeling pretty sure of course, that wherever there was a fire there also would be a little knot of Tommies gathered round it. And generally,

*unfortunately, they were right. So after several little disasters due
to trench fires, they were forbidden. If hot rations could always be
carried up to the trenches things, though bad, would not be so very
bad. But hot rations are not always practicable. For no rations
could possibly be kept hot over some of the difficult and slow
journeys that have to be made between front trenches and support
trenches. When it takes your food-party six or seven hours to get to
the rear to fetch rations, you could not expect them in really cold
weather to arrive back with anything even lukewarm. Cold drink
and 'iron rations'* [canned food] *are common fare in the trenches,
and precious cold comfort they must be. Rum is served out in many
divisions and very welcome it is. But not in all, for here and there
is a general who forbids the rum ration.*

*For your three or four days spell in the trenches then, you can
generally count on a chilling time. You may suffer perishing cold
that seems to defy all the leather and all the wool that you can pile
on to your poor anatomy. One excellent little idea is gaining ground
among the men, and it is one which I think the authorities might
look upon with a fatherly eye. It is the Primus stove club-custom,
which is spreading, especially, among the richer regiments. It is
simply that three or four of your pals of a company, club together
to buy a Primus stove. It has an oil reservoir, a little hand-pump,
and a burner. You heat up the burner with some*
oil to pump up the pressure, prod the burner
holes with a pin to clear them of burnt oil, and
away goes the stove-burner into a circle of blue
flame, which roars with a pleasing little drone
of its own that is quite companionable - and not
loud enough to be overheard by Fritz in the
enemy's trench. There is no smoke at all - just
a little ring of roaring, blue flame. Very
'devilish' it looks down in the blackness of a
trench on a dark night.

Basil Clarke.

*As these stoves and the fuel for them are not an Army issue, the
trouble is to get your oil fuel up to the front line.. You may carry up
a small supply, begged, borrowed, bought, or stolen, from someone
down at your rest billets; but there is nothing like regularity of
supply and private supplies tugged up to the trenches with infinite
labour soon give out. Paraffin is the right fuel, but, it is not easy to*

get and you find daring young campaigners using petrol begged, borrowed, bought, or stolen from a friendly motor-driver 'away behind'. The Primus in a trench is invaluable, not because you can warm yourself on a cold day by its modest heat, but because you can prepare on it warm drink, and can warm up 'iron rations' so that they in their turn warm you.

One little Primus club that I came across warmed up all their tinned food before they opened it. The method is to put the food tins into water boiling on the Primus.

Bully beef, Maconochie, stew, salmon and the rest were all served hot in this club. One genius of the party heated a tin of jam, vowing that no other food was really so hot and so warming as hot jam. They dipped their spoons into the tin and ate it so hot that the tears ran down their eyes. Still you can stand heat in quantities out on the Somme.

(Basil Clarke, war correspondent, *The War Illustrated*, 20 January 1917)

It was not always easy to heat up the Maconochie tins, as reported in the *Auckland Star*, 11 December 1915:

On one occasion, I saw a party of men with a tin of Maconochie, sitting round a fire. They had no water so they put the tin on the fire just as it was. Suddenly one of them exclaimed 'Blimey, Bill, look at that tin blowin' itself out.' The tin was swelling gently in the heat. 'Ere, prick it quick', said another, 'it'll go off'. The first speaker drew his clasp knife, knocked the tin off the fire and jabbed it with the blade. There was a shrill whistle and a jet of gravy steam shot in the air. The others danced with vexation at seeing the precious stew wasted. However, there was nothing for it and nature had to take its course. When the steam had worked off, the tin was cautiously opened and the men sat down to eat what was left of their meal.

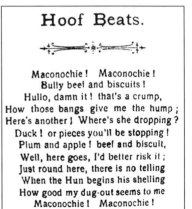

Hoof Beats.

Maconochie! Maconochie!
Bully beef and biscuits!
Hullo, damn it! that's a crump,
How those bangs give me the hump;
Here's another! Where's she dropping?
Duck! or pieces you'll be stopping!
Plum and apple! beef and biscuit,
Well, here goes, I'd better risk it;
Just round here, there is no telling
When the Hun begins his shelling
How good my dug-out seems to me
Maconochie! Maconochie!

The satirical troops' magazine, the Wipers Times. 1 May 1916.

Before the war, Sydney Hounsom worked as a secondary school teacher in Eastbourne, where his family had been involved with the resort's tourism industry for some time. John Hounsom owned a bathing machine business – wheeled 'huts' which preserved the modesty of Edwardian bathers. The bathers would enter the machine on the beach in their everyday clothes, change whilst being wheeled into the sea, and emerge in their swimming costumes. His grandfather had built the very popular Leaf Hall theatre in the town. In May 1916, Hounsom had just arrived in France with his comrades in 3 Company, 5th Battalion, Special Gas Brigade, Royal Engineers. It was one of the units responsible for firing poison gas at the Germans. He married Mary Bourne in 1912 and now wrote home to thank her for sending a Tommy Cooker.

> *I have just had a cup of OXO made by the cooker you sent. It is a most useful thing, dear.*[32] When he was not in action, Hounsom followed in his grandfather's footsteps and helped to arrange the Company's concert parties, acting as its stage manager. A few months later, he became one of the cooks. *The proud position was offered to me yesterday and I accepted it. So, this morning, I rose at 7am, helped light the fire and cut up all the bacon and helped make the tea. There was no fresh meat, so we had to make rissoles of bully, bread and onion – no light job for forty men.*

As mentioned by Hounsom, bacon would be a regular breakfast. The ration was four ounces – a couple of rashers – but there would be work to be done before cooking could start. The time around dawn was the most favoured for attacks by both sides and, in expectation that something may happen, the troops were ordered to 'Stand To Arms' each morning. For the same reason, there would be another 'Stand To' at dusk. Each soldier would be required to man his allotted position on the fire step with his rifle loaded and ready. Perhaps thirty minutes would pass by; perhaps sixty – until it became clear that there would be no enemy attack that day. The troops would then stand down and the process of cooking breakfast could start.

> *8 December – Still raining. On fatigues all day. The thing we most wanted was fresh water. I would have given anything for a glass of English water. What we had to do was get it from a shell hole and what do you think was in it? A dead German! We could see his skull.*

It was the recognised drinking place though. Of course, we had to boil it thoroughly before using and then it had a funny taste. I am now the section's cook, whilst in the trenches. Each section has to cook its own food and one man is detailed off to cook it whilst the rest are on duty. There are braziers supplied in the trenches and also fuel. It's some job getting breakfast ready for fifteen hungry men. For breakfast in the trenches we get bacon, a wee bit of bread and jam and a cup of tea. I slept a little better at night as the number was reduced to six in the shelter. I didn't get over three hours though.

(Private Ernest Holden, 20th Battalion, Royal Fusiliers)

Holden's letter home was published in the *Stockport Express* on New Year's Eve, 1915. He had been in France for a month. Earlier in the year, his older brother, George, was killed at Gallipoli serving with the 6th Battalion, Manchester Regiment. They came from a well-off family, living in the North Cheshire village of Cheadle. Before the war, they worked in the family shirt manufacturing business of Smethurst and Holden. In March 1918, Ernest Holden became an officer, serving for the remainder of the war as a Second Lieutenant with the Machine Gun Corps.

Also writing home to Stockport around this time was an unknown Territorial soldier serving with the 6th Cheshires.

We are at present on very important work behind the line – our battalion being on lines of communication - and are making the best of it. Thirty of our company [D Company] *were chosen to go further south and have now been away for two months, being billeted in a barn with beaucoup rats. We have just been treated to a tres gentil Christmas pudding which has expanded our body belts to a great extent. It must be admitted that it is rather early but it is a sure thing. Not a crumb left!*

Robert Holmes was an American who travelled to Britain at the beginning of 1916 to join the army. His account of his service[33] notes that,

I had the fondness for adventure usual in young men. I liked to see the wheels go round. And so it happened that, when the war was about a year and a half old, I decided to get in before it was too late. On second thought I won't say that it was purely love for

American Robert Holmes served as a lance corporal with 22nd Battalion, London Regiment.

adventure that took me across. There may have been in the back of my head a sneaking extra fondness for France, perhaps instinctive, for I was born in Paris.

After training, he went overseas with the 22nd Battalion, London Regiment, subsequently being promoted to Lance Corporal.

I had the job of issuing the rations of our platoon, and it nearly drove me mad. Every morning I would detail a couple of men from our platoon to be standing mess orderlies for the day. They would fetch the char and bacon from the field kitchen in the morning and clean up the 'dixies' after breakfast. The 'dixie', by the way, is an iron box or pot, oblong in shape, capacity about four or five gallons. It fits into the field kitchen and is used for roasts, stews, char, or anything else. The cover serves to cook bacon in.

Field kitchens are drawn by horses and follow the battalion everywhere that it is safe to go, and to some places where it isn't.

Two men are detailed from each company to cook, and there is usually another man who gets the sergeants' mess, besides the officers' cook, who does not as a rule use the field kitchen, but prepares the food in the house taken as the officers' mess. As far as possible, the company cooks are men who were cooks in civil life, but not always. We drew a plumber and a navvy (road builder)— and the grub tasted of both trades. The way our company worked the kitchen problem was to have stew for two platoons one day and roast dinner for the others, and then reverse the order next day, so that we didn't have stew all the time. There were not enough 'dixies' for us all to have stew the same day.

Every afternoon I would take my mess orderlies and go to the quartermaster's stores and get our allowance and carry it back to the billets in waterproof sheets. Then the stuff that was to be cooked in the kitchen went there, and the bread and that sort of material was issued direct to the men. That was where my trouble started.

The powers that were had an uncanny knack of issuing an odd number of articles to go among an even number of men, and vice versa. There would be eleven loaves of bread to go to a platoon of fifty men divided into four sections. Some of the sections would have ten men and some twelve or thirteen. The British Tommy is a scrapper when it comes to his rations. He reminds me of an English sparrow. He's always right in there wangling for his own. He will bully and browbeat if he can, and he will coax and cajole if he can't. It would be 'Hi sye, corporal. They's ten men in Number 2 section and fourteen in ourn. An' blimme if you hain't guv 'em four loaves, same as ourn. Is it right, I arsks yer? Is it?' Or, 'Lookee! Do yer call that a loaf o' bread? Looks like the A.S.C. [Army Service Corps] been using it fer a piller. Gimme another, will yer, corporal?' When it comes to splitting seven onions nine ways, I defy any one to keep peace in the family, and every doggoned Tommy would hold out for his onion whether he liked 'em or not. Same way with a bottle of pickles to go among eleven men or a handful of raisins or apricots.

*   *   *   *

In 1865, the Liebig's Extract of Meat Company was formed in Britain. Its founder, a German chemist called Justus von Liebig, had developed a concentrated extract from beef. In conjunction with a Belgian engineer, George Giebert, a manufacturing plant was established in Uruguay. The product would become known as OXO and, during the war, around 100,000,000 cubes were produced for the military.

In 1873, the company began producing tinned corned (salted) beef. It became a popular import to Britain and was sold under the name of the town where the Uruguayan factory was established – Fray Bentos. The ease with which the one pound cans could be transported made it a good choice for army rations and the company became very profitable with sales during the Boer War. The troops called it 'bully beef', believed to be an Anglicised version of the French 'boeuf bouilli' (boiled beef), dating back to the Crimean War. By 1914, Liebig's was farming five million acres of land in Uruguay and neighbouring countries and, at the outbreak of war, held large stocks of Fray Bentos corned beef, which it immediately put at the disposal of the War Office.

Perhaps the best known product was Fray Bentos but it was not the only corned beef supplied to the army. At its Annual General Meeting in 1916, the Smithfield & Argentine Meat Company recorded that it had already supplied millions of tins.

Although corned beef would be a monotonous part of the rations, the troops generally found it fine to eat. Before enlisting, Basil Miles worked as a civil servant. In April 1918, he was a gunner in the Royal Horse Artillery and wrote home to his sister, Dorrie, knowing that there was now rationing in Britain and many foodstuffs were in short supply.

> *Do you have much compressed, or as we call it, bully beef? In case you don't know, it makes jolly fine rissoles. Lots of cold bully for dinner but now the cooks have taken to mixing it, adding ham, bacon, rice, etc and it makes rather a good dish. It's certainly filling, which is a great thing to be considered nowadays. It's very seldom we get potatoes and I, for one, can do very well without them as they are always served up in their jackets and after we've got ourselves into a mess peeling them, they are often uneatable.[34]*

It was not always in good condition. In August 1917, the Quartermaster of the 1/5th Battalion, King's Own Royal Lancaster Regiment, wrote to the senior officer of 98 Company, Army Service Corps, complaining that a large percentage of corned beef that had been supplied to them was not fit for consumption. It had been packed in Colon, Argentina, according to the tin and, when opened, was found to contain a foul smelling liquid.

In November 1915, John Hodge, the Labour MP for the Gorton constituency in Manchester, visited the Western Front. He returned to tell *The Times* that there were "thousands of tins of bully beef" lying wasted and spoiled in the trenches. He attributed it to what he considered to be the overly generous daily ration of 12oz of meat per man and that there was no account of men who had become casualties and were no longer with their unit. Unsurprisingly, his views were unpopular with many people and it continued later in the war. He became Minister for Labour, taking the view that all strikes should be dealt with as acts of treason. In 1917, he threatened striking boilermakers with prosecution under the Defence of the Realm Act. There was, however, some truth to his observation that tins of food went uneaten from time to time. This may be after a major attack where the order for rations had been submitted beforehand and could not take account of the casualties. There are accounts where the tins have been used for purposes for which they were not originally intended – such as lining the floor of dug-outs. There was, certainly, a lot of tins of meat, in Belgium and France, whether Maconochie or bully beef. The New Zealand newspaper, the *Northern Advocate*, reported that in 1918, 3.5 million tins were arriving on the Western Front each week.

Also in the November, John Cathcart Wason, the Liberal MP for Orkney and Shetland, had something to say about the waste of corned beef. Wason had previously been a member of the New Zealand House of Representatives before returning to his native Scotland. In a letter to the *Daily Chronicle*, he noted that the beef supplied to New Zealand troops at Gallipoli was inedible unless cooked and, even then, it was being partially wasted. He added that the troops had made it a point of honour not to complain but that it was the cause of digestive disorders. The general diet of soldiers fighting at Gallipoli will be discussed more fully in a later chapter.

William Bird was a Canadian. Born in Nova Scotia, he joined the army on 6 April 1916 and was assigned to the 42nd Battalion (the Black Watch of Canada), Canadian Expeditionary Force. He survived the war and returned to Canada where he became a well known author, often drawing on his wartime experiences. In February 1933, the *Lethbridge Herald*, in Alberta, published the following humorous article:

The Diary of a Tin of Bully Beef

Oct. 10. At last! Am at the front. Tomorrow I shall be in the trenches, where I expect a hearty welcome. I heard someone say: 'Golly! Bully again!' Won't the chaps be pleased.

Oct. 14. Disappointed. Too many of us, so I am left behind. But Quarter says I'll be issued to new draft as iron rations.

Oct. 15. Given today to a new officer who put me in his shiny new haversack. Now in the trenches. Can hear rifle being fired. Don't like Jones, my master's servant. He dropped me on the floor while looking for matches, and said "D——d that bully."

Oct. 16. Jones tried to leave me behind when the company was relieved today, but my master caught him. We are now at rest.

Oct. 18. Jones kicked me across the tent three times while sweeping.

Oct. 19. 'Groceries' a tin can, my friend, is ill. His sugar has burst out and he has a haemorrhage of Oxo. The three biscuits who have been with me are complaining of the damp weather.

Oct. 21. We are moving to the front. Jones buried the biscuits outside the tent, and 'Groceries' is losing tea.

Oct. 22. Horrors! My master has been wounded, and Jones has deliberately abandoned me.

Oct. 30. The rats are awful but my armor protects me.

Nov. 1st. A night of horror. Was pitched bodily through the door at a rat on the parapet. Am lying in the trench gutter.

Nov. 5. Cold, dirty, disgusted, wedged now between two sandbags.

Nov. 6. Dented on one side through being used to drive a peg.

Nov. 7. Now am a door weight. Everybody kicks me.

Nov. 10. With two bricks am supporting brazier. My solder is melting.

Nov. 12. Shell explosion has shifted dugout and all. Very much shaken.

Nov. 13. The end. My corner was torn off. I see a large rat approaching....

Tanks first appeared as weapons of war in the autumn of 1916. They were very unreliable at first but improvements were made and they became much more numerous as the war continued. F41 was a Mark 4 model, nicknamed Fray Bentos. On 22 August 1917, it went forward supporting an attack by infantry during the Third Battle of Ypres, which had started on 31 July. It was able to engage an enemy machine gun post before becoming bogged down in No Man's Land. The nine man crew fought off enemy attacks for the next sixty-eight hours before the men finally abandoned it on the evening of the 24th. All surviving members of the crew received gallantry medals, perhaps evidence that corned beef tins and their contents are always difficult to deal with.

On 1 July 1916, the British Army launched a large scale attack on German positions near the French town of Albert. The offensive would continue for 142 days and, later, would be officially designated as the Battle of the Somme. On the first day, over a quarter of a million men went 'over the top' along a fourteen mile front. The attack generally failed with the British encountering unexpectedly strong German resistance. It remains the bloodiest day for casualties in the history of the Army, with nearly 20,000 men killed and many more wounded. However, on the right flank, the Pals battalions from Liverpool and Manchester captured and held their objectives, albeit with heavy losses. Ernest Grindley was serving with one of the Manchester Regiment units. Born in February 1897, he was only just old enough to be on active service with the army. He was serving under the name of Grundy and had probably joined up underage, 'hiding' from his family with the assumed name and leaving his job as a clerk with a railway company. He was interviewed in 1992,[35] recalling that he had not taken part in the actual attack:

> *That night I was given a petrol can full of drinking water in one hand and a bag of corned beef in the other. My rifle was slung over my shoulder. I had on my waist belt a Mills bomb and a pair of signal flags stuck on the back of the backpack. There were many of us taking up water to the frontline for the soldiers who had advanced. They had had no food during the advance, so those who managed to get into the German trenches needed feeding. How we managed to get the food to them in the face of all the gunfire without becoming victims was just a case of 'You were lucky, mate'.*

*   *   *   *

Lieutenant Kenneth MacArdle was not fortunate enough to receive rations being brought forward by Grindley and others. Serving with the Manchester Regiment's 17th Battalion, he had led his men forward during the morning in the successful attack on the German positions at the village of Montauban. The Pals would not be relieved until 3am on the 3rd.

MacArdle noted in his diary,

Army biscuit.

> *We held on in spite of determined counter-attacks. For 60 hours, I had no sleep and all I had eaten was a handful of prunes and two biscuits. Day and night we were shelled by heavy guns, shooting on a known target and their aim was accurate. We lost very heavily. Sproat was killed, blown to pieces and several men were buried in the trench as they were digging. In my platoon, Sgt. Butterworth was killed and four men badly wounded by a shell, reducing our numbers to four men with no NCO. And still I haven't been touched.*

The biscuits eaten by MacArdle will have been those issued to troops as emergency rations or for those times when bread could not be supplied to the men in the trenches. 'Hard tack' biscuits had originally been eaten by the Royal Navy and had formed part of Army rations for some considerable time. The ingredients were just wholemeal flour, salt and water and they were baked to be very hard. Troops likened them to dog biscuits and, with the poor state of many men's teeth at the time, they were difficult to eat. They would often be broken up, or ground to powder, and added to whatever had been supplied for dinner.

"Good news, lads, we've got a change for tea tonight." "What is it?" "Round biscuits instead of square ones". Punch, 3 October 1917.

On 12 August 1914, the well known biscuit manufacturers, Huntley & Palmer Ltd, were awarded a War Office contract to supply the product. It was to be very lucrative for the company and the factory at Reading went into continuous twenty-four hour production. By the end of March 1915, £84,000 of orders had been supplied (over £5 million at current values) and, by November 1918, this had risen to £653,000 (£34 million). It still formed only a small proportion of the company's business, amounting to 6.5 per cent of turnover. The rest remained in the production of sweet biscuits. On 12 March 1918, the King and Queen toured the company's factory at Reading, as reported the next day in *The Times*.

The tour among the biscuits occupied over an hour. Before the War, the firm made over 400 varieties; today only 50 kinds, all comparatively plain, are manufactured and a large proportion of the output goes to the troops of the Expeditionary Forces. In 1914 more than 6,000 workers, of whom one-fifth were women and girls, were employed. The total has now been reduced to 5,000 and two-fifths of this number are females. No fewer than 1,680 men have joined the forces and 106 have been killed or have died on service. The tour of the works began in a department where Army ration biscuits are made. The mechanical kneading of the Government Regulation flour, the rolling of the dough, the cutting out of the biscuits and the disappearance of the uncooked material into capacious ovens were watched. In other rooms, the King and Queen saw the putting up of small packets for the Expeditionary Forces, the manufacture of biscuits for British prisoners of war in enemy countries and the manufacture of rusks. Wherever they went, their Majesties passed through lines of cheering workpeople. The girls, wearing white overall aprons and white handkerchiefs to cover their heads, delighted in assembling along corridors which connected one department with another and they sang not only the National Anthem but 'Rule Britannia' and other patriotic songs so continuously that music and hurrahs followed the Royal party without break in their progress.

One of the company's casualties was Ronald Palmer, the nephew and adopted son of the chairman of the board of directors. He joined the company in 1912 after studying engineering at Oxford University. A keen sportsman, he had captained the England rugby team and was also an officer in the Territorial Force, serving with the 4th Battalion, Berkshire Regiment. On the night of 4/5 May 1915, Palmer was in charge of a working party, strengthening dug-outs in the Ploegsteert sector of Belgium. It was a dark night and, no doubt, he thought it would be safe to heave himself up onto the roof of the dug-out to better supervise the work. A single shot was fired by a sniper and he fell back dead.

Ronald Poulton Palmer, killed in action, 5 May 1915.

The company had several designs of biscuit during the war. The No. 4 design was about four inches square and weighed 3 ½ ounces. Three or four biscuits would form a man's daily ration. They were often eaten at tea, in the late afternoon or early evening, with the day's ration issue of jam or 'pozzy' as it was known to the troops. The origin of the slang term is unknown but, unlike many army terms of the time, it is thought it probably did not come from India. The word was in use during the Boer War and is thought to pre-date that, as possibly a corruption of an African word for sweetmeat or preserves.

As mentioned, the large tins that the biscuits were stored in could be adapted and turned into trench cookers of various levels of sophistication. But they could easily be used for other comforts, such as somewhere to sit:

> *Imagine me, then, in an overcoat splashed with mud from collar to hem; boots thickly covered with mud; puttees invisible under it, sitting on an upturned biscuit tin with a large hot potato in one hand and a big greasy hunk of hot, fat mutton in the other, biting alternatively at each, occasionally putting one or the other down on a none-too-clean sandbag in order to have a drink of some mahogany coloured stuff the cook called tea. The meal was typical of many meals.*
> (Sergeant William Allen Rigden, 196th Siege Battery, Royal Garrison Artillery, writing about his first dinner in new positions near the Belgian village of Boesinghe.)

The daily jam ration would be supplied in one pound tins and was intended to be shared amongst six men. Memoirs tend to recount that the jam was always "Tickler's Plum and Apple". T.G. Tickler Ltd was, indeed, a major jam manufacturer with premises at Pasture Street, Grimsby. For most of the war, its managing director, Thomas Tickler also served as the Unionist Member of Parliament for Greater Grimsby. In fact, there were a number of suppliers to the Army and all manufacturers supplied a range of flavours through the year depending on what fruits were in season. They included companies, such as Chivers and Robertsons, which continue to trade a hundred years later.[36] At the outbreak of war, the Wigan based company of W.R. Deakin Ltd received a contract from the War Office to supply over 300 tons of jam to the army by the end of 1914. Between the two canning factories at Wigan and Toddington, Gloucestershire, 40,000 tins a day were produced and the total contract for 700,000 one pound tins was completed on time. The company supplied the Army throughout the war, producing jams and marmalades as well as corned beef.

The Eternal Question.

" When the 'ell is it goin' to be strawberry ? "

The Things that Matter.

Scene : Loos, during the September offensive.

Colonel Fitz-Shrapnel receives the following message from "G.H.Q.":—
" Please let us know, as soon as possible, the number of tins of raspberry jam issued to you last Friday."

Sergeant Robert Johnston joined the 9th Battalion, Royal Scots towards the end of May 1915, when it was serving in the trenches near Ypres. His memoir of service is now held by the Liddle Collection, University of Leeds and includes his reminiscences of his early weeks in Belgium, mentioning the plum and apple jam.

Feeding in Sanctuary Wood was a difficult matter. Rations came up every night. The horse transport had to cross Ypres which seemed always to have several houses on fire and was constantly shelled. The ration dump was in the clearing between Zouave and Sanctuary Woods, close to Battalion Headquarters. Ration parties from the reserve and support companies brought up our rations, which travelled in sandbags, sugar and tea being in the same bag with an ineffective knot dividing the two. The rations mostly consisted of bully beef, ration biscuits (exactly like large dog biscuits) although frequently there was bread – a loaf between six men or so, cheese, plum and apple jam, tinned butter (very infrequently) and often

soup powder – mostly Symington pea soup. My clearest recollection
of this period was making pea soup, using a tobacco tin of rifle oil
as a stove with a piece of four by two (flannel for cleaning a rifle)
as a wick and taking three hours to reach the lukewarm stage at
which it could be consumed.

> *Have you heard about our ration*
> *We do live – in a fashion*
> *Tea and sugar's very scarce*
> *And the butter is even worse*
> *Maconochie's a total loss*
> *Unless you chance to win the toss*
> *A full grown navvy could devour*
> *A section's bacon in an hour*
> *The orderly man is in a fix*
> *To cut a loaf up into six*
> *And it nearly gives him fits*
> *To slice cheese in fifty bits*
> *The record up to date has been*
> *One tin of jam between sixteen*
> *We used to get served out with meat*
> *That had a smell of sweaty feet*
> *And now, the bully is no good*
> *It's just like eating lumps of wood*
> *And the biscuits – they are great*
> *We sometimes use them – as a plate*
> *Gott strafe the army and its ways*
> *When biscuits are for seven days*

T B Clark, King's Royal Rifle Corps
"Composed in the trenches, July 1915" [37]

The empty jam tins were put to good use, particularly earlier in the war, when they were converted into 'homemade' grenades by the men. They would pack the tins with bits of metal and gun cotton, fit a fuse, and seal it all with clay, before lighting it and throwing it over the parapet.

The bombers made a grenade launcher with a plank of wood, 6″
nails and some strong elastic. As soon as this started firing, the

Taking a break. Photo: National Library of Scotland.

Jerries naturally took cover. One day, our bombing sergeant decided to have some fun. Instead of grenades, he sent the Germans a succession of tinned stuff – jam, pork and beans, bully beef. After a bit, he said "Now I'll make the Germans blow their bugles for their stretcher bearers" and he sent over a live grenade. Sure enough, we could hear the German bugle blowing.

(Private Thomas Easton, 21st Battalion, Northumberland Fusiliers – quoted in The First Day on the Somme, Martin Middlebrook)

*   *   *   *

Soldiers going into the trenches would carry an 'iron ration' intended only to be eaten in emergencies when other rations could not be got to them and, even then, only on the orders of an officer. At the beginning of the war, the ration was :

Preserved meat (such as bully beef) – 1lb
Army biscuit – 12oz
Cheese – 3oz

Meat extract (such as OXO) – 2 cubes
Tea – 5/8oz
Sugar – 2oz
Salt 1/3oz

However, by the middle of 1915, rations were reduced to just the meat, biscuit, tea and sugar. In October 1916, Private Albert Bullock was serving with the 8th Battalion, Royal Warwickshire Regiment. In his diary, held by the Imperial War Museum, he notes that, on the 2nd, they went into the front line near the French village of Hébuterne. They would be in the trenches until the 5th. During this time, the men only got one meal supplied by the ration parties and had to eat their issue of 'iron rations'. He was hungry and spotted some bags of rations on top of sandbags just into No Man's Land. Taking a big chance, he climbed over and ran to get one. Finding they were tied together in twos, he grabbed both and made it back to safety unscathed. The following year, with the Warwicks now in northern Italy, he noted that hot soup was brought to the trenches every night in vacuum containers strapped on the backs of the ration party.

French troops also carried iron rations and, as with the British, they could only be eaten on the orders of an officer:

Soldiers of the French 370th Infantry Regiment in 1917.

362. - En Alsace
Nos braves Poilus à la Soupe

French troops in Alsace, in 1915, eating their lunchtime soup. Photo: Gwyneth M Roberts.

In the afternoon the lieutenant reviews each man's supplies of food: his haversack, spread open at his feet, must exhibit to the officer's vigilant eye two tins of corned beef, a dozen biscuits, two little bags containing sugar, coffee, and two tablets of condensed soup.

One of our men has neither biscuits nor corned beef. Questioning glance of the lieutenant. Evasive gesture of the man, who immediately stands at attention.

"Have you eaten your two tins of corned beef?" A sign of assent.

"Your biscuits too, naturally?" Another sign of assent.

"Ah ! And why did you eat your tins of corned beef?"

"Mon lieutenant, one evening I was hungry. . . ."

"Better and better. If the men begin to eat their reserve supplies whenever they are hungry, there will be no army left!"

That evening we laughingly relate the incident to Belin. Being an old soldier, he cannot get over it. "Eat one's reserve supplies without orders! If he had been in the Foreign Legion he would have received eight days' prison for every biscuit missing. The lieutenant was right. . . . You have your dozen biscuits and two tins, at all events? [38]

(Jacques Roujon, 352nd Infantry Regiment)

*   *   *   *

It was, generally, uncommon for men to go hungry, even with the regular difficulties and dangers of supplying them in the front line. Certainly, they complained of the monotony of the same food day after day but, for many men, the food was more than adequate. Even when there were shortages, men accepted it as a fact of army life, albeit grudgingly. Before the war, 24-year-old Victor Braund had worked as an assistant in a men's outfitters shop. After training at Aldershot, he went overseas with the 8th Battalion, Rifle Brigade, on 20 May 1915. His letters[39] to his parents in Mitcham, in south west London, show a wry humour, as this extract from one written on 2 July.

> *We are living like fighting cocks. Bully beef and biscuits and a loaf between ten men and a 1lb pot of jam between five. Oh, it's grand! I only hope I shall find a parcel for me on my return to the rest camp, so as I can have something to eat. Food is jolly scarce about here, but I suppose we must grin and bear it..*

Braund was killed in action on 30 July 1915 when the Germans attacked the Battalion's positions at Hooge, on the outskirts of Ypres. He has no known grave.

Some of the complaints reached the ears of journalists. One of them wrote about a food issue at the height of the Battle of the Somme in 1916. The unknown author had his article published in a number of newspapers, including *The Press*, the local newspaper in Canterbury, New Zealand on 13 October under the headline, "Where Goes the Pork".

> *What becomes of the pork in pork and beans? The question has puzzled thousands and the answer is now at hand and it has taken a great war to bring it out. If it hadn't been for Armageddon we might never have known. Some people suppose that cans of pork and beans contain mostly beans and little pork, for the simple reason that the pork isn't put in. This is not necessarily true: it may be sometimes, but not always.*
>
> *What becomes of the pork in pork and beans is that the beans absorb the pork. So saith the British Royal Army Medical Corps in France after analytical investigation. So the beans get the pork first and the soldier gets the pork when eating the beans – and without knowing anything about it.*
>
> *In a certain fighting organisation in France, there was an outcry from the Tommies over the missing pork. These complaints reached headquarters and, in the midst of the big push on the Somme, the soldiers were pleased to receive the following from higher up:*
>
> *Certain complaints have been received that no pork can be found in the tins and further that the ration of 1/3rd of a tin per man is insufficient. The ration has been analysed by the medical authorities with the result that it has been determined that 1/3rd of a tin contains the same nutritive as the present ration of meat. Troops must not be misled by the name Pork and Beans and expect to find a full ration of pork: as a matter of fact, the pork is practically all absorbed by the beans.*

The reply to the troops is allegedly signed by an unnamed colonel on the headquarters staff of one of the Army corps. Whilst there is something of the tongue-in-cheek in the newspaper report, the story does seem to have some basis in fact. Second Lieutenant Julian Tyndale-Biscoe, Royal Field Artillery, wrote home saying his men had complained about the lack of pork in the tins.

> *I reported this and the reply came back that the complaint was not understood since the food value was the same as the bully and the pork was absorbed in the beans.*

Canadian 8th Battalion, May 1916. Photo: Library & Archives Canada.

It was reported, in the newpapers of the time, that the tins of pork and beans had been acquired via the Canadian Pacific Railway Company and were introduced to the rations, as an experiment, in March 1916.

The German Kaiser celebrated his birthday on 27 January and, in 1915, a German attack was anticipated, almost as a birthday present for him from the army. The Stockport Territorials of the 6th Cheshires were in the trenches near to the Belgian village of Dranoutre. In the event, no attack developed, although several men were wounded during the tour of duty. Writing home to his family at 33 Russell Street, in the Heavily district of the town, 19-year-old George Dickinson recounted,

> *We had rather a rough time, when we expected an attack. There was a fierce bombardment by the artillery on both sides, but it didn't come off. We had got tea ready for the Allemans and everything prepared.– some nice potted gunpowder and some chunks of shrapnel – and then they disappointed us! Well, 'nuff said about that. I had a "nutty" time as far as grub went – what with milk, sardines, cake, tongue – blimey, living like lords!*

Another man who viewed his wartime experiences with some humour was Thomas Smith, who served with the 1/8th Battalion, Durham Light

Infantry. In 1971, he recounted his experiences in an interview, a transcript of which is held by the Liddle Collection, University of Leeds.:

> *I would say we were more comfortable in the French sector than in Belgium. The French seemed more friendly than the Belgians. If you had two or three tins of bully beef, you were alright with the French. You could get bread or a bottle of wine for a tin of beef. We did a lot of trade like that.*
>
> *We were going up one night and I put my hand up to my respirator like that and I was shot right through my hand by a sniper and that was what you had to be wary of going for rations. You used to get the lads some lovely soup. You used to boil the soup at the bases, put it into petrol cans which had never been washed out and the lads used to enjoy it. It used to put new life in them. The petrol used to make them fiery because you could taste more petrol than soup. The biscuits were so hard that you could make flags with them. We used to boil the biscuits up and make jam roly poly. We were the hardest up army in the world for rations. We could see Americans getting loaves of bread. Australians well provided with better wages and the poor old Tommy rattling away for a tanner a day and all you could get at the end, when you came out on rest, was five francs for your pay. Well, that couldn't buy you a bottle of wine. It made the lads steal. Break into estaminets and pinch. The same where we had a lad who broke in where there was a lot of pigs. He wanted to kill one – a little one – and because it started to make a noise, he said he couldn't kill the little thing.*

Shallett Raggett, serving with the Royal Fusiliers, wrote that, when away from the front line, he spent his spare time wandering round in search of extra food to supplement the bully beef and biscuits.

> *There are two words I never want to hear again. One is 'bully beef', and the other is 'Maconochie'. How I loathe these two words. They say a bull goes mad when it sees red, show me the little square tin and small round one and that bull would look sane beside me. We built a dug-out with bully beef and the following week I had a tin of it in a parcel. I would not ask a man in the army if he liked bully beef any more than I would ask him what he thought of stew.*

No dining room, but the table's still in use. Photo: National Library of Scotland.

Also on the scrounge for food was Private Frank Ridsdale.[40] In November 1917, he was a stretcher bearer, serving with the 89th Field Ambulance, Royal Army Medical Corps. Unlike the modern use of the name, the Field Ambulance was not a vehicle and the unit operated Advanced Dressing Stations and a Main Dressing Station, both staffed by army doctors, some way behind the front line. Other than a battalion's own medical officer, this would be where a wounded man would start to receive treatment, including the possibility of emergency surgery. Tanks had made their first tentative appearance in battle in September 1916, but on 20 November, they would be in massed strength. Deployed in support of a major infantry attack, the Tank Corps' full strength of 476 tanks would go into action, supporting six infantry and two cavalry divisions, south west of the French town of Cambrai. The attack started at dawn. Unlike most previous large-scale attacks by the British, this was extremely successful, breaking deeply through the German lines,

> *Saw the boys going over and the tanks in action, a splendid sight.....advanced with HQ over recaptured territory. Very few dead*

lying about. Entered Marcoing 1.30pm, after many kilometres march. Had a look round. Souvenir hunting. Brookes wounded. Many troops going up. Very tired at night – had to lie down in an old kitchen, very cold and damp but glad of a rest. Scrounged some German bread, cigars, matches, beer, coffee beans, tea, sugar, bacon, etc and had a feed. Some of the boys killed chickens and rabbits and enjoyed them. Everybody scrounging for food. Fritz shelling round the village at night.

Corporal Stapleton Eachus.

Corporal Stapleton Eachus went on active service with the Warwickshire Yeomanry – a cavalry unit of the Territorial Force – landing in Egypt on 25 April 1915. He is believed to have seen action at Gallipoli and, in 1916, was transferred to the Royal Engineers and attached to the Fourth Army Signal Office in France. It was a transfer that probably suited him well as, before the war, he had worked as a Post Office clerk. He kept a diary[41] throughout the war. As with many soldiers, his contains regular references to food:

29 July 1916 – Bully beef for breakfast this morning. The food we get here is simply abominable and, in fact, makes me ill.

31 July 1916 – On fatigues at 2pm with three others. Our work was to load a lorry with heavy logs of wood and distribute same to a number of places for cooking purposes.

16 August 1916 – For breakfast we rarely get more than a piece of bacon about 3" in length and about an inch wide. Our diet too frequently takes the form of bully beef and biscuits, now there is absolutely no reason for the greater part of all this. Hard times are only natural under war conditions and when they occur are always faced with equanimity by all the troops. But that they should exist here is inexcusable, that the men should be deliberately forbidden to buy things for themselves to fill the big gap in army rations is a crime against justice, common sense and decency.

By spring of the following year, he was still complaining about the monotony of bully beef but things did seem to be starting to improve.

3 March 1917 – Our dinner consisted of stew which was quite a change from the eternal bully beef and biscuits which had been our lot for a long time. We sadly miss vegetables though. For tea yesterday, we had one slice of bread per man and a handful of dirty currants. This is the sort of food which we have had to endure for some time now.

2 May 1917 – After dinner which was, by the way, the best that I have had for sometime – it consisted of boiled mutton, desiccated vegetables and cauliflower with bread to mix with the gravy. It was both good and liberally supplied. I walked over to Villers-Carbonnel which lies to the rear of our camp.

William Shanahan also found the food improved by 1917. Born in Llanelli in 1897, he worked in the local Co-op shop until he enlisted in the army. After the war, he returned to Wales and continued to work for the Co-op until his retirement. In a memoir,[42] written shortly before his death in 1971, he recalled his service with the 15th Battalion, Welsh Regiment – the Carmarthenshire Pals:

In late 1916 to early 1917, the ration was much more liberal. Corned beef, white bread and jam were in fair supply....Not much finesse was required to qualify as a cook. To make a hot dinner, the Dixie was filled with water. It held four or five gallons and, when piping hot, the water would have been added to a dozen or so tins of Maconochie rations. This was a tin containing already cooked

Corporal William Shanahan, 15th Battalion, Welsh Regiment – the Carmarthenshire Pals.

beef, potatoes, peas and gravy. All this was emptied into the Dixie, stirred about, then dinner was ready. Other times, we had stew made from handfuls of dried vegetables, all shredded. All this boiled away in the water, the flaked vegetables would swell and, with a good chunk of beef, that stew would have been first class for the troops. Flavour it, yes – the top of the stew would be covered with a thick film of yellow grease, but beggars cannot be choosers. Eat or go hungry, as simple as that.

Canadian Highlanders, 1916. Photo: Library & Archives Canada.

Men who kept diaries or wrote regular letters home generally went into some detail about their 'new experiences' – the first days after arriving in France, first time in action and so on. Samuel Chandley was no exception. Born in the North Cheshire village of Gatley in 1896, he had tried to join the Manchester Pals in September 1914 but had been rejected on medical grounds. However, trying again some weeks later, he was successful in enlisting into the local Territorial battalion – the 6th Cheshires and left his job working as an assistant in a local stationery shop. The Battalion went on active service in the November and Chandley trained with its reserve unit. He went overseas as part of a large group of reinforcements, leaving Britain for France on 9 May 1916.

> *12 May - We marched through the town of Rouen at about 8.30am just as people were going to business and we arrived in camp at 11 o'clock. Again we marvelled at the wonderful organisation, the British Army, as up till now we had had nothing but bully beef and biscuits since we left England so we were thankful for a good dinner and, for tea, cheese, honey and bread.*
> *14 May - I have had some mix-up dinners in my time but nothing like today. Bully and biscuits, boiled meat, potatoes boiled in*

*jackets, Maconochies, curried stew and boiled rice. They all went
down very well and I enjoyed it all with a little bread.*
(Samuel Chandley, diary entry)[43]

For most of its active service in France, the 6th Battalion had been
undertaking duties in the reserve areas and, as such, had little need for
replacement troops. As a consequence, at the end of May, this group of
reinforcements were re-assigned to other battalions of the Cheshire
Regiment and, indeed, to other Regiments. Chandley and many of his
comrades now found themselves with the Regiment's 5th Battalion – the
Territorials from Chester. His new unit was different from the old one, in
that it was a pioneer battalion. The men had been trained to fight and
carried weapons as did the other infantrymen but their main role was in
construction. They would undertake such duties as digging new trenches
or creating strongpoints in captured parts of the German line after an
attack.

Canadian Highlanders drawing rations. Photo: Library & Archives Canada.

The 5th Battalion was not a happy unit. Its commanding officer, Colonel Groves, was despised by many of his junior officers for his petty attitudes and his inclination to avoid the front line. Second Lieutenant Tom Heald recorded in his diary that he was,

> *An absolute coward* [he] *dare not go to the trenches,* [he] *also does not know his own mind. An absolute wash-out.*

Like Groves, Second Lieutenant Adrian Hodgkin was a pre-war officer serving with the Territorial Battalion. After a tour of duty in the trenches near Ypres, in the summer of 1915, the Cheshires moved back to the reserve area for a week of much needed rest. Hodgkin wrote in a letter

> *The march was a rather hectic performance: the whole of the Officers' Mess Cart was taken up with the CO's baggage and he had the grace to declare that he didn't much care a damn what happened to the Company's mess boxes....This will give a hint as to the relations existing between him and the other officers. It is a great pity, as the efficiency of the battalion is greatly affected by it.*

In October 1915, Tom Heald contrasted the daily lives of the junior officers and the men with that of Colonel Groves:

> *The CO is living in luxury. Carpets, sofas, fires and beds just the same as at home. He sits down and carves his joint and has his wine at night. No wonder he does not want to move out.*

Samuel Chandley was soon put to work building roads. The task was a vital part of the preparations for a forthcoming major attack by British and French forces on German positions near to the River Somme. It was feverish work as the deadline, although not known to the junior ranks, was less than a month away. The new roads would allow the better movement of men, artillery ammunition and other supplies to reach the forward areas.

> *3 June - Our food is excellent here. Bacon for breakfast. Good scilly [sic] for dinner. Bread, pure butter, jam, cheese and extra fine tea. Our food is far better than we had in Blighty.*
>
> *7 June – Today I had my baptism of fire and a real baptism it was too. We went in the trenches to repair a communication trench. The Allemandes were sending shells down all the time. I was sentry and nice little piece of iron went flying over my shoulder. That was my first souvenir. We were in from 9 till 4 o'clock and got back for a jolly good dinner about 4.30.*

Australians from the 22nd Battalion take a break from fatigue duties near the Somme village of Montauban in December 1916. Photo: Australian War Memorial.

A quick snack while it's quiet.

On 21 June, Chandley and the other pioneers marched to Grenat, a village about eight miles away. Here, they practiced their part in the attack on a life size model of the area around the village of Gommecourt. The main British attack would be just to the south of this position. The Cheshires and the other battalions of 56th (London) Division would attack Gommecourt as a diversionary exercise, intended to ensure that the Germans could not move troops away from this sector to assist their other comrades.

> *I am billeted in a big barn. The farm is about the size of Gatley Hill and people still live in it. We can get milk and eggs here, very cheap.*

At 7.30am on 1 July, the whistles blew and the leading battalions of the 56th Division 'went over the top'. Like Chandley, the men were serving with Territorial units, from the London area. The attack was initially successful and, as planned, the Cheshires got themselves across No Man's Land and got to work consolidating the gains – removing trench barricades

A reviving mug of tea. Photo: National Library of Scotland.

and starting to dig communication trenches. It was not long before the Germans recovered from the shock of the initial assault and started to counter-attack, supported by their own artillery. In this sector, as almost everywhere apart from the southern end of the battle, the assault had failed. The Cheshires lost forty-eight men killed in action and many more wounded. Samuel Chandley came through the day unscathed and joined the rest of his comrades, withdrawing to the village of Foncquevillers.

> *This is a better class village than the others – plenty of big houses. Plenty of gardens with red and black currants, gooseberries, raspberries and cherries. I have had plenty.*

By the end of the month, Chandley was in hospital but it was not a wound that confined him but 'trench fever'. This was an illness that baffled the army doctors. The symptoms could be varied, including those similar to typhoid and influenza or headaches, inflamed eyes and rashes. It was not until 1918 that it was established that lice were the cause. Men would usually need hospitalisation for periods ranging from a few days to a few weeks. Samuel Chandley reported sick on 27 July. *Admitted with trench fever. In till August 3. I had the time of my life there – chicken, oranges and everything.*

Men less seriously ill than Chandley, or those who had only sustained minor injuries, might be treated at a Corps Rest Station. These were units, well to the rear of the front line, to which a man might be sent if he required some continuing medical treatment that was not sufficiently serious to have him evacuated to a field hospital or a general hospital on the Channel coast. In October 1917, 3rd Highland Field Ambulance operated the Rest Station for VI Corps, at Gouy:

The work of the CRS was largely concerned with giving all these men a chance to recuperate during their stay in the back area. The patients had breakfast, dinner, tea and light supper. A large hut served as dining hall, three different sittings were held for each meal. The menu was arranged from the usual ration issue, but was supplemented by various extras such as salmon, tongue, sardines, biscuits, tapioca, rice, sugar, tea, coffee and cocoa. The light duty men got a small extra meal during the forenoon. It was quite possible to give considerable variety to the diet, which was so arranged that those getting roast one day would get stew next.
(3rd Highland Field Ambulance war diary. National Archives WO95/2859/1)

Photo: National Library of Scotland.

The three sittings would be served as follows:

    7.00am   – Porridge & milk, sausages, bread, jam, tea
    7.30am   – Bacon, bread, jam, tea
    8.00am   – Bacon, bread, jam, tea
    11.45am – Roast meat, potatoes, peas, rice, fruit
    12.15pm – Irish stew, peas, onions, rice, fruit
    12.45pm – Irish stew, peas, onions, cornflour, fruit
    4.00pm   – Bread, butter, jam, cheese, tea
    4.30pm   – Bread, butter, jam, veal loaf, tea
    5.00pm   – Bread, butter, jam, sausages, tea
    7.30pm   – Cocoa, biscuits

Patients on a light diet could expect porridge, bread, jam and tea for breakfast, followed by cocoa in the middle of the morning. There would be soup and cornflour at midday and bread, butter, jam and custard for tea.

Percy Jones' struggle with ration boxes has been recounted earlier in the chapter. He arrived in France with the other members of the 16th Londons on 1 November 1914. On the evening of the 20th, No. 2 Company, of which Jones is believed to have been a member, went into the trenches for the first time, near La Houssoie in Northern France. The Germans were 300 yards away, across No Man's Land. They relieved the Battalion's No. 1 Company which had been there since the 18th. The Battalion history notes that the men of No. 1 Company received instruction from the regular soldiers of the East Yorkshire Regiment, which included the art of keeping a charcoal fire alight in a bully beef tin and cooking a dinner over it in a mess tin.

Breakfast rations were drawn – a very good sized rasher of cold boiled bacon, two large thick army biscuits, jam for biscuit. We also have some OXO cubes from grocery rations. Priest and I worked together and made a fire for our tea and OXO. This made a pretty good breakfast.

Private A.G. Townsend, Australian 46th Battalion, May 1918. Photo: Australian War Memorial, E02185.

A dinner ration of two biscuits, 12oz bully beef and cheese was issued at midday. I found later that Mr Swainson had taken the next dug-out and Priest, as his servant, was busy making him OXO, or would have if the fire had not refused to light. However, we managed to get it good but the smoke from the damp wood produced a regular hail of bullets. Fortunately, Mr Swainson himself then turned up with some very dry wood and the OXO was pronounced a huge success by all three of us.

Tea consisted of two more biscuits and jam but we saved our tea and sugar for the morning. The second night passed without incident.

It was evident that our Saturday's bacon was a special treat, as the one we had for breakfast was so very small that I tossed a penny with Priest to decide who should have both and, of course, lost.

For dinner we had a Maconochie meat and vegetable ration in place of corned beef. The issue was one tin between two men and the contents, cooked beef, potatoes, peas, beans and carrots. The directions are to boil the tin in water for 20 minutes but, of course, this was out of the question, so we opened the tin and let the stuff stew in its own juices over a wood fire. The result was a very good hot stew, but frightfully rich and indigestible.

This chapter has concentrated on the experiences of men in the front line. But eating was, of course, the end of the story of food. The next chapter will tell something of how the food was produced and how it arrived at the front.

*   *   *   *

Devilled Sausage Pudding
(Thrift for Troubled Times, 1915)

One pound of beef sausages
One teaspoonful curry powder
Half level teaspoonful dry mustard
Salt to taste
One tablespoonful vinegar
Two pounds potatoes

METHOD
1. Remove the skin from the sausages and put the meat in a basin.
2. Mix in well the curry powder, salt, mustard and vinegar.
3. Form into a roll.
4. Cook potatoes, mash them, adding one ounce dripping and one gill milk.
5. Put a layer of potato in a pie dish and rest the sausage roll on it.
6. Put the rest of the potato on top and tuck it all round the sides
7. Cover with a piece of greased paper
8. Steam 1½ hours
9. Serve with a thickened brown gravy poured over
Sufficient for six people

Stew made of preserved meat and vegetables
(British Army Field Service Pocket Book, 1914)

Cut up the meat, removing all fat and jelly, powder up the vegetables and put them in a kettle or mess tin with water, cook until done, strain off most of the water, add meat and jelly and season with pepper, salt, and a teaspoonful of brown sugar. Put on the lid and allow to heat through, then serve. The secret of making palatable dishes with preserved meat is only to heat it through as cooking spoils it.

Macaroni Pudding
(Simple Cookery for the People, 10th edition, circa 1916)

2oz macaroni
1 pint of skim milk
1 egg
1 tablespoonful sugar
A little grated nutmeg or lemon rind
Average cost, 4d

Break the macaroni into short pieces, simmer it in the milk for ½ an hour, mix in the sugar and, when a little cool, the egg well beaten or the macaroni may be cooked separately and put straight into the pie-dish. Flavour with the nutmeg or lemon rind, put into a greased pie dish and bake for about 15 minutes.

CHAPTER 3

Supplying the Front

❖

Working behind the front line were thousands upon thousands of soldiers providing the vital supply support services that, today, we would call logistics. There were companies of Royal Engineers building and maintaining roads and railways. There were the Horse and Mechanical Transport Companies of the Army Service Corps delivering supplies to divisional dumps near the front. Other troops maintained stores or worked in specialist units such as bakery and butchery. Many thousands more came from parts of the empire or other places, such as China, and were engaged on various labouring duties. By the end of the war, no less than eleven separate labouring organizations were involved:

    South African Native Labour Corps
    Cape Boys Corps
    Egyptian Labour Corps
    Indian Labour Corps
    Chinese Labour Corps
    Fijian Labour Company
    Canadian Labour Units
    Non-Combatant Corps
    Middlesex (Alien) Infantry Labour Companies
    Russian Labour Companies
    Prisoners of War

In 1917, they were joined by the Army's Labour Corps, newly formed of men who were not sufficiently fit for combat duties. Many of them had previously served in the front line and had returned to this duty after recovering from wounds. By the end of the War, the Corps numbered some 390,000 men, almost half serving in the UK.

The supply lines on the Western Front – lines of communication in Army parlance – stretched back to the Channel ports but the supply of food for the army often started thousands of miles away. Britain had not been self sufficient in food since the early part of the nineteenth century and, by its final quarter, nearly 50 per cent of all food was being imported. The reasons were complex but partly reflected a move of people from rural agriculture to working in the new factories in urban areas. For example. the north-west town of Stockport grew from a population of 67,000 in 1861, to 160,000 over the following fifty years. In conjunction with this move, the cost of importing food plummeted in the late nineteenth century. The opening up of the American prairies meant wheat and other grains became easily available and the development of steam powered ships allowed the crop to reach Britain much more economically than in the days of sail power. Large quantities of foodstuffs, including meat, came from the British dominions of Canada, Australia and New Zealand.

William Vestey and his younger brother, Edmund, were born in the Liverpool area in the middle of the nineteenth century. Their father owned a provisions business in the city, mainly dealing in products imported from North America. The brothers joined the family firm and, still in his teens, William was sent to Chicago. There, he established a factory which canned corned beef. In 1890, he travelled to Argentina where he was able to take advantage of the newly developed refrigerator ships to send back meat to Britain. In Liverpool, the Vesteys opened a cold storage facility, which traded as the Union Cold Storage Company. Trade directories from 1900 show the facility at Banastre Street was large enough to accommodate 230,000 sheep carcasses. The company also had storage plants in Manchester and London with total capacity for another 380,000 sheep. The facilities also had separate chambers so that other products, such as cheese, fish and eggs, could be stored at optimum temperatures. By the time of the war, the company had acquired its own small fleet of refrigerated ships, which operated as the Blue Star Line. It also owned vast farmlands in Argentina and Venezuela as well as the freezing plants there. They were in an ideal position to become a major supplier to the War Office and, very quickly, their cold storage plant at Le Havre, only completed in 1913, was turned over to military use, for which the War Office would pay a fee. Further facilities at Boulogne and Dunkirk were soon constructed.

As a result of the cost of the war, in 1915, the Government introduced a Finance Bill which would increase the level of income tax. There was also a new tax on 'excess profits'. This would gain additional revenue from companies which, by the nature of their business, were profiting from the war.

The Vesteys tried to seek exemption from the provisions of the Act but, unsurprisingly, were refused. As a result, the two brothers left Britain and moved to Buenos Aires, where they remained until 1919, administering their business through offices in America. In 1922, William Vestey became a peer. Officially, it was in recognition of the company's services during the war but it was widely believed that Vestey was one of many who had purchased his peerage from Prime Minister David Lloyd George in the 'cash for honours' scandal of the time. It was said Vestey paid £20,000 (approximately £1 million at current values). It prompted the King to write a scathing letter, criticising the award to a man who, he felt, had evaded his national duty to pay taxes during the country's wartime crisis. He concluded his letter to the Prime Minister saying that the matter constituted an *evil, dangerous to the social and political well being of the State.*

With Britain so dependent on imported food, it was inevitable that German submarines would play an important part in the war. In response to a British declaration in November 1914, that the North Sea was now to be considered as a war zone, the Germans responded in February 1915.

The waters around Great Britain and Ireland, including the whole of the English Channel, are hereby declared to be a War Zone. From February 18 onwards every enemy merchant vessel encountered in this zone will be destroyed, nor will it always be possible to avert the danger thereby threatened to the crew and passengers.

Prior to this, the Germans had followed the accepted 'Rules of the Sea'. These required a submarine to surface and order a ship to stop, allowing the crew to take to their lifeboats before the vessel was torpedoed. Now, the submarines were firing their torpedoes without warning. Within weeks, Allied merchant vessel losses were exceeding 100,000 tons per month. In May 1915, the passenger liner, *Lusitania*, was sunk with the loss of many lives. The Germans claimed at the time that the ship was carrying war material and was, therefore, a fair target. It is a claim which has been substantiated in recent years. Following the international outcry, the Germans temporarily abandoned their tactic of unrestricted warfare and

The officers of SS Brodholme. *Second Engineer Denis Owens sits cross-legged on the right.*

returned to following the Rules. However, at the beginning of 1917, the Germans returned to attacking all ships, usually without any warning. During the course of the war, approximately 15,500 merchant marine seamen were killed by enemy action.

It had a serious effect on British food supply, both for the army and the civilian population at home. Between the beginning of April 1917 and the end of June, over two million tons of shipping was lost, with many neutral nations becoming reluctant to put their merchant ships to sea.

Vestey's Blue Star Line now had twelve ships in its fleet and four of them were soon to be attacked by submarines. The first was *Brodmore* which was torpedoed and sunk off the coast of Libya on 27 February 1917. She was carrying a cargo of frozen meat from Madagascar to Britain. There were no casualties and the crew were taken prisoner. The next month, on 31 March, *Brodness* was sunk near to Port Anzio in Italy, by submarine UC-38. She was on her way to Port Said. Again, there were no casualties. On 15 August, the *Brodstone* was sailing to Argentina to collect meat when she was torpedoed without warning by UB-40. Second Engineer James Walker was killed, together with four of the Chinese crew – Yee Ping, Ah Tai, Ah Yao and Ah Sing. The following year, *Brodholme* was attacked and torpedoed by UC-53 on 10 June. She was sailing from Naples to Syracuse in Sicily. The captain was able to beach her and the ship was later refloated; but four men were dead. They included another Second Engineer, Denis Owens, Fifth Engineer Ernest Fowler and two crew members, Chu Ah Ching and Ng Fook.

In the early months of the war, the responsibility for unloading supply ships arriving at the main French ports of Boulogne, Calais and Le Havre lay with the French civilian dock workers but this soon proved to be unsatisfactory, as labour was not reliably available when ships docked. The solution was to recruit British dockers and stevedores into newly formed Labour Companies of the Army

A SLOPER, Esq. M F KO M I E
(Mid Engineer Killed Out Men on Farage)

Ally Sloper.

Service Corps. The ASC was often derided by the troops in the front line for having an easy life of it. They were nicknamed 'Ally Sloper's Cavalry', after the comic strip character portrayed as a lazy schemer. Soon there were Labour Companies at each of the ports. The men continued to be supervised by their civilian foremen, now given the ranks of corporal and sergeant. The change was a great success. The operation of the ports was now controlled by the Docks Directorate of the Army Service Corps. In January 1917, the tonnage per hour being unloaded averaged 12.5 but, by September, it had more than doubled to 25.8.[44]

The quantities of food being transported were vast, as indicated by the following 1918 volumes.[45]

Biscuits	129,204,000 lbs
Margarine	52,203,000 lbs
Sugar	167,234,000 lbs
Meat and Vegetable Ration	38,262,000 tins
Preserved meat (bully beef, etc)	168,745,000 rations

The Liberal MP for Haggerston, Henry Chancellor, was something of a champion for the men of the Labour Companies, asking questions in Parliament about rumours that their rations were insufficient and that they were needing to buy additional food. On 21 August 1916, Henry Forster, the Conservative Financial Secretary to the War Office, replied that the men received the same general rations as other soldiers in France although, in fact, men in the fighting units received larger rations than those in the rear areas. Chancellor also raised a question about the *Ortolan,* a ship owned by the Pacific Steam Navigation Company. He claimed that the ship had taken on a cargo of 500 tons of potatoes at Dublin and then taken five weeks to deliver them to Dieppe. He alleged that the heat in the hold had ruined 50 per cent of the cargo and, that when the ship docked at Dieppe, the goods were off-loaded and then covered with a tarpaulin, which caused further rotting, such that when the potatoes were finally rebagged and ready to be sent to the front only 80 tons was fit for human consumption. Forster replied, dismissing Chancellor's claim and stating that the *Ortolan* had arrived in Dublin on 31 May, left on 2 June and arrived at Dieppe on the 9th and was back at Dublin on the 21st.

*   *   *   *

From the ports, meat would be taken to one of the army's Field Butchery units. These were small units – one officer and around twenty other ranks – located near to the ports. They would have the task of dressing the carcasses, skinning, gutting and preparing them for delivery to the troops in the front line. Few official records survive of the Field Butcheries but

Animal carcasses being taken for butchery. Photo: Australian War Memorial.

it is known that the expectation for each unit was to prepare enough meat for 20,000 daily rations. Even when a war diary still exists, the content is usually very sparse, as this complete entry for September 1917 for 4th Australian Field Butchery, based at Dieppe:

> The month of September, as regards the above unit, there is nothing to report. The month in question was an uneventful one, being just a continuation of many similar – doing our bit by carrying out general supply duties to No. 4 Base Supply Depot.

The butchers would usually be dealing with cattle or sheep carcasses but, in late 1917, it was decided to issue rabbits as an occasional substitute in the meat ration. These often arrived from Australia and New Zealand as frozen carcasses. Rabbit fur was popular in the garment trade for trimming coats as well as in the manufacture of gloves. It presented the War Office with an opportunity to recoup some of the costs. During the war over 5.5 million rabbit skins were sold, raising £123,000.[46] It was not the only food recycling initiative. From 1916, the army started to recycle carcass bones, together with a systematic collection of waste fats from the major camps in Britain and troop concentrations in the reserve areas in Belgium and France. These were sold to soap manufacturers who were able to extract crude glycerine from the waste products. In turn, this was resold to the Ministry of Munitions which used it as propellant in artillery shells. In 1917, approximately 1500 tons of glycerine were produced – sufficient propellant for 15 million 18-pounder shells.

The Manual of Military Cooking subsequently included a recipe for rabbit stew for one hundred men. It needed seventy pounds of rabbit, six pounds of bacon and three pounds each of flour and onions. The rabbits needed to be jointed and the bacon cut into slices.

> Clean and cut up the onions into small pieces. Place a little stock into a steaming dish and add the onions. Place 3 lbs flour, ½ oz pepper and 2 oz salt into a bowl and well mix, add the rabbit and bacon, well flouring. Next place the rabbit and bacon into the dish with the onions, barely cover with stock, stir well together, replace the lid and steam for 2 hours. If this is cooked in a camp kettle, the flour, pepper and salt should be added as a thickening agent about 30 minutes before required.

Butchers of the Australian Light Horse, probably in Egypt. Photo: Australian War Memorial, J02229.

The Manual suggests serving this with mashed potato, for which fifty pounds of potatoes would be needed.

On 15 June 1915, questions were asked in Parliament by Lancelot Sanderson, the Conservative MP for Appleby, about the training and recruitment of army butchers. Responding was the Under Secretary of State, Harold Tennant, as recorded by Hansard:

> *Mr Sanderson asked the Under-Secretary of State for War upon what principle promotion is given in the butchers' section of the Army Service Corps, at Aldershot; whether appointments to the field butcheries are now given to men who are merely cutters in preference to fully qualified butchers; and, if so, whether he will see that the services of qualified butchers are in future utilised to the full extent?*
> *Mr Tennant: 'All butchers undergo a course of field butchery instruction at Aldershot, at the end of which they are classified as to suitability for promotion. In allotting the men to units no preference is given to cutters over butchers. The services of fully qualified butchers are already utilised to the fullest possible extent.'*
> *Mr Sanderson: 'May I ask the right hon. Gentleman whether he is aware that at the present time fully qualified butchers who have*

Roadside butchery. Photo: National Library of Scotland.

given up their businesses for the purpose of assisting the State with their skilled knowledge are put on fatigue duties not connected with butchering at all, and whether he will take steps to see that their knowledge and skill are in future utilised in the best manner?'
Mr Tennant: 'Do I understand the hon. Gentleman to suggest that these men have enlisted for the purpose of being professional butchers?'
Mr Sanderson: 'Yes.'
Mr Tennant: 'If the hon. Gentleman will be so good as to give me the instance which he has in mind, I will have inquiries made.'

3rd Field Butchery was at the port of Le Havre and, amongst its men, was Staff Sergeant Arthur Matthews. Born in Stockport in about 1886, he had served his

Staff Sergeant Arthur Matthews, from Stockport. Died on Christmas Day, 1916.

butchery apprenticeship with the local Co-operative Society. Once qualified in his trade, he emigrated to America in about 1907 but returned as soon as war was declared and joined the army. He was able to keep to his trade and was soon promoted from private to his senior NCO rank. Matthews went overseas on 17 April 1915. On Christmas Day, 1916, he died from an injury which had fractured the base of his skull. There are no details of what had happened to him or, even, if this happened during the course of his work.

Away from the Western Front, butchery duties appear to have been combined with other supply functions in Lines of Communication Supply Companies. They also slaughtered live cattle, as well as dealing with frozen meat. During 1917, the 24th Company was based at Alexandria in Egypt, taking over the local abattoirs there on 4 February. Its war diary noted[47] *Frozen meat for troops being displaced by fresh local killed Sudanese cattle from 5 Feb onwards*. The writer was its commanding officer, Captain Edward Bagley. Born in London in 1877, he had worked in the Manchester area as a paid official and agent for the Conservative Party before joining the army.

Ten days later, Bagley wrote to all abattoir officers asking them to indent for more hooks if they had insufficient to hang all the meat. He told them that fresh meat must be hung up on arrival and not stacked on the floor, as was frozen meat. By the beginning of April, the Company's operations were well established and they were feeding around 28,000 people each day, including 22,495 Europeans, 209 Indians, 3,804 Egyptians (presumably from the Egyptian Labour Corps) and 2,070 refugees. On the 9th of the month, he went to inspect a consignment of condensed milk being stored at the depot at Mustapha Barracks, where he discovered that it had been sent to East Africa, in error, before arriving in Egypt and that the contents of many tins had coagulated or turned sour. He would be back at the depot in November on another inspection where he discovered that many tins of bully beef had been punctured during a faulty repacking process.

Much of the war diary is taken up with routine personnel matters and Bagley notes that on 17 April 1917, he demoted Staff Sergeant Price to corporal for drunkenness and being out without a pass. The day after Bagley had inspected the bully beef tins, there was a sad discovery. The Company's butchers are believed to have been allocated into sections and one of these was based at Sollum, near to the border between Egypt and Libya. Amongst them was 24-year-old Private Thomas Peters Lee. He had lived in Devon all his life prior to joining the army, undertaking his apprenticeship with a butcher in Exeter. For reasons not known, Thomas Lee had committed suicide by hanging himself.

Edward Bagley returned to politics as soon as he could when the war ended and was elected to Parliament in the 1918 general election for the Farnworth constituency. He was defeated at the next election in 1922.

The 25th Lines of Communication Company was also at Alexandria and its war diary contains almost nothing about its activities, recording only the movement of troops in and out of the unit, together with disciplinary and other similar matters. For example, it notes that, on 26 November 1916, Quartermaster Sergeant Henry Frost was placed under close arrest for allegedly stealing seventy-two bottles of whisky. He was convicted of the offence and sentenced to two years in prison with hard labour. It is not known if he served all of this time as his medal entitlement records indicate he was later reduced to the rank of private and transferred to the 19th Battalion, London Regiment.

Corporal Henry Wilkinson, 25th Lines of Communication Company. Died on 30 December 1917, when the troopship Aragon *was sunk outside Alexandra harbour. Before the war, Turner was a butcher, living in Chatbourn, Lancashire. His body was never recovered and identified.*

Staff Sergeant W Dean also served with the 25th Company, arriving in Egypt in November 1914. He was a married man and, fairly unusually, his wife had been allowed to accompany him, as Egypt was not regarded as a war zone at that time. They lived in married quarters at Mustapha Barracks. In late 1915, or very early 1916, the couple had a son but, sadly, he died on 16 August 1917 – an event noted in the war diary.

The men of 68th Field Butchery left Britain on 7 February 1916 and it would take them five weeks to sail to their destination of the port of Klindini in Kenya. After two weeks acclimatisation, the troops moved to Taveta, in northern Kenya on 29 March. This small town near the border between the British protectorate of Kenya and the German colony of Tanganyika had seen some fighting two weeks prior, when British forces retook the town from invading Germans. The next day, the men set up gibbets so that they could start slaughtering animals the following day,

Commenced killing. Previous to this date, killing was done by a S. African Butchery, the beasts being dressed on their hides on the ground. This was unavoidable as the S.A. Butchery was not in possession of such a complete set of equipment as issued to an Imperial Butchery. Without an attempt at flattery, I think it should be known that the comments one heard of our methods were of a commendatory nature. We made a start with 1500lbs, which increased to 4000lbs on April 6th. In addition to actual killing, there are somewhat large herds of cattle and sheep for which the Butchery is responsible. From time to time, consignments from these herds are despatched to Himo and New Mischi. The greatest difficulty experienced up to date is the language, which the various tribes of natives speak but I daresay this will be overcome as time goes on. People who are no strangers to this part of the world tell me that it is not at all easy to make themselves understood.

During the fortnight ending 15.4.1916, the average daily kill was: Cattle, 8; sheep, 20. Average weight 285.4lbs and 25.6lbs respectively.

(Lieutenant H Tomlinson, 68th Field Butchery. War diary entry – National Archives WO95/5378)

*   *   *   *

Usually working in reasonably close proximity to the butchers were the men of the Field Bakeries, also part of the Army Service Corps. Like the butchers, they each supplied a division of the army – about 20,000 men. Until the middle of 1916, each bakery comprised one officer and ninety two other ranks. For the latter part of the war, the units were amalgamated so that each bakery would supply three divisions with an increased establishment of two officers and 255 men. Fred Osborne, a regular soldier, arrived in France with 4th Field Bakery on 13 August 1914 (see Chapter 1). He is believed to have served with that unit, at Boulogne, until the reorganisation. It is then thought he served with the new 8th Field Bakery, at Dieppe, until the spring of 1918. On 21 March 1918, the Germans launched a devastatingly successful attack on the British along a wide front in France. Within hours, the Tommies were in full retreat and, within days, most of the gains of the previous two years had been lost. Many men were dead or wounded. Many others were taken prisoner. It was a desperate time, with real fears that the war would be lost. There was

8th Field Bakery, Boulogne.

8th Field Bakery's football team in 1917. Photo: Antony Osborne.

an immediate need for men and the 'back area' units were scoured for able-bodied troops, even though they might have only had their basic army training and, even then, it was some years prior. Fred was one of those who, after five years as a regular soldier baking bread, found himself an infantryman overnight. His arrival with his new unit, the 8th Battalion, Royal Berkshire Regiment, was noted in its war diary.

> *On 28th March 1918, a draft of 37 OR* [Other Ranks] *joined Battalion. These were men who had been compulsorily transferred from the ASC (bakers) and had received practically no training whatever.*

Within a month, Fred's war would be over. On or about 24 April, the Battalion was in the trenches at L'Abbe Defences, near the city of Amiens. Their position was shelled with both explosives

Fred Osborne, 8th Field Bakery. Photo: Antony Osborne.

and gas. Fred was affected by the gas and was also wounded in his left arm and it was necessary for it to be amputated.

In 1916, the *Holmfirth Express* published a poem written by a local baker, H Hubbard, then serving with 47th Field Bakery 'somewhere in France':

> *When Honour is divided, and victory is won,*
> *Don't think the only hero is the man behind the gun,*
> *What corps of men work harder than the happy ASC.*
> *With their labourers, clerks, and butchers, not to mention bakery?*
> *While Tommy's in the trenches, and Jack is on the sea,*
> *They labour at the bases, and their work is hard maybe,*
> *But you never hear them grumble, though they toil both night and day,*
> *To prepare the food for others who are fighting in the fray.*
> *The baker at the oven toils hard throughout the day,*
> *To give Tommy bread, not biscuit, to cheer him on his way.*
> *It is brought to him by transport, sometimes motor, sometimes horse,*
> *And helps to keep him happy and prevent the heavy loss;*
> *So when the boys come marching home just think of what I say,*
> *The ASC have helped to rob the Kaiser of the Day.*

Like the Field Butchery units, there is little surviving detailed documentation about the Field Bakeries. None of the war diaries remain for those British units which served on the Western Front and there is only very scant information about a handful of units which served in other theatres of the war. The Bakeries are unusual in one respect and that is they appear to be the only units in the British Army that were not commanded by fully commissioned officers. Instead, the senior rank was a Quartermaster, who held only an honorary rank of Lieutenant or Captain. Quartermasters were men who had usually been promoted from the ranks and, whilst they were considered to be 'officers and gentlemen', they would rarely be promoted further, nor would they ever be expected to lead men in combat situations.

In the early part of the war, the bakers would use an 'Aldershot Oven'. This was in kit form, weighing 374 pounds, and could be assembled quite quickly, although it would take a couple of days 'firing' before it was ready for use. The Oven had been in use by the army since the middle of the nineteenth century and each oven could bake around fifty four two-pound loaves at a time. The Army's 'Manual of Military Cooking', 1910, describes the process for setting up and using the oven.

> *Select a gentle slope on clay soil if possible and avoiding marshy or sandy ground, the mouth of the oven to face the prevailing wind, as the oven heats more quickly and the smoke is blown away from the bakers or cooks.*

British and Australian bakers, probably at Calais. Photo: National Library of Scotland.

*Bakery Work. Photo:
National Library of
Scotland.*

*The site should be cleared and smoothed and the sods should
be cut to build up the back, front and sides of the oven. The bars
are then placed over the site already prepared, the back one
overlapping the front, the back of the oven placed in position, the
plate forming the bottom of the oven is then placed against the front
portions and firmly fixed, the sods are then built round the front,
back and sides, a trench is next cut for the cook to work in, which
is 18 inches deep, 2 feet wide and 6 feet long, leaving a space of 12
inches between it and the oven. The clay or soil from the trench
being mixed with water and grass rushes, etc, to assist in binding
it is then thrown on the oven and well beaten down. The depth of
clay or earth should be at least six inches. The roof should slope
backwards slightly to carry off the rain.*

The directions for use suggest that wood should be laid in the oven each
night, so it was kept dry for lighting the next morning. Once lit, the wood
would be allowed to burn for thirty minutes before the bread dough was

Yeast stores. Photo: National Library of Scotland.

put in as, otherwise, the heat would be fierce enough to burn the top of the loaves, although if the oven was being used for roasting meat, then that could commence straight away. Once the oven was filled, the door would be fitted and wedged shut with a length of wood. The Manual suggests that improvised ovens could be constructed using the Aldershot Oven as a guide and that suitable materials would be corrugated iron, barrels or biscuit tins beaten out into the shape of an arch.

The rapidly expanding army meant that it quickly became necessary for 'proper' bakeries to be established, equipped with commercial ovens. The war diary of the 2nd Australian Field Bakery describes the unit's arrival at Calais, joining existing British Field Bakeries:

The bakery then consisted of 10 Field Bakeries and 8 Regular Bakery Sections. The arrival of the 2nd Australian Field Bakery made a total of twelve Field Bakeries at work in the one building. This was a large four storey building which had been a German paper mill before the war, now fitted out to meet the requirements of a bakery. The working of the bakery was run under the supervision of only two officers (O.C. Bakeries & O i/c Bakery) and a time serving Staff Sergeant Major, who was the Master Baker, and under whose sole direction the bakery was controlled and all details made out. This system of working proved unsatisfactory as far as the Australians were concerned who, for some reason or other, appeared to be unfavorably received by the Master Baker and the English Bakeries.

The conditions under which the men were working were very severe. Two shifts were working; the morning shift had to be marched to the bakery at 4am and very often were baking bread until 2 and 3pm in the afternoon and then had to carry the next day's requirements of flour (an average of 3000 bags) from the flour store or trucks off-loading, a considerable distance to the different dough rooms in the bakery. This very often took the men until 5 & 6pm, making a long days work of 12 & 13 hours. The afternoon shift had to march to the bakery and report to the Master Baker at 11am daily, whether he was ready for them to start work or not. This very often meant the men had to be marched back to Camp and wait until the morning shift vacated the Bakery. Another thing that caused discontent amongst the skilled practical bakers was that rigid rules were laid down as to the time and baking of doughs, etc. Although many of the senior NCOs were master bakers in civil life and could have turned out an excellent commodity, they were not allowed to exercise their discretion in the production of the baked article, although they were held responsible for the bread turned out.

It may be stated here that the Australian bakers acquitted themselves in a very capable manner. The bread manufactured by them was very creditable and their pace at work was much ahead of the English bakeries, but this was discouraged by the fact that the Master Baker, owing to his stereo-typed methods, insisted on every section waiting in the bakeries until the last section had finished, and then all the sections were marched away together. This meant the Australians often had to sit down in their damp doughy clothes and wait one or two hours.

The above remarks will suggest how essential it is, if possible, that Australian units should work separate from other Armies and under the control of their own officers. This has always been the feeling and desire of all ranks. An average output of 26,000 bread rations daily has always been maintained by the sections of the 2nd

Perkins ovens on their way to France.

> *Aust. Field Bakery and not a day has elapsed since arrival in France that this unit has not baked their days supply.*

The building was equipped with coke fired Hunt's steam ovens, with each Field Bakery unit having four large ovens, each capable of baking 150 loaves at a time, and four smaller ovens baking twenty eight loaves. In 1916, when the Australian unit arrived, the building was also fitted out with thirty nine Perkins ovens. However, these were not in use, as the Hunt equipment was meeting the needs of the 400,000 pounds of bread being produced each day by the 950 men there. The Australian war diary report continues:

> *The sections are organized in such a way that any neglect of duty, either in dough making or baking of bread can be immediately traced to the individual concerned. The dough is made on the upper floors and sent down chutes on to a table in the moulding room. The number of the section sending down the dough is called out and a man from that section carries it to the moulding table of that particular section. Each dough maker is given a certain number of doughs to mix. Each trough is numbered and the NCO in charge*

inspects the various doughs and if any neglect or bad work is discovered, the individual is warned and a complaint is entered in the 'complaint' book and, on a second entry in the book, the man is warned for orderly room.

The loaves, before being placed in the oven are 'docked', i.e. the number of the section is pricked on top of the loaf. This answers two purposes. It allows the gas to escape, when the bread is rising in the oven and, furthermore, if any bread is improperly cooked, it can be traced to the individual responsible. It is very seldom, considering the large amount of bread baked in this bakery, that any complaints are made of neglect or bad work.

By the spring of 1917, the need for fighting troops meant that consideration was being given to introducing women workers to the bakeries. They would probably be members of the Queen Mary's Army Auxiliary Corps which had just been formed. In due course, the Corps would number 57,000, of whom some 6,000 served in support positions on the Western Front. Captain John Miles, promoted from command of 2nd Australian Field Bakery to be in charge of the whole of the Calais facility, wrote to his superior officers recognising that it would be possible to replace 25 per cent of the workforce with women but *it is most undesirable to appoint women to positions of responsibility in the bakery which necessitates work of superintending and of giving detail for work to be done.*

Captain John Miles, in charge of the Calais bakers. Photo: Australian War Memorial, H00114.

Flour for the bakeries would arrive from England, being despatched by railway from the entry port, if necessary, and stored nearby. The Calais bakery used over 1,000 pounds of yeast and a supply from England would arrive daily. The railway formed a vital part of the Army's supply chain and, for the Field Bakeries at Rouen, loading was a relatively easy process, as the tracks had been laid adjacent to the breadstore. The war diary of 5th Australian Field Bakery notes that

Usually the daily output is divided amongst two trains, with an average of six to eight trucks each train. The railway line is on the

quayside and the first duty performed by the breadstore staff is the placing of the required number of trucks for the first train on the turntable and pushing them onto the siding alongside the store. The next duty is bagging the bread.

Until July 1918, the bread was put in large bags, capable of holding fifty loaves (one hundred ration portions) but there had been a change to using smaller bags, with half the capacity. This had been introduced because the increased number of 'low fitness' category men struggled to carry the large bags for any distance. However, it did not find favour with *the Australians employed on this work. The handling is exactly double, the cutting and tying of the bags is duplicated, also the carrying and packing in the trucks. It is easy to carry one of these small bags, but two, which would represent the weight of one of the former style used, would be impractical, due to bulkiness.*

The scale of the bakeries at the French ports can be imagined when it is known that the highest combined daily output during the war was 1,735,418 pounds of bread.[48]

John Miles, now an Honorary Major, had moved to Rouen by 1918 and was commanding the units, based south of the River Seine, designated as 'Bakeries South' (there was another group of field bakeries north of the River). There were thirty-six Perkins ovens, each capable of baking 150 loaves, every ninety minutes, with a daily output which averaged 64,000

Australian field bakery at Rouen. Photo: Australian War Memorial, E03460.

Bread inspection Photo: Australian War Memorial, E03489.

pounds. It was a smaller operation than at Calais but was an entirely Australian facility.

Perkins Ltd was an engineering firm located at Peterborough. For many years prior to the War it had traded as Werner, Pfleiderer & Perkins Ltd. During 1914 and the beginning of 1915 there were strong anti-German feelings in Britain, which culminated in serious disorder, after the sinking of the *Lusitania*. German owned businesses were attacked by mobs in several towns and cities. No distinction was made about companies which were owned by families which had long been naturalised in the country. Indeed, little distinction was shown between German names and those which were just 'foreign'. It prompted the company to change its name to Perkins Engineers Ltd in July 1915. A London based company, Joseph Baker & Sons Ltd, had been in negotiation with the War Office for some time, eventually persuading them to develop a more industrial approach to bread making than that offered by the Aldershot Oven. In due course, a contract was agreed and Baker entered into a partnership, sub-contracting work to Perkins. The work was divided between the two companies, with Perkins concentrating on the ovens, whilst Baker developed the ancillary equipment, such as mixers and moulders.

The Baker family were Quakers and the history of the company notes that the requirement for the factories to produce munitions as well as baking equipment did not sit well with their convictions. In 1914, Allan and Phillip Baker organised the Friends' Ambulance Unit at a Quaker centre in Buckinghamshire. Sixty Quakers were trained in ambulance duties and were quickly sent to the Ypres area. Further ambulance units were trained throughout the war, with several hundred men working overseas. The conscience of a third brother, Joseph, took him in another direction and he was commissioned as an officer in the Leinster Regiment. Rising to the rank of major, he was badly wounded in the knee. Returning to duty several months later, he was attached to the Army Service Corps, undertaking inspections of Field Bakeries.

The British 18th Field Bakery is believed to have spent 1916 in France, moving to Port Said, in Egypt, in the early weeks of 1917. Its war diary[49] for March 1917 recorded that bread production was increasing steadily, despite some minor problems with the locally built ovens. The Perkins ovens were giving no problems and average daily output was 340,306 pounds. This was three times the average amount produced in February.

On 24 March, Private Peter McGarrachie, of 18th Field Bakery, was reported missing, presumed drowned. He was acting as a conductor on a Suez Canal barge, travelling between Port Said and Kantara, some fifty kilometres south of the Port. It was, presumably, delivering supplies of bread to the troops. Reports from other troops on the barge suggested that McGarrachie had been wearing nailed boots and had slipped on the sheet iron deck of the barge, falling into the water. His body was recovered by the Port Police the next day. He was 26 and came from Ayr where, before joining the army, he had worked for Hall's Bakery.

In August, Lieutenant & Quartermaster Frederick Bear recorded that eight ovens were out of use and were being repaired and, in consequence, average daily production had dropped to 282,000. Bear was a regular soldier, going overseas to France on 14 August 1914. Born in London in about 1875, he held the rank of staff sergeant major at the outbreak of war, being promoted to the honorary rank of Lieutenant shortly after.

British and French troops landed at Salonika (now Thessalonika) in northern Greece in October 1915 with the intent of supporting Serbia, which had been attacked by a joint force of Germans, Austro-Hungarians and Bulgarians. The intervention came too late to be of any use but it was felt that there was some strategic relevance to the troops remaining. After developing the port defences, the troops advanced northwards but it was towards the end of 1916 before there were any significant offensive moves. French and Serbian forces had success at Monastir in November 1916. A second offensive, also involving British forces, took place in the spring of

German field bakery.

1917 but it had little effect on the Bulgarian defences. The front would now remain static until September 1918 when another Allied offensive was launched. This time it was successful in breaking the Bulgarian lines. Bulgaria surrendered on 30 September. The campaign was marked by more casualties coming from malaria and other illnesses than from combat.

The suburb of Lembet was on the northern outskirts of Salonika and was home to 20th Field Bakery in 1917. Another unit, 22nd Field Bakery, is thought to have been located nearby. Between the two, they supplied the bread needs of the six divisions making up the British Salonika Force.

In February 1917, 20th Field Bakery was using twenty-eight Perkins ovens and the 251 men working there were able to produce 97,000 bread rations per day. Demand had fallen by June to 78,000 rations. Of these, the war diary[50] notes that, on 3 June, 51,000 rations were sent north to the divisional railhead at Guvesne. The remaining loaves were for troops in the base area at Salonika.

*　*　*　*

As at Salonika, food arriving in France would leave the ports on its journey to the front line by rail. Once unloaded from ships, or released from the Field Bakeries and Butcheries, produce would be stored within the Base Depot at the port, being broken down into railway wagon loads. A day's

Train & horse transport. Photo: Australian War Memorial, H08746.

Potato ration. Photo: Library & Archives Canada.

production of bread would take up six wagons. For the first two years of the war, railway operations were undertaken by the French. By 1916, as the British started planning for the offensive which would become known as the Battle of the Somme, the increase in railway usage highlighted growing deficiencies in the arrangements. Rolling stock and the permanent ways were falling into disrepair and were in a very poor condition. This, coupled with the conscription of railway employees for the French army, meant that arrangements were negotiated whereby the British would take on an increased role. The new system worked well until the German spring offensive of 1918 captured land over which a number of the supply line railways ran. Fortunately, for the British, by that time the use of lorries had been much developed.

During the last two years of the war, some 80,000 loaded trains would be operated each year by the Railways Directorate of the Royal Engineers. In 1915, the British were only responsible for twenty-one kilometres of track, but this had increased to 1,384 kilometres by 1918.[51] The scale of the enterprise is shown by the number of wagon-loaded kilometres worked in the single week ending 3 October 1918 – 7,267,972. By then the Directorate had nearly 1,500 locomotives and 18,500 personnel.

Meat rations. Photo: Library & Archives Canada.

Albion lorry. Photo: Australian War Memorial, E05412.

The trains would initially deliver to the two Regulating Stations at Abbeville and Riviere-Neuve, near Calais, where the goods were reorganised into mixed loads for each army division. The construction of the Calais facility was reported to have involved the movement of 100,000 cubic metres of earth and the laying of fifty kilometres of track. From there, the trains would deliver to the Divisional Railheads, usually located about 10 – 15 miles behind the front line.

The goods would then be loaded onto the lorries of the Divisional Mechanical Transport Company of the Army Service Corps. For 39th Division, which included the Stockport Territorials of the 6th Cheshires, this would have been 374 MT Company. Like the other MT companies, it had five officers and 337 other ranks. The company operated 45 3-ton lorries and 16 30-cwt lorries.[52] The lorries would bring the supplies forward to the Divisional Refilling Point. Up to this point, the roads were in relatively good condition. As with the railways, it had been the responsibility of the French to maintain them but, from 1916 onwards, the British army took over and, by the end of the war, was maintaining nearly 4,500 miles.[53]

Movement of goods from the Refilling Point to a battalion's 'dump' behind the front line was the responsibility of the Horse Transport Companies. There were four companies assigned to each division – one for each brigade and one for divisional headquarters. Collectively, they were known as the Divisional Train. Each company had five officers and 185 other ranks. For transporting goods, they had three carts and twenty-two 'General Service' wagons. These were pulled by the company's allocation of 104 draught horses. Unladen, the wagon weighed about 18 cwt and its maximum load was 30 cwt.

Although not as dangerous as being in the front line, serving with a Horse Transport Company was not risk free. The wagons used the roads leading to the front and these were well within range of the German artillery, which could target strategic points along the route with great accuracy. During the war, nearly 9,500 men died serving with the Army Service Corps, many of them killed or fatally wounded driving the horse drawn wagons.

Unloading at Le Sars, May 1917. Photo: Australian War Memorial, E00484.

1ˢᵗ Canadian Divisional Train. Photo: Library & Archives Canada.

Canadian Divisional Train. Photo: Library & Archives Canada.

When war was declared, 20-year-old Charles Mileham Lovell was working as a woodwork machinist in Burgess Hill, Sussex. In his spare time, he was a member of the Territorial Force, serving as a wagon driver. In September 1914, he volunteered for overseas service but it was not until 28 November that he was summoned to join.

Less than a month later, he was in France, as a driver with 95th Horse Transport Company. This was the unit delivering supplies to the Headquarters of 27th Division. On 27 March 1915, he wrote home to his fiancée, Mabel Walder, telling her that they have been under heavy artillery fire, near St Eloi, for several days. He was, presumably, writing about heavy fighting at St Eloi on 14/15 March.

> *We had taken refuge in our cellar and I was supposed to take rations to advanced HQ but it was too awful to venture out, so I had to wait to see if things would quiet down a bit, but about half past ten at night, a shell caught our stables on fire and we had to turn out and get them out of it. The shells were simply pouring over. We succeeded in getting the horses into fresh stables, although it was an awful time and then I had orders to hook in and get out of the place to the Headquarters. I got ready to start after fetching my own kit out of the stables and the roads were one mass of glass and bricks from fallen houses. However, I had luck and arrived there about half past twelve.* [54]

Lovell's bravery that night, and possibly other occasions, was recognised the following year when he was awarded the Distinguished Conduct Medal

Australian horse transport company. Photo: Australian War Memorial.

for *conspicuous gallantry when taking rations under continual shellfire to advanced headquarters of the Division* (London Gazette, 11 March 1916). In November 1915, the Division moved to the Salonika theatre of the war. Lovell's service file, at the National Archives, indicates he returned to Britain on leave in December 1918, after the Armistice. On 30 December, he and Mabel got married. They had a long and, hopefully, happy life together until Mabel died in 1973. Charles died the following year.

The whole process of feeding the army had grown from supplying thousands of soldiers in 1914, to millions of them by 1918:

Highest Daily Feeding Strength[55]

1914	324,879
1915	1,148,229
1916	1,932,552
1917	2,752,633
1918	2,973,690

Highest Monthly Issues of Bread (lbs)

1914	5,974,382
1915	27,112,776
1916	46,644,610
1917	57,865,024
1918	58,717,114

There were also dramatic increases in the supply of frozen meat from the Base Depots at Boulogne and Le Havre, although each recorded the information differently. Boulogne recorded its highest monthly issue in pounds, rising from just over 1 million in 1914 to 21.5 million pounds in 1918. Le Havre recorded in numbers of meat rations issued, rather than in weight and saw a rise from the 1914 highest monthly total of 165,000 to 1,230,000 in 1918.

By the early summer of 1918, there were signs that the war might not continue into the following year. In itself, this presented some difficulties for the procurement staff at the War Office.[56] Contracts to supply food were in place and could not easily be cancelled. Deliveries were still required. For example, seven million tins of pork and beans were being

Photo: Australian War Memorial, H08492.

Divisional train. Photo: Australian War Memorial, E04263.

purchased every month from suppliers in America. There was, as yet, no sign of an armistice. However, nine months notice was given at the end of June to cancel contracts in America for the supply of condensed milk. After the Armistice, contracts were cancelled as soon as possible. In some cases, this probably involved paying penalty charges. In other cases, foodstuffs continued to be delivered but were diverted into the civilian food chain – for example, twelve million tons of tea was so diverted.

As noted earlier, horses were extensively used by the army during the war. As well as pulling supply wagons, they also pulled the guns of the Royal Field Artillery. Other horses were used by the cavalry and were ridden by infantry officers. By 1918, around half a million horses were being worked by the army. They were cared for by the Army Veterinary Corps. From time to time, it was necessary for the Corps to put down animals which had been injured or were otherwise unable to continue in service. Nearly 50,000 of them were sold to French civilian butchers as meat for human consumption, with a small number being used as food for prisoners of war. It was a profitable enterprise, realising some £640,000[57] (approximately £24 million at current prices).

*   *   *   *

From early in the conflict, troops from the Indian Army saw action on the Western Front. The dietary requirements of these troops meant that it was not possible to issue the same rations to them as eaten by the British troops. In due course, the Army would farm goats and sheep in France so that live animals could be supplied for slaughter in the approved fashion dependent on the religion of the troops being fed. However, at the beginning of the war, it was necessary to acquire the animals from civilian sources. *The Times*, in its edition of 16 November 1914, published the following article, written by an unnamed Anglo-Indian who had recently visited Boulogne, where he had seen a flock of sheep and goats driven through the streets by "Punjabi Musulmans":

> *The Gurkha, the Rajput, and other Hindus will eat goat or mutton, provided the animal has been killed in a special and orthodox way. The disgust which the strict Hindu feels at physical contact with beef is so intense that he will sometimes vomit at the sight of it; the prejudice is so inveterate that Mahomedans who are the descendants of Hindu converts cannot reconcile themselves to the*

Bread rations. Photo: Library & Archives Canada.

Pickles – an important part of an otherwise bland diet. Photo: Library & Archives Canada.

taste. Happily pork, the Moslem abomination, does not complicate the question of army rations.

But the crux is not so much the nature of the meat to be provided as the manner in which it is killed and cooked. In the case of sheep, the Sikh villager's gorge will rise when he sees meat prepared by the Mahomedan butcher, who kills by the halal, or throat-cutting stroke, just as the Mahomedan feels it an outrage that meat should be hung up for sale that has been killed by the jatka – the stroke at the back of the neck affected by the Sikhs. In France now a certain amount of tinned mutton is eaten willingly by the troops, but the great bulk of commissariat meat must be sent alive to railhead and slain there in accordance with prescribed rites. Hence the herd of sheep and goats in the boulevard. I found an old abattoir full of them – goats from all the hills of France, from Corsica and Dauphine and the Cevennes, from stony Languedoc and Rousillon on the Spanish border and bearded giants from the Pyrenees.......

.......That the men may know whether they are eating clean or unclean flesh, units are detached to a point near the railhead, when each man, be he Mohomedan, Sikh or Hindu, dispatches his beast by his own peculiar sacrificial stroke, marks it as clean and sends it on to his comrades in the trenches.

No beef is killed at the front, as the mere proximity of a Mahomedan slaughterhouse might carry pollution to the Hindus.......The Gurkha is proverbially an accommodating person and gives his British officer, with whom he is on the friendliest possible terms, as little difficulty as possible. But, in Bombay, when a regiment was embarking the question arose as to whether they would eat frozen meat. A conclave of officers decided that it would be better to put the case to the men. The Subadar was called and, after a little wrinkling of the eyebrow, said "I think, Sahib, the regiment will be willing to eat the iced sheep provided one of them is always present to see the animal frozen to death."

The meat ration for Indian Army troops, in 1914, was much less than for the British – only 4 ounces.[58] They were also issued with 4 ounces of *dhal*, in the form of dried lentils, chickpeas or beans and 1.5 pounds of *atta* (flour) from which they would have made flatbreads such as *roti* or *chapatti*, together with a small range of spices such as turmeric, garlic, chilli and ginger.

Marseilles was the Base Depot for the Indian Army troops and it received the animals ready for slaughter.[59] The highest monthly totals of sheep and goats received and processed confirm this was a large scale operation:

1914	16,537
1915	26,096
1916	6,203
1917	13,049
1918	7,833

The goat farms were established near Marseilles and at Le Grand-Quevilly, just outside the city of Rouen, on the bank of the River Seine. The animals were kept in sheds but also had attached outdoor pens. The farms were run by Indians, possibly civilians, who lived on the sites.

These were not the only examples of livestock farming on the Western Front. In early 1917, a pig farm was established near to the base camp at Étaples, on the Channel coast. The animals were fed on the men's food waste and they were kept in pens with outdoor space and shelter. It was such a success that the Directorate of Works designed and supervised the

Australian troops gather vegetables from market gardens deserted by their French owners at Camon, May 1918. Photo: Australian War Memorial, E04824.

construction of further farms at each large Army camp. Each one would have a slaughterhouse capable of processing a hundred pigs per week. At a more local level, several front line units kept chickens in their reserve areas, mainly for eggs.

A number of the more static units, along the lines of communication, had started growing vegetables quite early during the war. When 3rd Highland Field Ambulance moved to Maroeuil in 1918, it took over from a Canadian Field Ambulance unit which had been there for some time. They were one of the units which had started a vegetable garden to help supplement the rations. The Highlanders maintained the plot, planting crops in the June. The men of 192nd Siege Battery, Royal Garrison Artillery, also took up gardening after they moved to new positions south west of the Belgian village of Boesinghe in August 1917. Prior to leaving there in February 1918, the Battery's war diary indicates they spent a couple of days digging over the allotment and preparing it for planting by whichever unit was taking over the gun positions.

However, in late 1916 and early 1917, serious consideration started to be given to significantly expanding these operations. If it would prove to be a success, it would mean smaller quantities of food would need to be brought across the Channel and food could be retained in Britain to feed the civilian population.

The British Army Zone comprised some of the richest agricultural land in France, but the labour in these districts had been depleted by the calling up of men for military service. There came a time when the strain became too great for the women to carry on and the French Authorities made earnest appeals for assistance to be given by British units billeted in the vicinity of the farms.[60]

On a far larger scale, the army envisaged that 50,000 acres of French land would eventually come under British control for development for agricultural purposes, mainly growing cereals and potatoes. With assistance from the Ministry of Agriculture, a number of sites were assessed for suitability before a decision was taken to establish the farm near Roye, a town forty kilometres south-east of Amiens in the Department of the Somme. Planning continued through 1917 and, in January 1918, the War Office appointed the Earl of Radnor as Director of Agricultural Production. He inherited the peerage in 1900 while he was serving with the Army in South Africa, during the Boer War. At the time of the Great

War, he was a Brigadier General commanding the Indian Army's Dehra Dun Brigade in India between 1914 and 1917.

Work started at Roye on 2 February 1918. There were already considerable quantities of machinery on site – fifty-nine tractors, seventy-four rollers, forty harrows, fifty cultivators and thirty-three tractor ploughs. Further equipment had been landed in France and was ready for despatch to Roye. The men needed to undertake the work would come from six Agricultural Companies of the Labour Corps, each comprising one officer and 169 other ranks, and one larger Labour Company of the Corps. Each of the Agricultural Companies would farm 5,000 acres, with the Labour Company farming the remainder.

Everything went well until 21 March 1918. Nearly 7500 acres were under cultivation and double that were almost ready for planting. The German spring offensive, which was launched that day, brought everything to a halt. The advance captured much of the land taken by the British in the previous two years of war, including some 3,500 acres of the farm. As the attack petered out, the remaining farmland continued to be cultivated and made an appropriate, if much smaller than expected, contribution to

Potato growing near Béthune. Photo: Australian War Memorial, H09609.

Seaforth Highlanders gathering potatoes, Photo: National Library of Scotland.

food supplies. Towards autumn, a further attempt to develop large scale farming took place near Corbie. However, with the Armistice signed in the November, little progress was made with this project. There were similar large scale farming operations on the Salonika and Mesopotamia fronts.

Providing for yourself was not confined to growing vegetables. Units would often 'adopt' livestock which had been abandoned by Belgian and French farmers when they were obliged to leave their farms due to the war. Chickens would provide a small but regular supply of eggs but the 6th Battalion, Seaforth Highlanders went one better and kept a cow in 1915. The men were Territorials from Morayshire and had arrived in France in the May. Shortly after arrival, they took over positions from the French near the Somme village of Thiepval, as described in the Battalion history.[61]

Battalion Headquarters, in the middle of the wood, presented a beautiful sylvan aspect, boasting a little arbour with rustic table and benches for afternoon tea. The dug-outs, it is true, were not very strong, but luckily only light shells were ever fired at them and only very few of them. An excellent communication trench, afterwards named Elgin Avenue, led up from Headquarters to the

*centre of the front line. From the point of view of the Quartermaster
and the Transport Officer too, the sector was excellent. Everything
could be brought up by road to the Battalion dump near
Headquarters, from which all the companies had excellent
cookhouses sheltered from view by the convenient slope. The padre
also made his home at Battalion Headquarters, where he ran a
canteen for the men. Being Mess President, he was also made
responsible for the Battalion cow, which had been handed over to
us by the French. By day it used to graze on the meadows near the
river, while at night it came up to its own dug-out in the wood and
daily provided Battalion headquarters with fresh milk.*

The history of the 5th Seaforths also records the cow, noting that one day
she was being led down to graze when *a few bullets went over her head
so she turned, pulled the rope out of her attendant's hand, bolted for her
dug-out and absolutely refused to stir abroad for some hours after.*

In the middle of April 1915, the men of 1st Battalion, East Yorkshire Regiment, discovered a cow grazing near their trench at Ypres. William Gardiner, who joined up as a regular soldier in 1910, recalled the incident for the Regiment's journal, The Snapper, in 1926. Permission was given for the cow to be killed and Corporal Ike Croft, another regular, was called on to do the deed.

Ike shot the cow through the head but finding he hadn't killed it, he put on a field dressing and went back to the trench for more ammunition.

Another one for the pot.

The cow in the care of the 18th Battalion, Durham Light Infantry was regarded as part of the official trench stores, to be handed over to whichever new unit came into the front line sector. On 21 May 1918, the Durhams returned to the front line near the village of Caestre. During this tour of duty, the enemy shelling was heavy and there were direct hits on the front line trench and Battalion HQ, a little to the rear. A number of men were wounded, as was the cow, although the Battalion history notes that the injury, from a shell splinter, did not reduce her milk supply.

Ultimately, when things were getting too hot, as we were not likely to be able to replace her by indent if she was killed, we sent her to the Aid Post, which was not in so dangerous a place.

The German army's offensive, launched on 21 March 1918, drove the British back many miles over the following days. By the 30th, they had reached a defensive line, held by Australians, dug-in around the Somme village of Sailly-le-Sec. At about 11.30am, the men of the 42nd (Queensland) Battalion saw the Germans advancing over the crest of a hill in front of them. There were small groups of troops, closely followed by machine gun crews, who set up their weapons. Behind them, was a large body of German infantry. To reach the Australians, they would have to come down the hill slope, cross a valley and then climb another hill to the defences at Sailly-le-Sec. As the enemy massed, the German machine guns opened fire, quickly followed by the Australian guns. Fire, from both sides, was maintained for about an hour but the difference was that the Australians could shelter in their trenches whilst the Germans were in open ground. The Germans were pinned down all day, taking what shelter they could find by scraping in the ground. They took very heavy casualties until they could retire under cover of darkness.

The 42nd Battalion speaks of this fight with special memory of a mutton-stew which was brought into the firing line to at least one of the companies during the course of the fight. To the diggers, cheering and making bets with each other as they shot down the Huns, the appearance of the cook with this stew was a mighty tonic, though of tonic they needed none. The incident hinges on to the particular regard the battalions had for Sailly-le-Sec village in those days. They would have fought to the last gasp to defend it. The shooting the men had of the Huns was not the only attraction, though the position was admirably situated for that.

The departed villagers had left their sheep, rabbits, and a few cows as well in Sailly, and the result was that each company staked out its own little area in the village and appropriated as extra to rations the livestock and vegetables found in that area. The line had grilled chops and rabbit or mutton stew, such as Generals in most exalted messes never saw, and civilians in most countries beyond the zone of war would find impossible to obtain. The line had an extra breakfast at four in the morning, and an extra dinner at nine at night. They had fresh cows' milk for their tea. They regaled on succulent beefsteaks — and chuckled over them as they read in the newspapers of the Lord Mayor's appreciation of whaleflesh at a Mansion House luncheon. The result was that they worked day and night as few battalions were ever known to work. In the defence of that little valley of milk and honey they dug defence lines, support lines, switch lines, they built strong points and erected wire entanglements, and it is credibly stated that for the number of men engaged the length of line dug and wired in the time is near a record on the western front. Their patrols roamed Nomansland every night and swept it of all Germans who should as much as gaze upon this Australian valley. One battalion declares that when a brother battalion came in to relieve it, the men hid the cows in cellars, well camouflaged with debris, and milked them stealthily by night; and

*in similar dark recesses they pastured what remained of the sheep
and rabbits.*
(The Australians, their final campaign, 1918, an account of the
concluding operations of the Australian divisions in France. F.M.
Cutlack, 1919)

There was also food for free for the embattled troops on the Turkish
peninsula of Gallipoli, as recounted by Captain Frederick Walker, 2/4th
Battalion, London Regiment.[62]

*A favourite occupation when off duty was to go down to the pier off
Gully Beach and throw bread into the sea. Fish of the whiting type
came after the bread and then a Mills grenade was thrown in. The
fish were stunned by the explosion and two or three men, with the
help of a net, were sure of getting a good haul. The fish seemed to
recover after a few minutes, unless they had been actually hit by a
piece of the bomb.*

*   *   *   *

Although the vast bulk of rations were centrally supplied from Britain or
arrived direct from overseas to the Base Depot ports, there were also
significant local arrangements to purchase food in the countries where the
British Army was fighting. These arrangements were co-ordinated by the
Supplies Purchasing Department of the War Office, and much of its work
was reimbursing local unit funds for expenditure incurred, rather than
negotiating supply contracts. It was a significant operation which, during
the period of the war, amounted to the equivalent of 149,189,329 French
francs. Of this, some 90,000,000 was spent in France and Belgium, with
the remainder in the various other theatres of war. The total figure equates
to approximately £205 million at current prices.

Rowland Luther was born in Llanelly in 1895 and, prior to enlisting in
September 1914, worked as a coal miner in Bedwelty. After the war, he
wrote a memoir recounting his experiences of serving as a driver with C
Battery of the 92nd (Howitzer) Brigade, Royal Field Artillery.[63] The
Brigade had arrived in France in July 1915 and, a year later, was heavily
involved in the Battle of the Somme.

*I reported to the gun pits and was interviewed by Lt Armstrong who
said "I want you for a very special purpose. I understand you can*

speak a lot of French." "Yes, sir." "Well, I have fifty francs here and a special permit for you to be absent for 24 hours. You are to visit the village of Bray and buy all the French bread you can. You can take my horse and saddle so as not to interfere with the gun team horses, in case we want them suddenly." No-one ever questioned my credentials and I scouted this village and bought two big sacks of French loaves. They were about 18 inches long and about 6 inches in diameter. They contained no salt, so we used our own.

It is, perhaps, surprising that the young miner would be able to speak 'a lot of French' but perhaps this was in comparison to Armstrong. Three weeks later, Luther was sent off to the nearby village of Corbie with 100 francs to buy Quaker Oats which *helped our rations out during this period. Nicknamed "Bingo" and mixed with jam, it made a meal which we gobbled up at every opportunity.* Luther's recollection was slightly awry – porridge was nicknamed "burgoo" by the troops.

Also serving with the artillery was Frank Carter, a teacher born in 1892 in Sowerby, Yorkshire. He was a gunner with 160th Siege Battery, Royal Garrison Artillery. The Siege Batteries fired some of the most powerful guns in the British Army, usually howitzers of much greater calibre and destructive power than the

Gunner Frank Carter, 160th Siege Battery, Royal Garrison Artillery.

easily transportable ones used by Rowland Luther's brigade. He went overseas in 1916 and, in a quiet period in October 1918, he had time to write home telling the family that in his 'shack', he had accumulated quite a collection saved from food parcels and purchases from the Battery Canteen.

On one side, is a tin of sausages, a tin of Quaker Oats, a packet of flaked rice and a tin of condensed milk, while on the other side is a jar of honey, a packet of cream cheese and some biscuits. [64]

Although Carter's medal entitlement records indicate he was never promoted from the lowest rank of 'gunner', by 1918 he appears to have taken on responsibilities for extensive local purchase arrangements, something that would be expected to be usually undertaken by the Battery Quartermaster Sergeant.

Shopping for the Battery is quite different from shopping at home. For 120 men it consists of (1) fifty or sixty loaves of bread (2) 14 lbs of jam (3) 7 lbs margarine (4) 14 lbs cheese (5) 9 tins milk (6) 24 lbs bacon (7) 60 lbs beef (8)14 lbs sugar (9) 4 lbs tea (10) rice and oatmeal (11) potatoes and onions (12) dried vegetables and tins of cooked meat and vegetables (13) bully beef and biscuits (14) salt and pepper (15) mustard (16) coal (17) candles (18) tobacco.

I put my rations into separate bags, sometimes using one bag for two articles which require to be kept separate. For example I put my tea in a sandbag, tie it up and then put sugar in the top half. When I have got the Battery's rations I also draw them for Brigade Headquarters, whose strength is about 60. They require forage (hay and oats etc.) for their mules. I have only been doing this work for two or three days but shall soon get used to it. I made a few blunders such as putting packets of margarine on top in a bag containing tins of pork and beans, the result being that the margarine got badly knocked about and was mostly only fit for mashing potatoes. I also used the bottom half of a bag for sugar and the upper part for oatmeal but did not tie the string tight enough in the middle consequently some of the oatmeal got among the sugar so I expect we shall have porridge floating about on the top of the tea. Besides this I have the mail to see about – six bags full I had two days ago – registered letters, outgoing mail, returned letters and incoming mail provide quite good memory exercises. It is not at all a bad job but I shall not be able to stick to it when the Bombardier comes back from leave as he has been doing it now for about 2½ years. Such things as potatoes and onions are never weighed, they are simply calculated. Tea and sugar is roughly measured as well as rice and meal. On some days we get short weight owing to shortage at the Railhead whereas at other times we may get above weight. There is nothing to pay for it and a lorry to carry the stuff home. How would that suit you? Supposing you could go to Halifax in that manner. Today, after I had been round with the rations, the Brigade cooks came with a pitiful tale that they

Buying extra supplies at Étaples.

had no tea and sugar or spuds. That made me sweat for a bit as I know that I had drawn them and put them on the lorry but I afterwards found that they had gone to one of the other batteries so I got them back alright.

Sometimes the ration train comes early, sometimes late and I assure you it is no joke sharing them out in the dark in an open field. We are generally a day or two in hand so if it misses a day we make up the next. If the rations are poor or there is no mail you should see the long faces I have to meet when I get back. Today my meat was a whole sheep. If you just think of the food required for about a hundred men you will understand what marvellous organisation is required to feed the millions of men out here. If anything goes wrong we soon grumble but don't often think what a tremendous job it is to ration a modern army. Let me say just a few words about ammunition. I calculate that since we came out [in Sept 1916] our battery alone has fired at least a hundred thousand rounds of shell. That means that we have used nearly five thousand tons of steel. One battery, remember, out of thousands that are out here. Isn't it marvellous where it comes from and how we get it. I won't say any more as it may not be very interesting to you but the figures seem to me almost bewildering—

Carter returned to civilian life, as a teacher, in January 1919. Three years later, he became headmaster of Newsome National School, a post he held until he retired in 1952. He died in 1966.

*   *   *   *

Corned beef and vegetable omelette
(Housekeeping on 25/- a Week or Under,
National Food Economy League, 1915)

1 cup chopped raw onions
1 cup cold boiled potatoes, roughly chopped
1 cup cold cooked corned beef, not too finely chopped
¾ cup milk or any kind of stock

Mix all together and bind with the milk or stock. Form into a flat cake an inch thick and fry in 2oz hot dripping or margarine, browning first one side then the other. Cold chopped cabbage or other vegetable can be used instead of the onion or in addition to it.

[Author's note – the absence of egg in this "omelette" is not an error]

Preserved Meat Soup
(British Army Field Service Pocket Book, 1914)

Take four ounces of meat and half a biscuit per man with his allowance of preserved vegetables, cut up the meat, and powder the biscuit and vegetables. Put the vegetables in a camp kettle containing ½ pint of cold water per man, boil slowly and add the meat and biscuit, and continue the boiling for ½ hour, season with pepper and salt, if required, and serve. A quarter of a teaspoonful of brown sugar for each man may be added to improve the flavour.

Baked Apple Dumplings
(Simple Cookery for the People, 10th Edition, circa 1916)

6oz flour
2oz dripping
½ teaspoonful baking powder
4 apples
Moist sugar
Average cost 6d

Mix the flour, baking powder and a pinch of salt, rub in the dripping and add enough water to make a smooth paste. Peel and core the apples. Roll out the paste about a ¼ of an inch thick, cut out four rounds, each large enough to enclose an apple. Put 1 teaspoonful of moist sugar and 1 apple on each round of paste. Wet the edge of the paste, fold over until the apples are quite covered. Take care that the edges are well joined, brush over with water, sprinkle with caster sugar, place on a greased baking sheet and bake for about 25 minutes.

CHAPTER 4

Officers' Food

In March 1914, Britain's Regular Army consisted of 10,547 officers and 233,218 other ranks and the Territorial Force of 11,233 officers and 301,167 other ranks.[65] Many of the Regular Army officers were men from families which had a tradition of military service or came from the country's elite families – the aristocracy and others from the upper middle class.

Within days of war being declared on 4 August 1914, many thousands of men had joined the army and the rush to enlist continued through the next two months, as *The Times* reported on 2 September.

> *Yesterday, there were all the indications that the young men of London have been thoroughly aroused to the country's needs for their services and that a great "boom" in recruiting has set in. At all 42 stations, hundreds of young men were enlisting for the Regular Army. The scene at St Paul's Churchyard, the station for the City, was very remarkable. It was crowded all day with enthusiastic contingents of young clerks, eager to exchange the pen for the rifle and hoping they may be so lucky as to share in the adventures and risk of 'going to the front'. Over 4,000 men altogether were enrolled in London yesterday, a number far in excess of any previous day.*

By midway through the month, The Times was able to report that half a million men had enlisted and, by the end of the month, a further 250,000. This was enough men to form the equivalent of an additional 750 infantry battalions. Each one would have urgently required thirty officers – a total of 22,500. They would come almost exclusively from the middle classes and this selection process would continue until much later in the war, when casualties forced the army to commission some experienced working class soldiers.

In general, the officers would be young men, in their early to mid 20s, and, in that respect, they were similar to the mainly working class men joining up as privates. But that would be about the only similarity. With the constraints of Edwardian society, the two classes would not mix socially and would have had only scant contact on any level.

The future officers would have a remarkably similar family background. Most of their families were sufficiently financially 'comfortable' for them to employ at least one live-in servant. The author's grandfather, a fireman at a gasworks, served as a private with the 17th Battalion, Manchester Regiment – one of its Pals battalions. The Battalion went overseas at the beginning of November 1915, slightly under strength with regard to officers. Of the twenty-six officers who left Britain, it has been possible to identify eighteen of them in the 1911 Census. That shows that all but two of them came from families which employed servants.

Employing servants, even if only the one 'maid of all work', was a characteristic of Edwardian middle class life. The 1911 Census shows that the North Cheshire village of Gatley had 240 homes and, of these, forty-two of them employed servants. A tram line to Stockport opened in 1904 and, in 1909, the village railway station opened. The social character of the village was changing quickly and there were signs that it was becoming a 'dormitory suburb' with men travelling the few miles into Manchester to work in its commercial centre. Whilst some of the main income earners were wealthy company directors, most of them were working in jobs that, for the modern reader, it may be surprising to find that they would have servants. They were salesmen and buyers, estate agents and engineers, shop keepers, university lecturers, managers in commercial enterprises, as well as the village's vicar, doctor and bank manager. The census shows that there were 1.7 million people employed as domestic servants, almost all of them being women. Nearly 600,000 were employed as clerks in commercial undertakings, more than double the number in 1881. Over 80% of them were men. The differences in wealth between the middle and working classes were stark. At the beginning of the twentieth century, only people earning more than £160 per year paid income tax. Less than a million were liable for this payment of one shilling in the pound.[66] In contrast, a maid would be fortunate if she earned £25 a year, although she would usually have board and lodging provided by her employer.

Industrial workers were a little better off. At the beginning of 1914, men loading coal onto wagons, for delivery to homes in the London area, were paid at the rate of one shilling per ton and might earn 35 shillings a week. In Burnley, 40,000 people worked in the cotton mills, earning an average of two pounds a week.[67]

The new officers would generally have attended boarding school. Depending on the family income, this may have been one of the well known public schools or, alternatively, one of the many small boarding schools that opened in the latter part of the nineteenth century. They were likely to also have attended university. There, if they had shown any interest in a future career in the army, they may have joined the school or university Officer Training Corps. The Inns of Court, which housed many barristers' chambers in London, also operated an Officer Training Corps. During the war it was based at a camp at Berkhamstead, where men were given basic instruction in drill, musketry and other skills likely to be useful to them as potential future officers. In September 1914, its commander, Colonel Errington, wrote to *The Times*, saying that they had room for 200 – 300 recruits *with the proper qualification – i.e. either university or public school men or members of the Bar.*

Most of the men had been working in 'white collar' positions for commercial or governmental concerns. Others came from the education sector, either they were teachers or were still students. Many men who would later become officers had enlisted as privates into one of the so-called 'Public School Battalions' of the Royal Fusiliers. Some would receive commissions very quickly but others would see brief active service in France from late 1915 until the spring of 1916, when they also became officers and were posted to the newly formed battalions.

Geoffrey Potts typifies the young men who quickly became officers at the beginning of the war. Born in 1893, in Bolton, he was the son of William and Acksah Emily Potts. William Potts was a successful architect and his income allowed the family to employ two live-in general servants. When Geoffrey and his sisters, Jane and Barbara, were younger there was also a governess to look after them. In 1911, when a national census was taken, Potts was attending The Leys boarding school in Cambridge. It is not known what he did between the census and the beginning of the war but, on 28 September 1914, he received his commission as a Second Lieutenant and was posted to the 17th Battalion, Manchester Regiment. During the Battalion's training period, he commanded its 13 Platoon and, after qualifying as a signals instructor, also became the unit's signals officer. He went overseas at the beginning of November 1915. By the beginning of February, the Manchester Pals were at the village of Suzanne, near to the River Somme in France. They were undertaking tours of duty in the trenches, alternating with periods in reserve in billets in the village. On 10 February, Potts took over the duties of Quartermaster, following the wounding of the original postholder. It was an unusual decision by the commanding officer to move a commissioned officer to this job. Traditionally, the Quartermaster would be a man who had been a senior non-commissioned officer, such as a sergeant major, and who would be promoted with the honorary rank of Lieutenant.

Potts would often write letters home.[68] These were usually to his sister, Joan, and were often written in a "tongue in cheek" style. But, on 29 February 1916, he wrote to an unknown woman called Dorothy, with whom he was clearly very friendly.

> *This morning the Bosch did not realise that a Quartermaster was indulging in a late breakfast at 10am and, thinking everyone had had breakfast, put a shell over. I sighed as I left my untouched porridge. No more coming over in a few minutes, I returned to my porridge, finished it and was just about to tackle my bacon when again (rather near this time), I had to retire cellar-wards. In the event, I finished my bacon and was contemplating my marmalade when "crash" !!!! And some more glass in my windows was shattered. I was determined not to leave my freshly poured out cup of tea so took it with me only to be baulked by three wounded men being brought in from next door to await the stretcher bearers.*

As well as those wounded, the German shelling killed three men. Potts remained as Quartermaster until the middle of March 1917, when the Quartermaster Sergeant was promoted in accordance with the usual tradition. In a letter to Joan, he wrote that he expected to be put back in command of a platoon but nothing happened for several weeks. Towards the middle of April, the Battalion moved forward to take up positions in the front line, near to the village of Héninel, in preparation for an attack scheduled for the 23rd. It seems as though Potts was going to remain in the rear areas, along with the new Quartermaster, but he asked the Colonel to be allowed to go forward. Colonel Whitehead appointed him as his liaison officer. Whitehead later wrote to Potts' father telling him what happened next.

Lieutenant Geoffrey Potts, Manchester Regiment. Killed in action on 23 April 1917.

Geoffrey Potts grave at Wancourt British Cemetery. Photo: Author.

We attacked at dawn yesterday and the situation being somewhat obscure, I took him forward with me and two runners to make a personal reconnaissance, which was entirely successful – the information obtained was so urgent and important as I had such implicit faith in him that I sent him back to convey the result of our work to the Brigadier in person. As he was approaching my battle HQ in rear to telephone the information, he was hit in the groin by a sniper's bullet and died in the arms of the Regimental Sergeant Major a few seconds later. Before he passed away, he passed on to the RSM the most important part of my message and nobly died doing his duty. His loss is heavily felt in the Battalion and all ranks sympathise most sincerely with you in your deep sorrow. He was buried last night on the battlefield.

Captain Joseph Maclean, Scottish Rifles, was another man who enjoyed his breakfasts, even in a front line trench in the spring of 1918:

The morning breakfast was cafe au lait, bacon and sausage, bread and marmalade, which is pretty good going in a place like this. Breakfast is the best meal of the day. For dinner we have to fall back on bully beef, while tea is generally tea, bread and jam, or cheese, perhaps with sardines or something like that. Of course, everything is more of less filthy. During the night the men get stew and tea, which is brought up for them in hot food containers, and also rum, and I take a share of each.[69]

* * * *

Officers would receive the same rations as the men they commanded. There were, however, important differences. Firstly, they had a servant (a batman in later army parlance) to prepare food and undertake other 'domestic' duties, such as maintaining the officer's kit. Usually, for junior officers, a servant would attend to several officers. These were fully trained soldiers, who would undertake combat duties along with their other comrades, but would also receive a small weekly payment from the officer for looking after him. The second difference centred on the relative wealth of most officers. Parcels from home were welcomed by all soldiers. Those for the 'other ranks' might include a homemade fruit cake or chocolate but, as the war progressed and rationing was introduced, it became a strain on family resources to send food regularly. For the middle class families, there were few financial constraints and officers may well receive very regular parcels, perhaps weekly. And they were likely to contain tinned meats and vegetables that the servants could prepare for their officers. Although heavy food hampers could not be taken into the trenches they would be waiting for the officers, in the reserve area, when they finished their tour of duty. As well as receiving parcels from home, officers would have the income to be able to order food hampers from the country's premier suppliers, such as Fortnum & Mason in London, which offered a special 'war catalogue' for just such a purpose. The company's hampers would include relatively mundane items, albeit scarce in the trenches, such as tinned peaches, biscuits or French beans, along with more interesting items with which an officer might supplement his rations. They included tins of potted grouse or devilled ham. A popular item was a tin of real turtle soup.

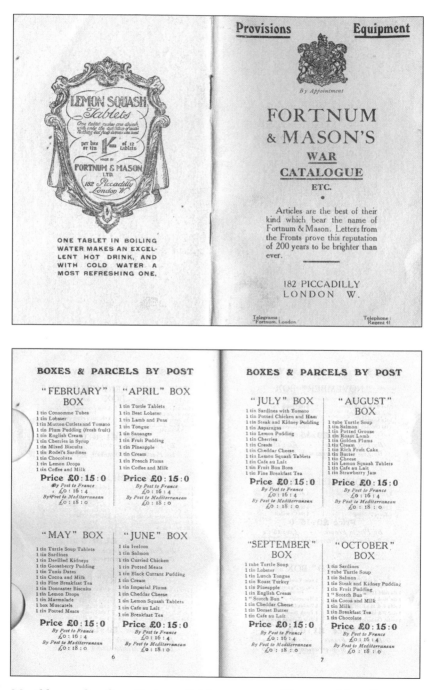

Monthly supplies from Fortnum & Mason meant officers could easily supplement their diet.

Fortnum's also sold large hampers, intended for a group of officers who had clubbed together to buy it. One box, in 1916, weighed a total of fifty six pounds and cost £3 7s 6d. Intended as a week's supply for six officers, it contained:

1 tin pressed beef	3 tins Dorset butter
1 tin soup squares	1 tin cheese
3 tins Oxford sausages	2 tins Quaker Oats
6 tins potted meats (assorted)	1 tin Bath Oliver biscuits
2 tins sardines	1 tin chocolate
1 tin salt	1 tin cakes
1 tin mustard	100 cigarettes
1 tin pepper	2 tins tobacco
1 bottle Worcester sauce	1 packet Special Stearine
1 bottle assorted pickles	2 tablets carbolic soap
1 tin blended tea	1 packet toilet paper
1 tin cocoa	1 tin apple rings
2 tins Ideal Milk	1 opening knife
4 tins jam and marmalade	

The Times, 16 May 1917.

We did supplement our rations when we could, extras like sardines and tinned fruits – pears, apricots, peaches, pineapple chunks. Otherwise we ate exactly the same rations as the men, brought up usually at night by a ration party. Of course, they didn't always

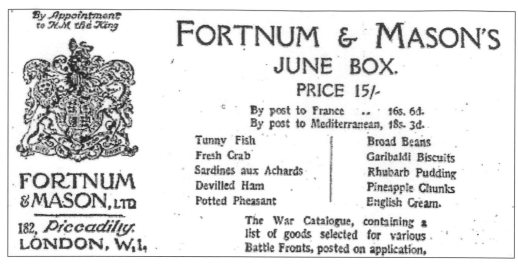

The Times, 11 June 1917.

*reach the front line. I remember once living for nearly three weeks
on bully beef and biscuits (hard square half-inch thick, as sold for
very large dogs) and jam (always plum and apple in the army).*
(Lieutenant Bernard Martin, North Staffordshire Regiment)[70]

John Reith is better known for his career after the war, when he became
the first Director General of the British Broadcasting Corporation and was
later raised to the peerage as Lord Reith of Stonehaven. However, in the
winter of 1914/1915, he was serving as a lieutenant with the 5th Battalion,
Scottish Rifles, a Territorial Battalion from Glasgow. He later wrote that
he was receiving parcels every few days:

*One evening a splendid box of candy arrived from a girl of whom I
had never heard; others followed from her at regular intervals. It was
not until the spring when, being invited to tea at my home, she
explained the mystery to my parents. Shortly after we had gone
overseas, a photograph of the officers was published in a Glasgow
newspaper. This young lady and some of her friends allocated us out
among themselves with this highly satisfactory result. I never met her.*[71]

Away from the front line, officers might head for the nearest large town in
search of entertainment and good food. Lieutenant Thomas Nash, 16th

Battalion, Manchester Regiment, went to Amiens in early March 1916. He had just finished a tour of duty in the trenches which had seen one of his men mortally wounded. *Poor Keeling was killed. A triangular piece of shrapnel had cracked the skull and chipped a large bit off, without lacerating the brain. Death was due to the exposure of the nerve centres.*[72] Once in town, he bought some duck pies and *marrons glacés*. Later in the month, he was able to return to have lunch at the Café Godbert.

> *This was a very exclusive restaurant frequented almost solely by French officers of high rank. The English usually went to feed at the Hotel du Rhin, where the food was not of the best, charges very high and service poor. At the Godbert the cooking was wonderful and every meal a work of art. It was not cheap, but it was jolly good. This particular day, I met Papa Joffre having lunch there and mine was the only British uniform in the place. He returned my salutation very graciously and gave me his left hand to shake.*

At the time, Joseph Joffre was commander-in-chief of the French Army.

On 1 August, officers of the 2nd Battalion, Royal Welsh Fusiliers also dined at the Godbert. They included the Medical Officer, Captain J C Dunn, who wrote of the day in his memoirs, published as 'The War the Infantry Knew'.

> *Dinner at the Godbert was good, even at the money, and decorous, although Colonel P, lamenting after the sweet that he had not had any dressed lobster, did get down on all-fours to stalk an unwatched dish on another table and he devoured it with help.*

The Colonel's behaviour is, perhaps, explained by Dunn's comment that, prior to the meal, they had been in every bar on or off the Rue des Trois-Cailloux.

Most of the equipment for the officers' dining arrangements when the battalion was in the rear area was carried on its own wagon, or mess cart. This was generally equipped with twelve camp kettles, enamelled plates and cups, knives, forks and spoons for thirty-five officers and three mess staff. Regulations stated that whilst these would come as army issue, any additional equipment must be arranged by the individual units. Captain Gerald Burgoyne and his officer comrades in the Royal Irish Rifles clubbed together in April 1915.

my platoon of sixty men was issued with a solitary loaf of bread a
week, the rest of the ration being made up with biscuits. The usual
procedure was to fill a mess tin with the very, very scarce drinking
water, bring it to the boil on the brazier and then add the very hard
biscuits. When there was a nice porridgy consistency we stabbed
open a tin of Tickler's jam, called 'pozzy' and mixed it all together.
This was then eaten with a spoon and was usually accompanied by
some cold slices of corned beef.[74]

The brazier could be something of a double-edged sword as men
scavenged any pieces of wood they could find in the trenches:

The wooden crosspieces of the duckboards and the boarding of the
hurdles burned well and, once the discovery was made that these
materials could be prised off, they quickly disappeared. Little could
be done to stop these depredations to which blind eyes were turned.
No one would admit responsibility. It was worse in severe frosts.
'You won't suffer for this as long as the cold spell lasts', people

Officers having breakfast near Pozières. Photo: Australian War Memorial,
EZ0075.

An officers' dug-out.

would be told, 'but after the next thaw these trenches will be impassable and you will have casualties on the top.' And so they did. But not necessarily those who despoiled the revetments. (Lieutenant Carlos Blacker, 4th Battalion, Coldstream Guards[75])

Lieutenant George McGowan, 5th Cheshires, also enjoyed the efforts of his servant as noted in a letter home, on 10 May 1915:

I received the parcel the first night here and very acceptable it was. Thanks to it and some of the grub I had left, out of the last, Bass & I have had some excellent meals out here in the open. The crab by the way was delicious. Not the least bit thirst provoking, quite the reverse in fact. We are going to have some of the Huns' beans tonight along with our usual Irish Stew, which my servant has made for us each evening while here. It's my own recipe and consists of Maconochie (I described what that was some time ago I think), bacon, bully beef, an Oxo cube and potatoes of which there is a plentiful supply in a ruined farm close by. I hope the colonel and adjutant don't disturb us in the middle of this evening as they have done the last two days.[76]

In the November, McGowan was seconded to the staff of 114 Brigade as a signals officer:

I'm fairly moving about in high circles at present and a very fine education it is too to be dining each day with a General to say nothing of Brigade Majors and Staff Captains; of course I say little except when spoken to but there's always plenty of interest to listen to. General McClintock is a dear old man who has seen service in quite a lot of places. He's short, stout and enjoys his food but is none the less very energetic and very considerate to those under his command. You should see some of the meals turned out by the cook of the 114 – soup, fish, meat and 2 vegs, boiled pudding and milk pudding, entree, cheese, dessert, coffee and everything. Of course, we have to pay for it, something like 6 francs a day but I suppose we can well afford it.

Born in Salford, in 1893, Arthur Patrick Burke lived at 1 Encombe Place, where his mother, Letitia, ran a beer house. Prior to enlisting in the army around November 1914, he worked as a clerk for a local firm of provision merchants. He joined the 20th Battalion, Manchester Regiment – the fifth of the city's 'Pals' battalions. He regularly wrote home, signing himself as 'Art', until late 1916 when he started to call himself Pat or Paddy[77]. He took part in the Battalion's attack on 1 July 1916 – the first day of the Battle of the Somme - and saw many of his comrades killed or wounded. Private Burke trained with 3 Platoon, 'A' Company and was probably still serving with those comrades. The Manchester's attack on the German positions at the village of Fricourt was scheduled for 10.30am, part of a second phase and some three hours after the advance had commenced elsewhere on the battlefield. In the event, it was postponed until 2.30pm. It meant that Burke and his comrades would be 'going over the top' and crossing No Man's Land in the full knowledge that the attack was anticipated by the enemy. As they went forward, the men of A Company came under heavy machine gun fire, together with rifle fire from snipers, and there were many casualties.

Private Arthur Patrick Burke, Manchester Regiment.

Burke was fortunate. He did not advance as part of the first wave, being held back as a reserve machine gunner, but followed later. Immediately afterwards he wrote to his brother, Reg, about the Germans he encountered:

> *In one dugout, there were about 25 in and we set the place on fire, we spared them no mercy, they don't deserve it. They continued sniping as we were advancing until we reached them and then they thro' up their hands, "Merci Camerade", we gave them mercy, I don't think.*

Unscathed, Burke came through the rest of the fighting on the Somme during the summer and autumn of 1916 and, by April of the following year had become servant to Second Lieutenant Henri S Gros.

> *[I] made the dinner tonight, am getting a first class cook, & to crown all the Capt. complimented me on same. Soup, Salmon, Fried Steak & onions & beans. Pineapple, tea cheese biscuits etc etc. Its now about 9.30 pm just going to get my kit down after concluding this, shall be up doing the bacon & eggs for breakfast at 8.30 in the*

Canadian officers' cooks, June 1916. Photo: Library & Archives Canada.

morning - and they say the officers rough it. Take it from me they dont & neither do their servants. Mr Gros has mentioned to somebody that he is trying to get permission to let me go with him to the R.F.C. stating 'He's a damn good servant to me'. You will begin to think I'm blowing my own trumpet a great deal - but its truth & I cannot avoid these things.

The next day, 2 April, he wrote to his sister 'Tot',

For lunch, I gave them stewed beef and beans, rice pudding and, of course, tea. As regards the result, it was top hole, especially the pudding. For tea, sardines on toast, chicken and ham paste, marmalade. Now, I'm just about to prepare their dinner (6pm) but I don't intend overdoing myself with trouble tonight so they are having the following. Lentil soup, Stew with veg, 'Chicago fritters', blancmange & apricot, and for savoury, bloater paste on toast.

The middle class officers will have been used to five course meals such as Burke had served up for dinner. The inclusion of the 'savoury', after the 'sweet' is very much in keeping with formal dinner parties of the times. In July 1917, he wrote home to his brother, describing another day's meals for the officers although, seemingly, with some more cynicism than previously.

We were up again at 7 - got the officers cup of tea ready & had breakfast (Bacon, Eggs, Toast, Marmalade) ready set for them at 9. Oh the poor chaps do go short in the line for lunch they had garden peas, new potatoes, fried steaks, Pears & Custard biscuits cheese butter & followed by tea & of course their drinks during lunch consisting of 'Lemon Squash', 'White Horse' & Sherry. For tea I've got sardines on toast for them & dinner at 7.30 pm. as follows. Household soup, salmon, roasted potatoes, Colliflower [sic], steaks, Rice pudding & fruit & coffee etc - thanks to their caterer I dont think they do so badly whats your idea when its an understood thing they ought to be roughing it.

Paddy Burke's time as an officer's servant was short-lived. On 9 October 1917, the 20th Manchesters were in the front line near the Belgian village of Broodseinde. Burke was one of the men who was detailed to go to the rear area to collect the rations. On the way back, a shell burst over them killing him. Captain Nicholl wrote to Mrs Burke saying he had been buried with his comrades. However, as with many men, the location of the grave was lost over the remaining year of the war. Arthur Patrick Burke is now commemorated on the nearby Tyne Cot Memorial to the Missing.

A little to the east of Burke's position on 1 July 1916, was Captain Wilfred "Billie" Nevill. He was commanding B Company, of the 8th Battalion, East Surrey Regiment. Born in 1894, in Islington, he was the son of Thomas and Elizabeth Nevill. Thomas Nevill died in 1903 and had previously been a successful coal merchant and, later, a publisher of

Captain Billie Nevill.

Kelly's Trade Directories. At the time of the 1911 census, Elizabeth Nevill was still living at the family home at Montpellior Road, Twickenham. She was still very financially secure and was able to employ two live-in servants – a cook and a housemaid. At the time, Billie was attending school at Dover College, where he was headboy and captain of the cricket and hockey teams. He left in 1913, to read classics at Jesus College, Cambridge. Both at school and university he was an active member of the Officer Training Corps and it was, perhaps, no surprise that on 5 August 1914, just one day after the declaration of war, he applied for an army commission. He became a Second Lieutenant on 27 November and appears to have been posted to the 1st Battalion, East Yorkshire Regiment. At some point, whilst still in Britain, he transferred to the 8th East Surreys and was promoted to captain. He went overseas with the Battalion on 27 July 1915.

A couple of weeks later, he wrote home to his sister, Amy:

We're near a railhead here, which means that after that point, motor supply columns take grub and ammunition up from the railways. They take it to the refilling point, where the Divisional Train meets them, sorts out the stuff into various brigades and carries it, in large horse drawn wagons, to the collecting points for each regiment. The regiment sends back its transport and carries the stuff up at night to the end of the long communication trenches and dump it down......

> *......I see our mess waiter-cook-manager (a charming Tommy named Potter) mawling* [sic] *two fowls who, ten minutes ago, were in the prime of life. One of them already has that peculiarly naked and indecent appearance which a plucked fowl always presents. I had breakfast with D Company this morning. It was quite a rag. We started with tinned peaches, then sardines and finally eggs and marmalade. All on the same plate of course.*[78]

On 4 September 1915, there was another letter to the family, in which he wrote his address as 'same billets, clean straw, no rats'. He had recently received a Tommy cooker in a parcel and was finding it *a great and roaring success. I've made myself, and two others as well, cocoa the last four nights on duty in the trenches and, by Jove, my old brewing hand from 'study days' had not forgotten his cunning. But I shall want refills fairly regularly and often when I am 'up'.*

As mentioned earlier, the 8th East Surreys attacked German positions near Carnoy on 1 July 1916. Shortly before, Nevill had been on leave and had bought four footballs – one for each of his platoons. He intended that they should help to encourage his men and offered a prize for whichever platoon managed to kick the ball across No Man's Land, during the attack, and be the first to land it in the German trenches. At least one was inscribed 'The Great European Cup-Tie, the Final, East Surreys v Bavarians. Kick off at zero'. The Battalion's war diary takes up the story.

> *At 7.27 a.m. B Company started to move out to their wire, Captain Nevill strolling quietly ahead of them, giving an occasional order to keep the dressing square on to the line of advance. This Company took four footballs out with them which they were seen to dribble forward into the smoke of our intense bombardment on the Hun front line. The first part of B Company's advance was made with very few casualties, but when the barrage lifted to the second Hun trench, a very heavy rifle and machine gun fire started from our front and left, the latter coming apparently from the craters and the high ground immediately behind them. At 7.50 am the Adjutant reported that the Battalion was in the German trenches. Hand to hand fighting went on for a long time in the German trenches.*

The East Surreys captured their objective in spite of heavy casualties and, by shortly after midday, the positions were relatively secure. A bottle of champagne was found and was shared out amongst the officers. Unfortunately, Billie Nevill was not amongst them. He was killed during the advance and is now buried in the military cemetery at Carnoy. Two of the footballs survive, one being held by the National Army Museum and the other by the Regimental Museum.

Although the position of cook was often thought to be a 'cushy number', working away from the dangers of the front line, Walter Lawrence was not at all keen on his new role when he was allocated to be the assistant to the officers' cook at the headquarters of 4th Cavalry Brigade in April 1915. He was a regular soldier and, before the war, had been serving as a private in India with the 69th Mechanical Transport Company, Army Service Corps, attached to the 3rd Lahore Division of the Indian Army. The Division, which comprised Gurkha, Sikh and British troops, landed at Marseilles on 26 September 1914 and was soon in action. By the following spring, Lawrence had transferred to the ASC Company supporting the 4th Cavalry Brigade which was near the French village of Pradelles. He kept a brief diary during this time:

7 April – This is my first day of being chef's mate. I let the fire out, twice.
8 April – I don't like my job over much.
9 April – Getting fed up with job
12 April – Getting a little better
14 April – Chef left me in the lurch, so I had to go and cook the General's dinner. A fair success.
15 April – Had to cook breakfast. Started cooking lunch when chef turned up.
16 April – Have started today as officers' cook. A fairly successful lunch.
18 April – Not much doing. Getting on with my cooking.
20 April – Had some fun. Served up a crab for lunch. Uncooked.
22/4 – Cooked my second chicken. Got praised for it.[79]

There is no record of what the General thought of being presented with a raw crab for lunch. Brigadier General Cecil Bingham was the son of the 4th Earl of Lucan. He had had a distinguished military career, joining a regiment of hussars in 1882, before transferring to 1st Life Guards four years later. He saw action in the Boer War and had commanded 4th Cavalry Brigade since 1911. Later in 1915, he was promoted to command 1st (Cavalry) Division with the rank of major general.

That Sword.

How he thought he was going to use it——

——and how he did use it.

Walter Lawrence remained in his post until August 1915, when he caught typhoid and was evacuated to a hospital at Boulogne and, eventually, back to Britain, where he spent more time in hospital in Oxford. His medal entitlement records indicate that he returned to duty and was transferred to the Royal Garrison Artillery. As far as is known, he survived the war.

The 14th Battalion, London Regiment, was a pre-war Territorial unit known as the London Scottish. It was one of the first Territorial battalions to go on active service, arriving in France on 14/15 September 1914. Amongst the men was Private John Stewart Thomson. Born in about 1893, he lived in Wimbledon with his parents and, as a young man, studied to become an architect, with the intention of joining his father's practice. On 31 October, the 14th Londons became one of the first Territorial units to engage the Germans. They had been rushed forward, travelling to Ypres by bus and then deploying to strengthen a sparsely held front line along the road between the Belgian villages of Messines and Wytschaete. Already in position and under pressure from the Germans was General Bingham's 4th Cavalry Brigade, now fighting dismounted as infantrymen.

They arrived just in time to help the 6th Dragoon Guards repel an attack on the British line. According to the history of the London Scottish, the Germans attacked *in a dense mass, cheering loudly, with bands playing.* There would be further attacks during the following hours. All were repulsed with, on one occasion, the Londons leaving their trenches to engage the oncoming Bavarians with their bayonets. In the early hours of 1 November, the weight of numbers of the German assault finally compelled the London Scottish to withdraw. When the roll was called, only 150 men answered but others rejoined later. Final losses were calculated at around 400 men, dead, wounded or missing.

Thomson remained with the Battalion until July 1916, when he was commissioned as a Second Lieutenant and was posted to 112 Brigade, Royal Field Artillery. Artillery officers were often men with a technical background, who could quickly get to grips with matters such as range finding and trajectory. Shortly after arriving at his new unit, he wrote home to his parents

> *Our mess here at the wagon lines usually consists of four of us. We manage to do ourselves pretty well. Dinner consists of very excellent soup, meat (beef or mutton), vegetables (potatoes, asparagus, etc), tinned fruits, savouries (sardines on toast), cheese, coffee and liqueurs, cigars, whisky and beer.*

Another man enjoying dinner in the mess was the future prime minister, Winston Churchill. At the beginning of the war, he was an MP and member of the cabinet, serving as First Lord of the Admiralty. However, he was effectively sacked from the position after proposing what was to become the ultimately disastrous invasion of the Gallipoli peninsula in Turkey. Churchill then sought to command an infantry battalion, drawing on his experience as a young man when he had fought in the Boer War. He briefly joined the 2nd Battalion, Grenadier Guards, as a major, before taking command of the 6th Battalion, Royal Scots Fusiliers. In the middle of December 1915 he had a lucky escape when he was called away from his dug-out, which took a direct hit from an artillery shell shortly after. He later wrote to his wife, whilst at the Army General Headquarters.

Here I am, after a glorious hot bath, between the sheets in this abode of comfort, resting before dinner. My departure from the 2ⁿᵈ Grenadiers was very different from my arrival. Then the Colonel thought it necessary to remark 'We don't want to be inhospitable, but I think it only right to say that your coming was not a matter in which we were given any choice.' But, today, all smiles and handwaves and pressing invitations to return whenever I like.

My dear – where are the bi-weekly food boxes? They can be my only contribution to the messes where I lived. We eat our rations and the officers have parcels of extras from home. So there are no mess bills. But I want to put something into the common pot. So do send me some useful and practical additions to our fare. Peach brandy seems to me to be a hopeful feature in the liquor department.

During 1916, Royal Navy guns that were usually fitted to ships, were brought ashore and mounted in concrete bunkers near the Belgian seaside town of Nieupoort, which was the northern extremity of the hundreds of miles which formed the Western Front. They were used as long range artillery, shelling German positions many miles inside the occupied territory, under the command of a unit known as Royal Naval Siege Guns.

No lessening of standards for these French officers.

German officers in the Vosges mountains. Photo: Gwyneth M Roberts.

On New Year's Day [1917] *another neighbour of mine, a French gunner captain from the Basque country, who inhabited the interior of a nearby dune and was noted far and wide for the excellence of his table, asked me to celebrate with him the Jour de l'An. He was somewhat of a gourmet and had the good fortune to enjoy the services of an hotel chef from Paris as batman. The five-course meal, deliciously cooked and ending with dessert and over-much sweet champagne, left me prostrate for the rest of the day. The soul of politeness, when he subsequently came to return the call, the marine cook had chosen, to my consternation and alarm, curried bully beef as the plat du jour followed by a bizarre specimen of la cuisine anglaise known to sailors as 'figgy duff'. With Gallic fortitude he did his best to stifle fears for his digestion when confronted with these formidable gastronomic obstacles, but I felt that the Anglo-French entente had been put to a severe test.* (All in the day's work, Lieutenant Commander Charles Kerr, Royal Naval Siege Guns, 1939)

A few weeks prior to the opening of the Battle of the Somme, in the summer of 1916, Second Lieutenant Thomas Nash was attached, for liaison purposes, to the French Army, dining with the neighbouring unit's officers. He was an ideal choice for the job as he spoke French well, noting in his later memoir, 'Diary of an Unprofessional Soldier', that he could also swear fluently in the language.

> *Some of their little ways were very funny. I remembered with difficulty to retain my knife between courses and that only after I had been reduced to eating with my fingers once or twice. Dinner was an elaborate affair even in the trenches and consisted of one sardine, half a boiled egg chopped in vinegar, a scrap of boiled liver then sauté potatoes as a separate course, followed by jam eaten with a spoon as a sweet and cheese. The Colonel's way of paying me a compliment was to offer me tit-bits from his own plate on his own fork.*

*   *   *   *

The Welsh Guards was a new regiment, raised in February 1915 and its 1st Battalion joined the Guards Division in France in the August. At the beginning of August, the following year, they were billeted at Bus les Artois, a small hamlet to the north west of the Somme town of Albert. The history of the Guards[80] mentions the officers' messing arrangements at this time:

> *At Bus les Artois there was a battalion mess, but all was so arranged by this time – nearly a year's experience in France – that the comforts of both officers and men, so far as comforts could be obtained, were enjoyed and arranged for whatever the resources of village or camp might be. There was no necessity to fuss because of a sudden intimation on arrival at new billets that no battalion mess could be found. Sergt. Marshall, the 'Universal Provider' of the battalion, issued food to company cooks, and in a very short time food was ready if wanted. The office of Mess President had by this time devolved on the second in command.*
>
> *On the subject of cooks much could be written. Goodman, of the Prince of Wales' Company, was probably the best, at least he was thought so by Arthur Gibbs and Bob Bonsor, both gourmets; but*

this was at a much later period. Geoffries, of No. 3 and Thomas, of No. 4, were at this time the best known characters. Geoffries was a man of many qualities, but no one could tell why or how he became a cook. Aldridge declared that he found him in the kitchen, a self-constituted cook; how he got there Aldridge never dared enquire – he just came. But he always seemed to have food ready at a moment's notice, and some of it was well treated. Thomas, on the other hand, had started as a cook in the battalion mess, but had been found extravagant. He passed rapidly to No. 4. There was never a more devoted servant than Thomas, but the culinary art he acquired had not the lightness of touch which gives distinction to great artists, which raises them from scullions to escoffiers, which gives them the name of 'genius', while they pass their own patronymic to a sauce. He was known to be in active correspondence with the chef of a Cardiff club and had been seen taking lessons in the mysteries of omelette-making from a fat lady in Wormhoudt. But who taught him to make what he called 'rimsoles' and why he boiled a galantine of chicken were two of the unsolved questions which disturb the soul of man.

Arthur Gibbs, mentioned above, was certainly a man who, today, would be called a foody. His letters[81] home are full of mentions of what he had eaten, or what he wanted to eat and hoped would be sent in a parcel. When war was declared, Gibbs was studying at Brasenose College, Oxford and was a member of the University Officers Training Corps. He received his commission on 9 September 1915 and joined the Guards on 19 December. In the Welsh Guards' History, Dudley Ward describes him as *"a dark, solid, round-faced, full-lipped, bespectacled and competent officer, still very young."*

Arthur Gibbs, 1st Battalion, Welsh Guards. Photo: Gibbs family.

Although not in the front line at the time, there do not seem to have been any Christmas Day celebrations but Gibbs wrote home, saying that they had just finished a tour of duty.

The rats and mice abound in the trenches. I wonder if you could get a catapult or 2, and some bullets, it would be great fun with the rats, then. When you send out slab chocolate will you please put it in a tin, otherwise the mice get at it, as I have already found out. It doesn't matter about any fancy chocolates, as they are eaten so quickly! We had the pheasant and the swiss roll up in the trenches: they were splendid.

There would, however, be New Year celebrations:

We feed much better up in the trenches than we do in the Battn. Mess, as we supply our own food in the trenches: this is a selection from the menus in the trenches.

Breakfast
Porridge and cream
Sausage and bacon
or eggs
Sometimes kipper
Bread, butter, marmalade, tea etc.,

Dinner (New Year's Eve)
Turtle Soup
Roast Pheasant etc.,
Home-made Xmas pudding and cream
Sardines on Toast
Krug 1904
25 yr. old Brandy

Lunch (New Year's Day)
Caviare (with hot toast and butter)
Consommé *Fortnum and Mason*
Hot Roast Pheasant
Chipped Potatoes
Onions
Stewed Pears and custard
Pate de Foie Gras

The pheasants had been ¾ cooked at home and were heated up by tying them to a string and revolving them near a brazier. We don't feed quite so grandly at every meal, but we don't go hungry very often. Our servants do the cooking for us: we have got a small oil stove and the rest is done in braziers, made out of any old tins, with holes knocked in them.

There would be further letters to his mother, over the following weeks:

6 January - *I am not particularly fond of shortbread: but I like honey, which we don't get out here. Our meals in the Battn. Mess are very dull and uninteresting: mostly stews or roast beef and milk puddings and stewed fruit: bacon and eggs for breakfast and tea to drink at every meal: chipped enamel plates and cups and rather ancient knives and forks, and only a few of them. But you soon get used to using the same knife, fork and spoon for the whole meal!*

28 January – *The half cooked sausages you sent were awfully good – about the best I've ever tasted. We had them up in the trenches at a lunch party – 6 of us – we had sausage and mash, pork pie, oxtail soup and champagne! Followed by fruit and chocolate cake. Your cakes are very popular out here. I can't remember if I told you that Uncle George sent me a big box of apples with about 100 in it. They are lovely apples, Newton Pippins, and arrived in excellent condition, only about 6 being damaged.*

12 February – *Your little aluminium saucepan is invaluable here. I use it for everything. Dinner is just coming. I am now eating some sort of soup, which is very good and hot and am writing this between sips. Bivouac cocoa is rather good stuff, there was a box of it in the parcel Grandpa sent me. It is made up into blocks, big enough for one cup and contains milk and sugar already mixed with it, so it is easy to make and very good to drink. Those 'Camp Pies' aren't particularly good: there's too much of the camp about them. Peter Crawford's dog seemed to recognise an old pal in the last one we had.*

18 February – *I received a big batch of letters last night, also parcel containing herring, tomato soup, cream, fruit pudding, chicken and vegetables and tooth powder. The best parcel yet.*

Early in March, Gibbs badly twisted his knee. He struggled on for a couple of days but the medical officer sent him off to the 4th Field Ambulance at Watou.

> *I have got my servant with me. I have just changed my servant and have now got a man called Edge, who was Nigel Newall's servant. He is an excellent man and used to be a butler. I was thankful to get rid of my other one.....Don't send any parcels for a few days as the contents will only get eaten by the other members of the mess. They give you good food here:*
>   *Breakfast – porridge, eggs, bacon, marmalade.*
>   *Dinner – soup, chicken & beans, mashed potato, jam tart and*
>   *coffee*
>   *Tea – bread & butter and jam*

Gibbs' new servant was probably Private Ernest Edge, who originated from Prees Heath, Shropshire. He was killed in action on 16 September 1916. His previous officer, Second Lieutenant Nigel Newell, survived him by just over a year, being killed on 12 October 1917

> 11 March – *Two splendid parcels arrived last night – containing cake, grapefruit, crystallised fruit, cigarettes, notepaper – in fact, everything I wanted. The chocolate biscuits (Bourneville) in an earlier parcel are very acceptable. Macfarlane Lang's chocolate biscuits are also very good. I always like fruit too – but it should be sent absolutely by itself. If it is packed with heavier things, the fruit gets squashed.*

He rejoined the Guards, now at Ypres, on the 16th. He wrote a brief letter to his mother concluding *I haven't got much time for writing, as I am busy arranging about food, etc.* On the 21st, he wrote from the front line trenches, near Railway Wood.

> *It is very difficult to get water or fuel up here so I shall want cold things sent, which don't need any cooking, such as tongues, ham, chicken, etc. We can't show any fires as the Bosche shells them at once. He is much more awake here than he was on the other line. A small Primus stove would be jolly useful.*

The Battalion History notes this was a particularly miserable time for the men. It was cold and wet with the trenches in poor condition and everywhere was thick mud.

Still in the Ypres area and after undertaking tours of duty in the front line, the Battalion was relieved to what its History describes as a '*nice camp*', near Vlamertinghe, at the beginning of May. The History continues

> *We went back to Ypres by train on the 7th and found the Huns were shelling hard the roads, the railway and the town. When we marched into the town, we found the roads blocked with traffic – a mass of transport wagons and artillery limbers. The Hun was pumping shells into the Square and the Menin Gate. Finally, we got across the Square and when we reached the Menin Gate found the Hun was shelling the road like mad.*

Once back in the front line, Gibbs wrote to his mother on 8 May, thanking her for a parcel.

> *The cauliflower and asparagus arrived in fine condition. Some of the officers are having lettuces and tomatoes sent out, which is an excellent idea. Of course, the tomatoes have to be packed when they are pretty hard.*

The situation in the Ypres trenches was no better than previously when the men went back into the front line on 18 June.

> *All the right half of the line was under water to the knees, and the trench and the parapet only about four feet high. The left was a straggling bit held by posts. From the start, casualties were heavy.* (History of the Welsh Guards).

Gibbs was now in command of a group of a hundred men, known as the Propping Company. They had the main responsibility for improving the trenches and maintaining the barbed wire erected in No Man's Land. It was *a fearful job. Round Turco Farm, there was a regular marsh and for some days enormous parties carried up quantities of T-shaped frames and hundreds of sheets of tin to try and make some sort of gutter through this marsh. It was, however, not a success.... This annoyed Arthur Gibbs very much, as he had put in some very strenuous hours over the work.*

Gibbs and his men were in positions along the canal bank, just outside of Ypres. He wrote again on 27 June:

I got in at 3.30 this morning feeling like nothing on earth. It had been raining hard all night, and I was thoroughly wet, as I hadn't got my mackintosh with me, it being fairly fine when I started out. I had my rubber boots on and slipped about all over the place. I had fallen down flat in the mud quite half a dozen times when the climax was reached. I slipped into a big shell hole, full of water. I went in up to my waist and fairly gasped for breath – it was so cold. Of course my boots got full of water, which I had to carry about with me for the rest of the night. (I didn't feel nearly strong enough to take the boots off and empty them!)

However, I got home eventually and found a lot of parcels and letters waiting for me. They bucked me up a lot, so I hurried up and got on some dry clothes, and then sat down and enjoyed my mail. There was a lovely box of peaches, which arrived in excellent condition: another parcel with biscuits, sardines, potted meat and another with a steak and kidney pudding and other excellent things. Olive sent me a box of shortbread.

I had some awfully good curried prawns the other day from Fortnum and Mason. The curry was not too hot.

The Bosch put a whizz-bang into the water just outside my dug-out during tea time. It was quite close in to the bank on the near side, so it must have been only about 6 inches from the top of my dug out, when it came over. I do not take Edge with me when I go out to work. He stays behind to get the rations. He and the other servant do the cooking between them. I get some food brought up by the mess corporal of the Welsh Guards: he brings up bread, fresh butter, wine, water etc. With the food that you send and what Newey has, we do ourselves jolly well!

As mentioned earlier, the Battle of the Somme had started with an artillery bombardment of the German trenches, from 23 June, followed by the infantry attack on 1 July, which cost so many casualties. The Welsh Guards remained in the Ypres area, holding the line.

It would not be such a wild stretch of imagination to say that the Guards Division first took part in the Battle of the Somme while they were at

Ypres. They were, at least, preventing troops and guns from taking part in that battle. (History of the Welsh Guards).

A move to the Somme was made at the end of the month, with the Battalion going into billets at Bus les Artois as mentioned earlier. Before the move, Gibbs had time for a letter home, on 25 July.

Many thanks for the parcel received last night containing tomatoes, lettuces, lavender water, acid drops and watch glass. We have just discovered a new dish – fish cakes made out of tinned salmon. I know you will be frightened to death at the words 'tinned salmon' but I'm afraid you will have to put up with it and think of the thousands of people who eat tinned salmon and don't die and must not think of the unfortunate one who gets Ptomaine poisoning. Besides there's always a chance of getting home if you get poisoned.

Advert in The Times, *21 August 1917. Note the availability of potted grouse, a few days after the opening of the grouse shooting season on 12 August.*

In a time when the causes of food poisoning were not as well understood as today, there was a belief that the decomposition of protein, ptomaine, was the cause of occasional fatal ingestion of food. The particular problem with salmon was that it could not be heated sufficiently, as part of the canning process, to guarantee killing botulism bacteria without making the fish unpalatable. The newspapers of the time did occasionally report deaths after eating tinned salmon, so it is understandable that Mrs Gibbs might be concerned for her son.

The Guards spent the early part of August in trenches in the area of Beaumont Hamel. The area showed many signs of the devastation caused by the artillery shelling of previous weeks, as well as the July fighting. The History describes the front line as

at best, indicated by bits of shallow, wide-open ditches, but mostly it was mounds and shell holes, broken bits of wood and splintered

An uncommon scene – officers doing their own cooking. Miraumont le Grand. Photo: National Library of Scotland.

> *rifles and the half decomposed dead. On a dark night, you could smell your way into the front line. Patrols reported quantities of dead in No Man's Land and companies buried scores found in their own front trenches.*

On the night of 9/10 September, the Welsh Guards went into the front line, near the village of Ginchy, taking over positions which had been captured only a few hours before. At about 7am, the Germans attacked in strength to try to retake their lost positions. There was hard fighting throughout the morning, some of it hand-to-hand, with much of it taking place in a wood on the outskirts of the village which was

> *a mass of deep shell holes – it had been bombarded by the British heavy guns for some weeks – and there were heaps of bricks from the demolished houses by the side of the road and large heaps of earth from German dug-outs; there were fallen trees too, and a great number of standing ones. It was a confused jumble and the men taking cover in one shell-hole could not possibly tell if anyone was in the next, or if it was friend or foe.* (History of the Welsh Guards).

There were further attacks during the afternoon but these continued to be beaten off, albeit with heavy losses amongst the Guards. All the officers of the Prince of Wales' Company became casualties and Sergeant Oswald Ashford took command. Earlier in the day, Ashford had carried Lieutenant Pugh to safety, under heavy fire, when the officer had been injured in the leg. He was awarded the Distinguished Conduct Medal, the official citation reading:

> *For conspicuous gallantry and skill in organising his company when all the officers had been killed or wounded. He also carried in a wounded officer under heavy fire.*

On the 11th, Arthur Gibbs wrote home again.

> *We really are on active service, and I don't dislike it at all! Our rations for two days are biscuits and bully, a bottle of water. I have got a cardboard box with extra food, which I am husbanding very carefully. I haven't got any tea, which I miss very much. I have got some bivouac cocoa, and soup and beef-tea squares, which are excellent, and really invaluable. Will you send a lot more of both as soon as possible? Even if I don't want them the men would be delighted to have them, as they haven't got any extra delicacies. The men worked marvellously last night. They knew that the position would have to be defended in the morning, and they worked for their lives, or rather for other people's lives.*

The Guards continued to be in action over the following two weeks, taking more casualties. The Prince of Wales' Company, now temporarily commanded by Arthur Gibbs, was reduced to just fifty two men – around 20 per cent of its full strength. In spite of their weakened state, the Guards received orders to support an attack by other units on 25 September. Gibbs' men and those from another company, commanded by Captain Dene, were soon rushed forward to support the flank.

> *Arthur Gibbs, in answer to Dene's repeated "Come on Arthur – can't you move?", arrived in a state of collapse, his round face pouring with perspiration, his eyeglasses dimmed and his lungs working like wheezing bellows.* (History of the Welsh Guards)

The remainder of the year was relatively quiet. October was spent well away from the front line at St Maulvis.

> *We have got a battalion mess now, and I am joint mess-president. We have to go 5 or 6 miles for food, so catering for 25 is rather difficult, as we can get very little in the way of fresh meat in this village. There is no mineral water to be had near here, nor eggs. There seems to be any amount of fruit round here, but it isn't ripe yet.* (Arthur Gibbs)

The early weeks of 1917 continued quietly, although there were tours of duty in the front line. On 8 March, Gibbs wrote home.

> *Many thanks for the two parcels received last night, containing excellent cake, bread, dried egg, which we are going to try tomorrow for breakfast, chicken, spaghetti, etc. Please don't send the bread and cake if they are coming out of your rations at home, as they are pure luxuries and I can easily do without them.*

At the beginning of the year, the Germans had returned to unrestricted submarine warfare and, within a few weeks, the reduction in food supplies in Britain was becoming noticeable. Formalised rationing was not introduced until 1918 and Gibbs must be referring to the various voluntary schemes that were being developed. In Stockport, the Council introduced such a scheme in conjunction with local churches and other bodies. The Mayor wrote to the *Stockport Advertiser* on 30 April, drawing attention to a national shortage of wheat.

> *People must eat to live, not live to eat. After all, it was asking very little sacrifice on the part of people compared with the sacrifice of our gallant men at the front. It was far better to have voluntary rationing than compulsion.*

A few days before Gibbs wrote home, the Guards undertook a tour of duty in the trenches which the History described as one of the hardest they ever had.

*Heavy guns, field guns and trench mortars fired continuously at the
British line; the line was blown in and the men occupied shell holes
where they could; enemy snipers waited to catch men moving from
one hole to another .....*

During this tour, Sergeant Oswald Ashford was badly wounded and
evacuated home for treatment. He had been Gibbs' platoon sergeant and
was now in hospital in Newcastle. Gibbs wrote to his mother asking her
to send Ashford a parcel of fruit, chocolate and biscuits. He was *a splendid
fellow. He was badly wounded by a Minnie last time we were up in the
trenches. I hear now that he has got 14 wounds and his arm is rather bad.*
Twenty-six-year-old Ashford was never able to return to duty and was
discharged from the army on 6 December 1917.

On 31 July 1917, the Welsh Guards attacked on the opening day of
what would officially be called the Third Battle of Ypres, but known to
many simply as Passchendaele. Their advance was generally successful.
Arthur Gibbs, now with the rank of acting captain and serving as one of

An officers' lunch. Photo: National Library of Scotland.

three officers at Battalion HQ, later wrote for the History *I am afraid we have not killed many Huns, as they ran too fast for us long before we came up to them.* The Battalion suffered casualties – 138 men dead, wounded or missing. Weeks later, a major attack on German positions near the village of Passchendaele was ordered for 12 October. Gibbs would lead his men of the Prince of Wales Company but, in fact, they were able to achieve their objective on 11 October, without serious loss, as described in the History.

> *Thanks to a patrol under 1795 Lance Sergeant Johnson – sent out by Arthur Gibbs as soon as he had taken over the line – who discovered that a blockhouse reported held by the enemy was vacant. Gibbs promptly occupied the post with a couple of Lewis guns and had several slight brushes with the enemy patrols, but no serious attempt was made by them to retake the place.*

December 1917 saw the Guards billeted in Arras where, on the 13th, Gibbs had afternoon tea in the officers' club.

> *I had tea with Himalaya Bonn at the officers' club this afternoon: it's really an awfully nice place. Clean, warm, bright, and excellent waiting – on the strength of the tea we ordered a tremendous dinner for tomorrow night. Perhaps the menu will interest you (and incidentally may allay any anxieties you may have about my health): it is – Hors d'oeuvres – Tomato soup – Filletted Plaice, sauce tartare, Mutton cutlets – Crème caramel – Scotch Woodcock – Dessert; perhaps chicken after the cutlets if we still at all hungry! And talking of food, what about that celery you were going to send to me, and have you any mince pies to spare?*

On Christmas Day, Gibbs and the other officers served a festive meal to the men, after a church service –

> *They got beef, pork, potatoes and onions, gravy and apple sauce: a very good helping of Xmas pudding, an apple, an orange, 3 packets of cigarettes and I gave them a cigar each: tonight I am getting up a concert for them, with free beer for the performers, so we ought to get a good programme.*

Their own dinner was in the evening –

*Soup, fish, turkey, Xmas pudding (not forgetting the brandy butter),
savoury and dessert. Champagne flowed like water!*

Shortly after New Year, the Guards moved from Arras, going into the front
line on 5 January, near Gavrelle. The weather was very cold and the
trenches were in good condition, until it started to rain. The previously
frozen earth on the parapets started to collapse and the men were soon
above their knees in mud. Gibbs wrote,

*have got a good cookhouse about ½ a mile behind the line and the
men get hot tea for breakfast, hot dinners and hot tea and cocoa in
the middle of the night, all of which is brought up in containers,
which keep the food really hot for an hour or two. They make their
own tea on the braziers, and are thoroughly happy.*

From this point, Gibbs letters rarely mention food and, although he
continued to serve with the Guards as a company commander, he is not
further mentioned in the History, except in passing. There are no letters
after 19 August 1918, when he wrote saying he would be returning to
Britain, on leave, on the 24th. He did not return to duty overseas but
continued to serve in Britain until he left the army in 1919.

This and the preceeding chapters, have mainly concerned themselves
with the Western Front, in Belgium and France. The next chapter will
examine food in some of the other theatres of the war.

*   *   *   *

Curry Soup from Fish
Thrift for Troubled Times, 1917

Three pounds of fish or fish trimmings
Two ounces of butter or fat
Three cloves
Two onions or leeks
One apple or a stick of rhubarb
One carrot
A bunch of herbs, thyme, marjoram, bay leaf & parsley

Three tablespoonfuls of flour
Two ounces of curry powder
Four quarts and half a pint of water

METHOD: Cut up the fish and wash it clean. Put it into a saucepan with the fat or butter, the apples and the vegetables, washed, peeled and cut up and the herbs. Let all this cook for about ten minutes. Then add four quarts of cold water and mix the flour and curry powder into a smooth paste with ½ pint of cold water and stir it into the soup. Stir till it boils, then skim it well and let it boil gently for 1½ hours. Strain it into a tureen and add to it one pint of cooked rice and some pieces of cooked fish nicely cut up.

Kebobs
The Times, 3 December 1915

Cut a sweetbread, two kidneys (the chilled variety are cheap) and two tomatoes into slices; put them alternatively on a skewer, add pepper and salt and toast them thoroughly. When done, cut open a roll (yesterday's for preference), take the kebob off the skewer and put inside the roll. Pour over a cupful of stock, a wineglass of claret, heat up and serve.

Gillege Pudding (a way of using up breadcrusts)
Housekeeping on Twenty Five Shillings a Week,
National Food Economy League, 1915

4oz stale crusts of bread
4oz flour
A pinch of salt
1 teaspoonful baking powder
2oz chopped suet
2oz sultanas
3oz sugar
1 egg
1 level teaspoonful ground cinnamon

Soak bread in cold water, when quite soft squeeze very dry (in a piece of muslin if you have it) and beat with a fork. In another basin, put all the dry ingredients, then mix contents of the two basins together. If too stiff, add a little milk or water. Put at once into a greased basin and steam three hours. (Ginger or pudding spice can be used instead of cinnamon).

CHAPTER 5

Away from the
Western Front

❖

During the course of the war, nearly 5.5 million British and Dominion troops fought the Germans in Belgium and France and it is often these men who are remembered in popular culture. But, sometimes forgotten, are the 3.5 million who saw action in other parts of the world, in what were often regarded as 'side shows' to the Western Front. These troops fought the Germans in Africa, the Bulgarians in Salonika, the Austro-Hungarians in Italy and the Turks in Mesopotamia, Egypt and Palestine, as well as on the Turkish peninsula of Gallipoli. The campaigns would have some similarities. There would often be extended supply lines with the inherent difficulty of getting good, fresh, nutritious food forward to the men, particularly in those campaigns where there was movement across considerable distances to engage the enemy. There would be extremes of weather – from the bitter cold of the Asiago Plateau in Italy to the heat of Mesopotamia and Africa. Disease was rife and there were times when there would be many more men reporting sick than there were casualties from combat.

War was declared on 4 August 1914 but the first troops into action would not be the soldiers of the British Expeditionary Force hurriedly preparing to go to France. On the 7th, a detachment of the Gold Coast Regiment crossed the border into the neighbouring German colony of Togoland, advancing towards the capital of Lomé. Originally a police force operating in what is now Ghana, the Regiment was formed in 1901 and comprised local troops and colonial British officers. The Germans had no

Troops and carriers advancing in East Africa. A campaign characterised by the long distances to be covered.

troops stationed in their colony but the local police force, numbering more than 600, was commanded by German sergeants and headed by a German officer, Hauptmann Pfaeler. As a party of Gold Coast men approached the village of Nuatja, they came under fire from the police. Alhaji Grunshi returned fire, becoming the first soldier in British service to fire a shot in the war. The next day, Pfaeler was shot dead after he climbed a tree to try to get a better view of the advancing troops. Resistance collapsed soon after and the colony had surrendered by the end of the month.

The number of British and Colonial troops in Africa was relatively small. In 1916, in East Africa, there were just three divisions, of which two were South African. There were immense difficulties in maintaining the very long supply lines, with most items being carried by porters on foot. Edward Paice, in his book *Tip and Run*, notes,

> *In order to maintain troops 450 miles from the railhead in Northern Rhodesia 16,500 carriers were needed to transport a single ton of supplies – enough to feed 1,000 askari and their camp-followers for just one day – for the simple reason that 14,000 men were required to carry the food for the 2,500 who carried the troops' supplies.*

The soldiers were the men of the 1st King's African Rifles, another unit of African troops with British officers. The supplies would have originated in South Africa, arriving at Durban or Cape Town. From Durban, they would have been shipped to Beira in Mozambique, then to Chinde, where they were loaded onto river boats for transport up the Zambezi, thence by railway and lake steamers to Northern Rhodesia.

Lieutenant John Cairnie started his military service with the Seaforth Highlanders, going on active service to France in June 1915. After recovering from illness, he was posted to the King's African Rifles and, in December 1917, was near Nairobi. On the 30th, he wrote in his diary,

> *Up at 5 a.m. Dawn just breaking. Breakfast in a hurry & marched into Nairobi, arriving there about 9 a.m. The men were fed on the hill, on mealie-meal, monkey nuts, dates & potatoes. Their methods aren't very clean, and the meal at least didn't seem half cooked. It must be very filling because there wasn't a great deal of it. They roll it into a ball in their hands & then eat it, after dipping it into a basin of melted 'ghee' – dirty greasy stuff. Brown and I walked down to the New Stanley for lunch.* [82]

A few days later, he had moved to Dar-es-Salaam.

> *Up at 6 a.m. and had a bathe in the bay, about 200 ft. from the tent. Water very warm, nearly tepid. Very bad mess here run by a Greek who would be making a fortune if so many officers didn't get their own back by going off without paying their mess bills. He charges 2R.75 a day, & draws our rations. Very hot and moist today; hardly able to do anything and it's worse if you sleep: you feel so rotten when you waken.*

On 26 January 1918, Cairnie's unit set out from Ndanda, in what is now Tanzania, heading for Tunduru. They took with them rations for what was expected to be a three week march.

> *Left Ndanda at 6 a.m. and marched till 9 a.m. Pitched camp at Tschikukwa......... Spent the afternoon devising measures for the men's rations - starting with a tin of bully as unit of measure, and a piece of stick with cups tied to it as scales. The Q.M. clerk who was with us turned back at Ndanda sick so we are left to our own devices. Pratley & Cairncross, & S. Major Addey have joined us. Our chickens are a bit of a nuisance: they require careful transport*

on a donkey, & as we let them run loose when we get into camp, it takes about an hour every night to catch them again. We had a grand dinner tonight - roasted monkey nuts, followed by bully, some green vegetable like spinach which the boys got, and boiled beans, rice & date pudding & coffee.

After spending several days at Tunduru, the troops moved on to their final destination, a further march of several days to Songria. Once there, rations were reasonably plentiful and were supplemented by shooting game.

Shot another hippo today as we were short of meat. I got him with one bullet, somewhere behind the ear, which was a much better show than last time especially as he was over at the other side of the river. Also hit a big croc. but he got away. Saw a few turtles perched on the rocks midstream. All the men and porters were down cutting up the hippo in the afternoon and we took away as much as they could carry, leaving the rest — one side — for the shenzis. The men are in high spirits in the prospects of a good feed.

*   *   *   *

Thousands of miles to the north of Cairnie's position, British troops had been on duty in Egypt since 1882 and it was, effectively, part of the British Empire, although technically still part of the Turkish Ottoman Empire. In the middle of the nineteenth century, the Suez Canal was built by a company jointly owned by French and Egyptian investors. Although the construction had originally been opposed by Britain, as it felt it might be a threat to its domination of the international maritime trade, it quickly became a vital interest for the country, offering quick passage to India and Australia. In 1875, the Egyptian ruler suffered a financial crisis and offered his shares for sale to Britain. It was, perhaps, the bargain deal of the century with Britain now owning a significant minority stake for less than £4 million. Six years later, Britain was asked to help to put down a rebellion. This was successful and resulted in a permanent military presence in the country, which lasted until 1954. The country effectively became a British protectorate – a status which was formalised in late 1914, after the Turkish declaration of war.

When war was declared, the most urgent need was to ensure the security of the Canal from an attack by Turkish troops based in Palestine.

Free movement along the canal was a vital component of British strategy, aiding the movement of troops from India and Australia to the Western Front, as well as being the established route for supplies coming from the Empire. As mentioned in Chapter 1, the Territorial soldiers of the East Lancashire Division (later 42nd Division) arrived in Egypt in September 1914, to take up garrison duties, allowing four battalions of the regular army to leave and head for the Western Front. Troops also arrived from India and Australia and, by January 1915, there were 70,000 stationed in the country, with nearly half of them deployed on the defence of the Canal.

The Turkish plan was to invade Egypt across the Sinai peninsula, capturing the Canal and then continuing the advance to Cairo. The British had plenty of warning of the Turkish advance, learning in the middle of January 1915 that large columns of enemy troops were making their way forward. Nearing the Canal on 3 February, the Turks came under fire from British and French warships that had sailed into the Canal to aid the defence. Reaching the eastern bank, the Turks attempted to lay pontoon bridges but quickly came under devastating machine gun fire from the 62nd Punjabis. The Turks broke off their attempt to cross and were forced to withdraw from the area on the 4th.

With the threat to Egypt now relieved, many of the troops in the country would soon be leaving to go into action elsewhere. In the previous chapter, mention was made of Winston Churchill's brief time in the infantry, following the disaster of the Gallipoli campaign of which he had been the greatest advocate in the British government. He had argued that capture of the Turkish peninsula would hand effective control of the narrow passage to the Black Sea to the Allies. This would allow free movement of supply ships to and from the Russian ports, thereby permitting that country to continue the war against the Germans on the Eastern Front. Churchill, as First Lord of the Admiralty, had argued that the assault could be undertaken solely by the Royal Navy and there would be no need for land forces until the peninsula was secured. A preliminary bombardment of the Turkish strongpoints took place on 19 February 1915, with the main attack being delivered on 19 March. Eighteen British and French warships opened fire on the Turkish positions, concentrating on the part of the Dardenelles passage where the seaway was only a mile wide. Although the area had been cleared by mine-sweepers some time earlier, the Turks had laid new mines some ten days before the attack and these caused considerable damage to the Allied warships.

Lieutenant William Wedgwood Benn, Middlesex Yeomanry, at Alexandria, about to taste biscuits that will be part of the Gallipoli invasion rations. He was the father of the late Labour politician, Tony Benn. Photo: Australian War Memorial, G00203.

It was now agreed that Gallipoli could not be secured by naval power alone and that an invasion by infantry troops would be needed. Planning took several weeks and the first landings were made on 25 April. The regular army troops of 29th Division landed at Cape Helles, on the southern tip of the peninsula and, further north, landings were made by Australian and New Zealand troops who had been in Egypt. There was a lack of decisive leadership and the attack stalled within hours, with little progress being made over the coming days. Still, in Egypt, the Territorial soldiers of 42nd Division were now ordered into action to bolster the attack. They landed on the morning of 6 May. During the evening of the 11th, the men of the 6th Manchesters went into the front line for the first time. Amongst them was Private Ridley Sheldon, who now had more serious matters to deal with than his division of mince pies, between comrades the previous December (see Chapter 1):

I had a terrible experience on Ascension Day, Thursday, May 13th, when along with a number of our fellows, I had to go on a ration party. There were ten of us detailed off for the work with the Quartermaster Sergeant and you may have some idea of the dangers connected with what we had to do, when I tell you that though we had only about half-a-mile to go for the rations, it took us from half past seven in the morning until half past two in the afternoon to get back – seven hours altogether. The explanation is that the snipers were so awful and you had to watch your chance, dodging just a little at a time, otherwise you were bound to be picked off. For about three hundred yards, we were forced to wade up to our waists, in mud and water and one of my chums, happening to put his foot on someone's dead body, found the bottom of his puttee covered with blood. There was one part, about fifty yards in distance, where we had to run the gauntlet, which was fully exposed to the fire of the enemy's machine guns and here we had to dash across, one at a time.

I managed to get across safely, but the Quartermaster and another man were both hit. Then somehow the rest of us got separated and there were only six left to go for rations and wherever we could not help exposing ourselves, the snipers were potting at us immediately.

Also serving with the 6th Manchesters was 18-year-old Private Charles Frederick Binns. Like many of the men who would later become officers during the war, Charlie came from a middle class background. The family lived in the Heaton Moor district of Stockport, where his father's employment as director of a cotton spinning company allowed the family to employ a live-in servant. Binns was educated at Manchester Grammar School and worked as a bank clerk. Like many of his contemporaries, he was a keen athlete and sportsman and enjoyed riding his motorbike. He had also found time to join the Territorials in about 1910. Not long after arriving at Gallipoli, he wrote home:

Private Charles Binns, Manchester Regiment.

We have just finished dinner – a fine stew made in our mess tins out of bully beef and desiccated vegetables. We have become expert cooks and have concocted some weird and wonderful dishes. For breakfast, we generally have pobs made of biscuits, water and sugar; bacon frizzled in our mess tins, bits of biscuit cooked in the bacon fat, bread and jam. The biscuits, by the way, are like dog biscuits but, all the same, very nice. For dinner, we have a stew if possible; if not a tin of corned or 'bully' beef and biscuits. For tea we have cheese and biscuits and, if there's a good supply of water, we have tea at each meal. We get it from a well for cooking and the water carts for drinking. In the second line, we get it from a spring and, in the firing line, we had to sink wells for it. It was muddy but had the advantage of making the tea look as though it had milk in it.

His letter was published in the *Stockport Advertiser* on 11 June 1915. By that time, Charlie Binns was dead. He had been killed during the Third Battle of Krithia on 4/5 June. The whole of the British line, stretching across the peninsula, attacked at noon on the 4th, with Charlie and his comrades in the middle of the battlefield. On their left, the attack of 29th Division and a brigade of Indian troops quickly stalled when they encountered intact defences and heavy Turkish machine gun fire. On the right, the Royal Naval Division had early successes but came under increasingly heavy fire when the French attack, on their right, failed. It left the Manchesters holding an untenable salient into the Turkish lines. Many of them lay dead in No Man's Land, cut down by heavy Turkish machine gun fire.

It is, indeed, terrible the first step you take right in the face of the most deadly fire and to realise that any moment you may be shot down, but if you are not hit, then you seem to gather courage and when you see, on either side of you, men like yourself, it inspires you with a determination to press forward. Well, away we went over the parapet, with fixed bayonets – one long line of us, like the wind, but it was absolute murder, nothing less……This however did not deter us and on we went.....we took six lines of trenches. (Private Ridley Sheldon, 1/6th Battalion, Manchester Regiment)

Sheldon got no further than twenty yards from the British trench before he was wounded in the left thigh. Whilst he was recovering in 1915 and 1916, he wrote the account which has been quoted here. In due course, he was able to return to duty but was transferred to the Royal Engineers and served with them until he returned to civilian life in 1919.

The Manchesters held their captured position from the early afternoon until early evening when, under increasing pressure from the Turks, they were ordered to withdraw to the original Turkish front line and consolidate there. Many were dead, many more were wounded.

Before the war, William Chorlton lived in the North Cheshire village of Northenden. He earned his living as a house painter, working with his older brother and father, both called Thomas. Another pre-war Territorial, he was serving at Gallipoli as a sapper with the East Lancashire Field Company of the Royal Engineers, where his construction trade skills would be put to good use. Writing at the end of June, he said

> We have had bread this morning for the first time in over a fortnight.
> I think we shall have it regularly now, as they have built the field
> ovens at the base.

Chorlton's comments illustrate the lack of planning that had gone into the invasion, with senior commanders thinking the peninsula would be quickly secured and that there would be no need for the infrastructure of a long campaign. It would leave the troops fighting in the heat of summer in southern Turkey with scant regard to the needs of water for drinking and basic hygiene and inadequate food supplies. The History of 42nd Division noted *Fruit – even good tinned fruit – and fresh vegetables would have done much to preserve the health of men during the intense heat of summer.*

Charles Watkins, from Rochdale, was serving with the 6th Battalion, Lancashire Fusiliers, also part of the 42nd (East Lancashire) Division. He later privately published 'Lost Endeavour', an account of his war service:

> The bi-weekly case of jam our sergeant was opening aroused no
> enthusiasm in us – except for the piece of wood the box was made
> of – handy for lighting a little fire for brewing a can of tea. The
> known contents of the box was such that we didn't dwell on thinking
> about it too long – those tins of green frog spawn masquerading
> under the name of plum and apple jam. We had grown to loathe it,
> and God knows – we of all people weren't fussy eaters.
>
> It was the sergeant's long whistle of surprise that first raised a
> gleam in our dull and unenthusiastic eyes. 'HELLO, HEL-LO,
> HEL-LO', he says, loud and slow. 'Wot the 'ell we got 'ere. Reckon

they've given us orficers jams by mistake. Best take it back, save a
bloody row, I spose.'

  By now we had crowded round the opened case and glimpsed
the Treasures of the Incas. Neat little rows of jam of all sorts –
blackcurrant, raspberry, strawberry, gooseberry – anything you
liked. You name it, we had it.

  'Nay, you can't take it back now, Sarge, wot wi' the box bein' all
broke.'

  'Nay, Sarge. They made the mistake – they must stand by it.'

  'Nay, you can't send it back.'

  The chorus of protests mounted. Still our sergeant hesitated.

The sergeant quickly bowed to the pressure from the men, saying that once
the jam was eaten there was nothing anyone could do about it, and it was
soon issued according to preference.

  'Wots thine, Cobber?' he calls to me, 'blackberry? – ee, but Ah
thinks tha's unlucky. Nay, howd on a minute, 'ere yare, blackberry
coming up.'

  All men have a secret vice - or weakness, if you like. Mine's
blackberry jam. For a tin or jar of this delectable conserve, I'd sell
my own grandmother down the river and my children into slavery.
It was Jimmy N who first cracked open the secret. He'd already dug
his bayonet into the soft tin top of the can and hooked out a bladeful.
'Reckon some silly little bitch at the factory put the wrong label on
this bloody tin. It's plum and apple, not strawberry like it says on
the tin.'

  Other tins began to be opened and there was a dead silence. I
didn't dare open mine. The silence was a bit of the silence of sudden
shock – a shock that there could exist anyone in the world who'd
play such a trick on blokes like us in our own poor straits. A few
mutterings later, then despair, hate, disillusionment, cynicism brittle
as glass – all the things that men are better off by being strangers
to – they all crystallised into one black devil of anger. But most of
all there seemed to be a sort of sadness, a sadness that anyone
would play such a trick on soldiers at the front.

  Then we flung the tins of this revolting pseudo jam over to the
Turkish lines like hand grenades. I often wonder if the Turks ever
got 'em.

Conditions for the men continued to deteriorate through the summer.

The seasoned veterans fared better than the new reinforcements, who succumbed at an appalling rate. There had been no break in the hot dry weather. Many of the wells had gradually become defiled, others had run dry and this no doubt contributed greatly to the amount of sickness. The insanitary conditions inseparable from the type of warfare waged in so confined and exposed a space, the continuous strain exacted from all, the lack of sleep, the tropical heat, the monotonous and unsuitable food, the lice and, above all, the plague of flies, with which no sanitary measures could cope, all were in their degree responsible for the deplorable results. The country was one huge graveyard in which hundreds of corpses of friends and foes lay unburied and the air was heavy with the stench. Flies clustered in noisome masses on everything that attracted them, on the food and in the mess-tins as these were carried to one's mouth, on sores, on faces and hands – blue and green monsters too lazy to fly or crawl away and to kill fifty was but to invite five thousand to attend the funeral. Under such conditions men lived and moved and even kept a stout heart. (History of 42nd Division)

Biscuits at Gallipoli.

The monotony of the food, particularly in the early weeks of the campaign, was bad for morale. Almost daily the ration was tinned bully beef and army biscuits and the men did the best they could to introduce some variety into what they were eating. One of the problems with the bully beef was that, in the heat, the contents turned into an unappetising liquid. Born in Somerset in about 1888, Frank Phillips was a proof-reader for a printing company in Frome before the war and, in his spare time, was a Territorial soldier, serving with the Royal Army Medical Corps. Corporal Phillips arrived at Suvla Bay, Gallipoli on 8 October 1915, attached to the West Somerset Yeomanry. The Yeomanry was a prewar cavalry unit but was now fighting, dismounted, as infantry. Phillips kept a diary of his time at Gallipoli:

Stores at Gallipoli, including crates of American corned beef – Rex brand from Cudahy Canning of Omaha and Supreme brand from Morris & Co of Chicago. Photo: Australian War Memorial.

A few recipes might be of interest:
1. Cut up a tin of bully beef in slices and fry
2. Cut up some bully beef very fine. Beat up some hard biscuits until they are like flour, cut up a little bit of onion, well mix with water, then roll into balls and fry in boiling fat.
3. Beat up biscuits and make into paste and fry
4. When flour is obtainable, which is not often, make pancakes of flour and water and a few currants when you can get them
5. Soak biscuits in water and then boil, adding milk and sugar (if any) or perhaps add a few raisins or currants (again if any) otherwise have them plain.
6. Stew raisins.[83]

In comparison with many other units there, the Yeomanry had a relatively easy time, with only eleven fatalities during their time on the peninsula. However, like the other units, they had many men reporting sick and, by 4 December, they had been reduced to just 111 men. They left the peninsula on the 19th, moving to the nearby Greek island of Imbros. Phillips survived those rigours only to be killed in action, on 6 November 1917, during the fighting against the Turks in Palestine. The precise nature of his death is not known but it is understood that his unit was involved in a successful attack on the enemy positions at Tes es Sheria, described here:

This attack was a fine performance, the troops advancing eight or nine miles during the day and capturing a series of very strong works covering a front of about seven miles, the greater part of which had been held and strengthened by the enemy for over six months. Some 600 prisoners were taken and some guns and machine guns captured. Our casualties were comparatively slight. The greatest opposition was encountered by the Yeomanry in the early morning, the works covering the left of the enemy's line being strong and stubbornly defended. (General Edmund Allenby, Despatch, London Gazette, 22 January 1918)

Jack Morten served with the 7th Battalion, Manchester Regiment, from September 1914 and had come through two hard battles at Gallipoli, losing friends on both occasions. With the losses mounting, he was promoted to second lieutenant on 1 September 1915 and now had an officer's servant to cook for him:

I always have my best sleep from 6.30 to 8.30 and as a rule don't waken up until my man puts the bacon and eggs (eggs are not an army issue) under my nose, then my latent energy springs up and I do full justice to it. Breakfast over, I have a good swill then at 10 o'clock I inspect the rifles and gas helmets of my men.

I don't have much for lunch as it so hot, but a favourite lunchtime dish of mine is to have one suet dumpling with Golden Syrup over it and two cups of tea (my man is a dab hand at making dumplings). In the afternoon, I do all my writing and have dinner about 6pm which consists of steak and eggs, or else a stew washed down with two cups of tea. My menu is not a very varied one but I always enjoy my meal. Then of course at times we can procure tinned fish and fruit from the canteen, but the demand is so great that usually by the time my man gets down from the trenches they have nothing left but eggs and milk.[84]

The 2/1st Battalion, London Regiment spent the early part of 1915 on garrison duty in Malta but was sent to Gallipoli as much needed fresh troops, arriving at Suvla Bay on 24 September. Among them was Private Harold Boughton:

Gallipoli Pudding was created as a diversion from the hard biscuits. We used to take two or three of these, lay them on a flat stone and bash them with our entrenching tool handles into a sort of meal or flour. If we were lucky enough to have any water, we would mix it up with the flour and make a ball about the size of a cricket ball. We rolled the ball in our khaki handkerchiefs , used or unused, and put them in our mess tins with some water. We built enough fuel to make a little fire, put the tin on that and boiled them in there. Of course, the khaki used to come out of the handkerchief and that was good because it used to give a Christmassy look to the pudding. When we thought they were done, we used to turn this horrible mess out and eat it. But it made a change.[85]

By the end of November, the Londons had been reduced to almost half strength. Only twenty-two men had been killed or had died of wounds and only fifty seven wounded but 445 men had reported sick – dysentery and jaundice being the main illnesses at this time on the peninsula, although the changing weather conditions meant that men also started to suffer from frostbite.

Live sheep being taken ashore at Gallipoli for issue to Indian troops. Photo: Australian War Memorial, C01662.

Ghurkha field kitchen at Gallipoli. Photo: Australian War Memorial, C00681.

The monotony of the food could be relieved by buying additional food at the divisional canteen. General Sir Ian Hamilton, commander of forces at Gallipoli, wrote in his diary on 20 August about the growing need to set-up canteens.

> *Put through a lot with Altham. Am pressing him to hurry up with his canteens at Helles, Anzac and Suvla. In May I cabled the Q.M.G. begging him either to let me run a canteen on the lines of the South African Field Force Canteen, myself; or, to run it from home, himself; or, to put the business into the hands of some private firm like the Mess and Canteen Company, or Lipton's, or Harrods or anything he liked. In South Africa we could often buy something. In France our troops can buy anything. Here, had they each the purse of Fortunatus, they could buy nothing. A matter this, I won't say of life and death, but of sickness and health. Now, after three months without change of diet, the first canteen ship is about due. A mere flea bite of £10,000 worth. I am sending the whole of it to the Anzacs to whom it will hardly be more use than a bun is to a she bear. Only yesterday a letter came in from Birdie* [Major General William Birdwood, commanding the ANZACs] *telling me that the doctors all say that the sameness of the food is making the men sick. The rations are A.1., but his men now loathe the very look of them after having had nothing else for three months. Birdie says, "If we could only get this wretched canteen ship along, and if, when*

she comes she contains anything like condiments to let them buy freely from her, I believe it would make all the difference in the world. But the fact remains that at present we cannot count on anything like a big effort from the men who have been here all these months.

The canteen ship arrived a few days later and, by October, Able Seaman Archibald Robert Peters, Drake Battalion, Royal Naval Division, had been able to do some shopping. He kept a diary of his time at Gallipoli and this is now held by the Imperial War Museum. In the collection of his papers, is a price list from one of the canteens, including the following items, in October 1915:

Apples (tinned) - 9d
Biscuits (packet) - 1s
Butter, 1lb – 2s 6d
Yorkshire Relish – 6½d
Rowntree's Fruit Gums – 1s 5d
Chutney – 6d
Golden Syrup – 6½d
Herrings (tin) – 8d
Herrings in tomato sauce (tin) – 11d
Sausages, 1lb – 1s 8d

Apparently the golden syrup and fruit gums were in short supply.

At last the Division have wakened up and opened a Divisional Canteen which opened last Sunday, so Woodward and myself thought of the early bird and the worm and sent a man off in the early hours of the morning to await the opening of it and, by Jove, we have fed like fighting cocks ever since.

The various luxuries we received were Cambridge sausages, tinned fruit and cream, potted meat, pickles, Worcester sauce, biscuits, Genoa cakes and last but not least a 1lb tin of Irish butter (the first since leaving home) so you can imagine how we have lived and you will not be surprised to hear that poor old Woodward has been troubled this last day or so with diarrhoea and tummy, but my old tummy is as good a pal to me as ever, so I think that the various mixtures which the Army has pushed down me for the last twelve

British field bakery, probably on the Greek island of Lemnos. The island was a major supply base for the troops at Gallipoli, just fifty kilometres away. Photo: Australian War Memorial, G00281.

Breakfast in Shrapnel Gully, in the north of the Gallipoli battlefield. Photo: Australian War Memorial, H15685.

months has made it absolutely proof against being upset with such delicacies.

(Second Lieutenant Jack Morten, 1/7th Battalion, Manchester Regiment)

Not long after this, Morten was evacuated away from Gallipoli after a relatively minor scratch to his hand turned septic. He did not return to duty until May 1916, by which time the Manchesters were back in Egypt. He wrote home on 17 September, telling the family that they were now in the desert but had celebrated the birthday of Captain Higham, the company commander. It was very much a scratch meal but, as Mess President, Morten was pleased to have ensured an eight course feast:

Soup made from OXO cubes
Tinned lobster
Tinned chicken, with peas bought from the canteen
Ration beef, with beans and new potatoes (also from the canteen)
Pears and cream
Gingerbread
Savoury – sardines on toast
Coffee

The Glasgow Territorials of the 5th Battalion, Highland Light Infantry, landed at Cape Helles on 2 July. They were soon in action, reinforcing the troops who had been there since April, supporting an attack by other Scottish battalions on the 12th. It was initially successful but the Turks then counter-attacked.

For a time the situation was critical. It looked as if "A" Company were to be driven back and the trench lost. But they soon steadied down to hold on. The Turkish grenade had a fuse which burns for 8 to 10 seconds; it therefore rarely explodes until some seconds after it has fallen. Recognising this, some of our bolder spirits began to pick up and throw back the enemy's grenades. Pte. J. Melrose and Corporal A.R. Kelly were amongst the first to attempt this and their example was quickly followed by others. It was a deadly dangerous game, for it was impossible to tell how long any fuse had still to burn and the grenade might explode at any moment, but though several men were killed and wounded in this way, the survivors persisted bravely and the Turkish advance was effectually checked.[86]

The men remained in the forward area until the 18th when they were relieved to a rest camp, where they remained for the rest of the month.

About 6 p.m. we reached our destination, a series of holes in the ground lying between the Pink Farm Road and 'X' Beach, and about a mile behind the Farm itself. The Quarter-Master, Lieut. T. Clark, and his satellites had a good meal of hot stew and potatoes ready for us, and lots of tea, after which we stretched our blankets on the ground, lay down and fell asleep......

.... The climate, the flies, and the experiences of the preceding fortnight had already begun to tell upon the general health of the Battalion. Diarrhoea and dysentery were prevalent throughout all the troops on the Peninsula, and we suffered with the rest. One factor which contributed to, if indeed it was not—as many of us believed—the primary cause of, the prevalence of these diseases, was the unsuitability of bully-beef and hard biscuits as the basis of our diet under the weather and other conditions in which we were then living. This was quickly recognised by the medical authorities and important modifications were soon introduced in the scale of rations. The toothsome Maconochie, rather rich for the average digestion under a tropical sun, disappeared in the meantime from the menu. Fresh meat—or, to speak more strictly, frozen meat—of excellent quality was substituted for bully, which latter was only issued on the rare occasions when, owing to transport difficulties, no frozen was available. The hard biscuits gave place to good bread; the ration of desiccated vegetables was increased; an issue of rice was instituted; cheese was reduced and preserved milk increased. The only rations which were never quite sufficient to satisfy the men were those of tea and sugar—especially sugar. They liked their tea very strong and very sweet, and quickly tired of rice unless boiled with lots of sugar, which the limited rations of sugar did not run to. Jam was plentiful and popular; marmalade only appealed to a limited circle. Some uncharitably minded fighting men were wont to insinuate that the best beloved brands of jam, such as strawberry and raspberry, never got beyond the Beach, the A.S.C. who handled the supplies being suspected of a nefarious weakness for these varieties. One hesitates to listen to such calumnious suggestions, but it must be admitted that for many long weeks we received an overwhelming proportion of 'Apricot Jam'

French field kitchen at Gallipoli. Photo: Australian War Memorial, G00478.

V Beach, Gallipoli. Fish were killed by exploding shells and became an occasional part of the diet. Photo: Australian War Memorial, G00329.

Australian field bakery on the island of Imbros. The island was ceded to Greece in 1912 and became a supply base for the Gallipoli invasion. Photo: Australian War Memorial, C04618.

> *with which, popular as it originally was, the men became so 'fed up' that they changed its name to 'Parapet Jam', because, they explained, it was so invariably thrown over the parapet instead of being eaten.*

Even in the rest camp area, the Glaswegians were still within range of the Turkish artillery but only

> *once in these weeks were we treated to a dose of high explosives. This happened about seven one morning when most of the officers were at breakfast in the swimming-bath mess room. Six big 'coal-boxes' were hurled on us in rapid succession. One exploded near our mule lines just beyond the Quartermaster's dump, doing no damage to speak of; a second landed and burst right inside a trench occupied by several of the Headquarters signallers. We thought they were all wiped out, but, miraculously, not a man was hurt. They were even laughing—somewhat nervously, it must be admitted—as they scrambled out of the ruined trench. Another shell exploded about 30 yards short of our mess, leaving a symmetrical saucer-shaped crater about 6 feet in diameter and a little over 2 feet deep in the centre. Its dust showered over us and covered our unfinished meal with a thick layer. It had been an unusually attractive breakfast too!*

There may have been some truth to the allegation that the Army Service Corps troops kept back items intended for the infantry. In 1974, Frank Woolmer Parker gave an interview[87] in which he mentions there was extra bacon and other items for 'friends'. Parker was a New Zealander who farmed at Blenheim, on the country's South Island, and had been commissioned as a lieutenant in the infantry in 1914, but was transferred to the Army Service Corps in Egypt before going to Gallipoli. He is believed to have served on the Peninsula with the ASC's New Zealand Divisional Train and had responsibilities for allocating delivery of foodstuffs to battalions.

> *I was calling out so much tea, so much sugar, so much biscuits and that sort of thing to the section which were issuing them out and when I come to bacon, so many pounds of bacon. 'Oh, if you please, Sir, We are Jews. We do not eat bacon. They are from an unclean animal.' I said, alright, all the more for everybody else and what they didn't have, the next day when the next unit came along, I gave them three or four pounds extra bacon to make it go round . We used it up. Anyhow, after three days I think it was, he came to me one morning and said we have had special dispensation from the rabbi to eat bacon. We are not getting enough to eat. We would like our bacon ration. So I said, right oh, and I called out the amount of bacon but he said, 'if you please, we would like our back rations as well. We can have them now.' I said, I'm afraid you can't. You are a bit late. They got on alright, I think.*
>
> *The Canadians had a terrible amount of bacon written off. He [The Canadian Medical Officer] would say 'unfit for human consumption, write it off.' The Canadian bacon used to come in great big long cases. It looked to me as if they just put salt in the bottom of the box and then as many sides of bacon on top and then covered them up with salt. Half the bacon was putrid. Where they over-lapped each other, they went bad and, of course, it would smell to high heaven and the doctor would say you can't issue that to the boys. Well, of course, after he had gone, we would turn it out and it would be about a quarter of the stuff was bad. The rest would be good. So, we had extra bacon for the rest of our friends. The same thing with cigarettes and rum. We had a lot of fun with the rum.*

The Canadians mentioned by Parker will have been the men of the

Newfoundland Regiment. At the time, Newfoundland had not yet joined Canada and its men fought as an individual battalion, for much of the time part of 29th Division.

> *In August, there had been a fair supply of vegetables and raisins, but as a general rule the onion was the only vegetable obtainable. A small consignment of strawberry jam actually reached the trenches. By one of those lucky accidents that occur all too rarely the labels had been removed from the tins and as the happy warrior enjoyed the unaccustomed treat his fancy toyed with the picture of the anguish and indignation of the profiteer and the conscientious objector on learning that their strawberry jam had been sent in error to the brutal soldier and on being asked if they would take 'plum and apple' instead. Plum and apple was now anathema. No longer would the poilu proffer his delicacies in barter and even the Senegalese declined to trade. The flies were less fastidious*
>
> *Cookhouses were now established in Gully Ravine; the battalion chefs made the most of the ingredients at their disposal; and as the nights grew chilly the hot well-cooked meals were more and more appreciated. Improvisation was the crowning art of that weird-looking soldier, the cook, and one essential qualification for the job was the ability to 'win' wood. In justice to him it must be admitted that he generally possessed this qualification and he did good work. Cookhouses were no safer than other spots behind the line and the cook's job was not a cushy one. In one cookhouse in the ravine a shell exploded when some dixies of rice were on the fire. The cook, uninjured in body but indignant at the mess made, gazed disgustedly at the debris. His only comment was 'Might have been a b..... wedding in here!'*

(History of 42nd Division)

* * * *

By September of 1915, it had become clear that the invasion had been a failure. It was now a matter of consolidating whilst preparations were made for an evacuation. Troops in the northern sector, around Suvla Bay and ANZAC Cove, were gradually withdrawn from 7 December and all were evacuated by the 20th. In the south, around Cape Helles, the final withdrawal of British troops was made on 8 January 1916.

On Christmas Day, we catapulted over a tin of bully beef for a bit of fun. Three or four days later it came back to us. It was weighted with mud and stones. Inside there was a message written in good English. "We are sorry you are leaving, we'll meet you again at Suez." They knew that we were leaving.[88]
(Trooper Edwin Pope, West Kent Yeomanry)

It could be argued that the withdrawals were the best planned and executed aspects of the whole campaign as, although large quantities of stores had to be left to fall into Turkish hands, the evacuations were carried out without death or serious injury to any of the troops. Many of the troops were withdrawn from the peninsula back to Egypt, where they had started out at the beginning of the previous year. They would find the fighting to be of a very different nature. Rather than months spent in trenches, often within grenade throwing distance of the enemy, large distances would now have to be marched to engage the Turks across Palestine.

Joining them were the men of the 16th Battalion, West Yorkshire Regiment – known as the Bradford Pals. Amongst them was Reg Oxtoby. In his mid-20s, Oxtoby had worked in the family business, manufacturing worsted cloth. Like many of the Pals battalions, the 16th was formed in September 1914. There was a long training period but, at the beginning of December 1915, the Pals were ready to go on active service. They arrived at Alexandria on the 22nd. Early in the new year, they moved to the town of Kantara, on the banks of the Suez Canal, where Oxtoby wrote home on 13 February.[89]

We have not had much scope for spending money here, but we manage to get through it somehow. The regimental canteen supplies bread, oranges, chocolate, soap and one or two extras at Egyptian prices (which are very high) and the transport bring the other things for their friends – jam, treacle, milk, butter, biscuits, etc. I have had all of these at various times, except butter which I do not care for. I have only tasted butter once this year and I did not like it – it is packed in tins like everything else and is very strong in flavour, almost rancid.

We had some very good jam this week – today's ration including a 1lb tin of Silver Shred marmalade which is a treat after the usual 'Household' and 'Mixed Fruit' or 'Plum and Apple' which are army favourites.

The Bradford men's stay in Egypt would be brief and, on 29 February 1916, they left, heading for France, where they would serve for the remainder of the war.

The East Kent Yeomanry was another pre-war Territorial cavalry unit that found itself fighting as infantry at Gallipoli, landing there on 24 September 1915. Among them was Private William Rawlins Bowden, from Margate. They were attached to the East Lancashire Territorials of the 42nd Division, taking their turn of duty in the front line before being withdrawn from Gallipoli on 30 December. They spent some time on the island of Mudros before moving to Egypt in the middle of January 1916. After a few days reorganising, 42nd Division took up defensive positions on the east bank of the Suez Canal, with outposts stretching a few miles further eastwards. The defences were quickly established in case there should be a Turkish attack.

> *The parcel mail arrived this evening. Of course, I didn't expect one. There are two in my tent so we are alright, the boys usually share them. We have also got parcels for boys who are still in hospital at Malta and some from three left at Gallipoli. Poor devils. The contents of their parcels are distributed between the other boys.*[90]
> (Private William Rawlins Bowden, letter to mother, 27 March 1916)

In late 1915, whilst Bowden was still at Gallipoli, British forces in north west Egypt came under serous attack from a force of irregular troops of the Senussi, a religious sect of tribesmen from neighbouring Libya. They had been urged to action by the Ottoman Empire and received support from it. On 21 November, the Senussi force crossed the border, attacking the small British garrison at the village of Sollum, forcing the defenders into a withdrawal. A much larger force was now assembled to retake the lost ground. It comprised three Territorial battalions and a battalion of Sikhs, supported by cavalry, artillery and armoured cars of the Royal Naval Air Service. There were several engagements over the following weeks. In all cases, these were successful and Sollum was reoccupied in the middle of March, with the surrounding area secured. Sometime after this, the East Kent Yeomanry was detached from 42nd Division and moved to Sollum as part of its garrison.

> *It would be alright here if only there was more shipping. Our boat never brings enough grub. We are always running short of potatoes*

Turkish bakers, possibly in Palestine. Photo: Australian War Memorial, P03093.

Turkish field kitchen in Palestine. Photo: Australian War Memorial, P00360.

and onions. Onions are scarce in Egypt. It's a good thing we are able to get things from the canteen. Our grub hasn't been fit for a dog this week. I have just finished making some rissoles. I felt so hungry, so I minced the bully up with biscuit crumbs and fried it in bacon fat and now I feel full up but the damn stuff repeats for an hour or two afterwards. They say we are going to get better grub next week so we have something to look forward to. Some of the boys are thin as rakes – one would think we were in a wild country [but we're] only 200 miles from Alexandria and being short of food! A month or two isn't bad on short rations but when it comes to nearly a year, I reckon that's a scandal. (Private William Rawlins Bowden, letter to his sister, Mag, 30 November 1916)

At the beginning of 1917, the East and West Kent Yeomanry were merged into a newly formed 10th Battalion of the East Kent Regiment and moved to France. Private Bowden remained with the unit until he returned to civilian life in February 1919, where he is thought to have resumed working in the Margate fruit shop owned by the family.

The 1/5th Battalion, Somerset Light Infantry, was a prewar Territorial unit, recruiting in the Taunton area. It was mobilised on the declaration of war and, towards the end of September 1914, was selected to go to India, where it would relieve regular army troops who would then go to the Western Front. They arrived at Bombay on 9 November, moving to a garrison at Jubbulpore. They remained in India until the spring of 1917, when they were despatched to Egypt, arriving at Suez on 11 May. For several months they remained in the rear areas undertaking garrison duty, later making several moves forward over the following weeks until, by mid-August, the Battalion *now, at last, found itself within range of enemy gun fire, and face to face with the rigours of active service conditions.*[91]

In the early part of the year, the Turks withdrew to defensive positions around Gaza. Attempts to dislodge them had taken place in March and April and planning for a third attempt was underway. It was expected to be another difficult assault. The Turkish defences stretched from the sea at Gaza eastwards about thirty miles to Beersheba. At the end of August the Battalion moved forward and went into the trenches under the instruction of an experienced battalion of Argyll and Sutherland Highlanders. On 3 September 1917 they suffered their first fatal casualties in action. A party of men from No. 4 Company were resting in a wadi when a shell burst among them, wounding twelve and killing Thomas Sear and William Webber, both from Bridgwater.

The expected offensive was launched on 31 October but, unlike the two previous attempts which had seen British forces attempt a frontal assault, the attack was successfully delivered on the Turkish flank at Beersheba. The Somersets were not in action that day, but were readied for an assault the next day on more central positions at Middlesex Hill. It would be their first time in significant combat. No. 2 Company was commanded by Lieutenant Harry Lincoln Milsom. His commission as a second lieutenant dated to 22 August 1914 and he had served with the Battalion since then. In 1930, he co-wrote the Battalion's wartime history. In the event, the attack was postponed until just before midnight on the 6th. At 11.30pm, the British artillery opened up, battering down the Turkish barbed wire defences in No Man's Land. A few minutes later, Milsom and the other company commanders led their men forward, storming the Turkish positions with ease. Only three men were wounded in the advance and the remainder were soon able to consolidate their gains.

Advert in The Times, *11 October 1917 – plenty of time to ship a Christmas hamper to the eastern theatres of the war.*

> *When things had quietened down a bit, I went into the village with a Sergeant Jennings and hunted out an observation post in order to get a better view of the surroundings. I also took the precaution of sending Bale, my batman, into the village also to see what he could forage and he later brought me a dozen eggs – a great luxury.*[92]

The Somersets were in action again on the 12th and, on the 16th, moved to near the village of Kezazeh, which had recently been taken. The troops were given to understand that there would be ten days rest there and, possibly, they would remain in the area over the winter. Milson wrote:

One or two small villages nearby were soon looted of all possible foods and my batman was unable to find anything to relieve the monotony of bully beef and biscuits which had been our sole grub hitherto. "D" Company were first in the field with the nearest village and in half an hour not even an old hen was left. The Lewis gunners created a diversion by trying to pick off the fowls with their revolvers. Not a bird was hit, though the poor inhabitants had narrow escapes. A few oranges could be got and most delicious they were too and very sweet though the skin was quite green.....

....I went off with Bale in one village but not a thing could we find except one pigeon which I commandeered and gave the owner half a piaster. That bird we boiled in a mess tin and never have I tried to set my teeth into anything tougher – it was not a success. Saturday night, I was invited to dine with Major Griffin, who commanded the battery I had been attached to at Lees Hill. The dinner was a revelation to a poor infantryman like me. It consisted of tinned salmon, fresh mutton, peas (tinned), fig pudding and a sardine savoury. For drinks, we had whisky and soda and an excellent liqueur brandy.

The rest period was shortened and the Somersets returned to action on 23 November, the Battalion history noting,

The enemy artillery put down a terrific barrage of high explosive shells and shrapnel. Through this inferno of shellfire the attackers advanced with the greatest courage, keeping perfect formation, as if on parade. But worse was to come, for on passing through the artillery barrage, the lines came under a veritable hail of bullets from enemy machine guns in front, the northern slopes of Nebi Samwil on the right and the high ground on the left. This devastating enfilade fire from all sides wrought terrible havoc and the lines seemed to melt away.

Forty Somersets were dead and Harry Milsom was amongst 141 wounded. As far as is known, his injuries were such that he was not able to return to duty and was later discharged from the army. The 5th Somersets continued to be engaged with the enemy until the Armistice in November 1918 and remained in Egypt on garrison duties until the autumn of 1919. Milsom married after the war and, in about 1920, the couple had a son. On 29

March 1940, Pilot Officer Darrell Milsom's plane collided with another in mid-air, killing both pilots.

*   *   *   *

The reader will return to the Middle East later in the chapter but, for now, it's time to look much further west.

The United States of America did not enter the war until 6 April 1917. There would be a slow build-up of troops arriving in France and it would not be until 4 July 1918 that four companies, totalling around 1000 men, were able to undertake the first offensive action by the American Expeditionary Force. Significant numbers of troops would not be in the field until the middle of September. They would see hard fighting for the remaining eight weeks of the war. However, a not inconsiderable number of Americans saw service much earlier. Many went north and joined Canadian forces. Others, like Harry Butters, travelled to Britain to enlist. A Californian from a middle class family, he had spent a year of his youth at Beaumont College, a Jesuit public school in Berkshire. He felt that Britain's cause was just and that he should be part of it. The *Cheltenham Chronicle* described his decision, in September 1916:

He put aside as fair a prospect of wealth, success, happiness and long life as could well open before a young man and determined to throw in his lot with the old country and the Allies in the fight for civilisation against all the armed might of lawless iniquity which had flung itself on Belgium.

Butters arrived in London in February 1915 and, after a day or so, went to live with friends in Stow on the Wold. His letters home were published in 1918 by his stepmother and they show that, immediately on arrival in Britain, he applied to become an officer. Originally commissioned into the Royal Warwickshire Regiment, Second Lieutenant Butters soon transferred to the Royal Field Artillery, going overseas in September 1915.

On 26 November, he wrote home to his stepmother:

The gorgeous package arrived today, also your postcard. Thank Heavens my letter two days ago will be an alibi against the charge that I only write in reply to parcels. Did you make the hot cakes? Had two Canadians to lunch and we polished off the whole lot –

Lieutenant Harry Butters – a Californian in the Royal Field Artillery.

hot, with butter and, luxury of luxuries – hot maple syrup. The corn formed the first vegetable course and was positively lovely; I've just thought that if you can get Campbell's tomato soup it would be nice – but nothing could top the corn. I'm saving the Huntley and Palmer biscuits for the road but am chewing a raisin right now.

Harry Butters was killed in action on 31 August 1916, aged 24. His friend and comrade, Captain Nelson Zambra, wrote to the family to tell them what had happened.

Harry and another officer were in the dugout at the gun position. The Germans were putting over a heavy barrage of gas shells and the air became very poisonous and oppressive. Harry said "It's time we moved out of this" and went out. Immediately he was outside, a gas shell hit him direct. Death must have been instantaneous and the officer with him removed his gas helmet to make sure. So, some little consolation remains to us that he was spared all pain. A Roman Catholic chaplain buried him beneath the Union Jack (we tried to get an American flag but one was not procurable).

Butters is buried at Meaulte Military Cemetery, Somme, France. He is remembered as 'An American Citizen' on the war memorial inside St Edward's Church, Stow-on-the-Wold.

The town of Andover, Massachusetts, was one of many small communities in America which initially viewed the European war as being very distant from their lives. But many of its inhabitants had British ancestry and, within a few weeks of the declaration of war in August 1914, letters were received from relatives in the 'old country' telling of family who were now on the Western Front. Even before America joined the war, the community had lost one of its members. William Pert originated from Dundee and had emigrated to Andover prior to the war, having previously served as a regular in the British Army, enlisting when he was eighteen. In 1914, Pert was on a visit to Scotland and rejoined his original unit, the Black Watch. He was killed in action, reportedly shot by a sniper at the Battle of Loos on 25 September 1915. Other relatively new immigrants to the USA also served with British or Canadian forces.

In anticipation that their country would soon join the conflict, the people of Andover formed a Committee on Public Safety in March 1917. It would quickly form sub-committees, including one to oversee the recruitment of a local home guard, and an aid committee which would be able to give attention to needy cases caused by men joining the army. Much of the Committee's time would be spent fundraising and

Private William Pert had been a regular soldier before emigrating to the USA but rejoined the Black Watch on the outbreak of war. He was killed in action on 25 September 1915.

encouraging the population to buy government bonds intended to help finance the war effort. The community was good at fundraising and, at

Christmas 1915, Andover sent one hundred pounds to the soldiers' 'comforts fund' at Brechin, where many residents had family ties. Of particular interest is the Food Production Committee which quickly met with the leading vegetable growers, mill owners and other local agricultural interests.

> *Patriotic citizens at once offered the use of land in different parts of the town, the purchase of seeds and fertilizer was undertaken by the Committee, the lands carefully ploughed, fertilized and divided into workable size gardens and a garden supervisor was engaged. The first year found the regular gardeners planting more land and devoting a larger portion of their land to potatoes, beans, cabbage and turnips. The small gardener, who cultivated his individual garden, was advised by the supervisor and seventy-eight of these gardens were planted and developed on lands donated by our citizens. The applicants for these gardens not using the entire land, the remaining portion was used by the Committee for potatoes and a crop sufficient to meet the expense was harvested and sold.*
>
> *The ladies of the town, working with the Food Production Committee, organized a Canning Club and were allowed by the School Committee the use of one of the basements of the Punchard School and there faithfully and successfully preserved not only vegetables but fruits and the sales of their products yielded a profit at the end of the season.*(Andover in the World War, Claude M Fuess, 1921)

Nearly 600 Andover men would serve in the forces during the war, of whom the book quoted above records fourteen who died in service. Many of the men who enlisted from the town found themselves in units of the newly formed 26th Division, comprised mainly of men serving in the National Guards of the various New England states. They were the second American division to arrive in France, with its various units coming together there at the end of October 1917. They went into the trenches for the first time at the beginning of February 1918. The Americans would soon be voicing the same complaints about food as the British had since 1914.

Lieutenant Jeremiah Evarts, commanding a platoon of the 18th Infantry, 1st Division, in trenches at Cantigny thought it was *the most extraordinary game of life and death ever invented. Men lived on their wits, their nerves and that sixth sense which combined all other senses and were assisted to live once each twenty-four hours – if the chow party was lucky – by a slice of meat, a spoonful of sour mashed potatoes, a canteen of water, a canteen cup of coffee, a half-loaf of bread, a beautiful country and sometimes a sunny sky.[93]*

On 17 July, the men of the 1st Division were in action near the village of Saconin-et-Breuil, to the south west of the town of Soissons. There was very heavy fighting and the Americans suffered many casualties, dead and wounded, though eventually generally succeeding in gaining their objectives.

Hunger got the best of us. All afternoon small groups wandered up and down the valley, searching discarded enemy packs for food. I went into the deserted village on our left, Saconin-et-Brieul, if the signs spoke correctly, and found some wine. This, plus some salvaged crumbly sausage and some dark hardtack that I found on a dead German, helped my hunger. (Gerald V Stamm, 26th Regiment[94])

Three Andover men would die between the beginning of September and the Armistice. Charles Young, serving with the 101st Regiment, was reported to have been wounded in the hand during fighting in July. Although in hospital, blood poisoning set in and he died on 2 September. A comrade, Sergeant John Murphy, was also serving with the 101st Regiment when he was killed by a shell on 27 October. And finally, Second Lieutenant Tom Carter, 9th Regiment, was killed by machine gun fire on 4 November, just one week before the war ended.

*   *   *   *

Charles Young, from Andover, Massachusetts, 101st Regiment, US Army. Died on 2 September 1918.

In the relatively short period that American troops were in the combat zones, 3602 were taken prisoner.[95] They would join over two million other Allied soldiers held as prisoners in Germany. Some had been there since the early days of the war. Private Alfred Whistler, originally from the Paddington area of London, was a regular soldier serving with the 1st Battalion, Cheshire Regiment. As described in Chapter 1, the Battalion was in action on 24 August 1914. Many were wounded and captured, including Whistler. He would soon be joined by other men serving with the Cheshires who had a connection with Stockport. On 22 October, George Ainscough and his comrades were preparing trenches near the village of Voilanes, when they were surprised by a heavy German attack. The Germans captured the position with a bayonet charge which left 200 men dead, wounded or captured. The following month, the Cheshires, now at Ypres, came under another attack which forced them to withdraw 150 yards to reserve trenches. Another thirty men were dead, wounded or missing. Sergeant Edmund Kelly was taken prisoner.

The internationally agreed rules for the humane treatment of prisoners of war were governed by the Hague Convention of 1907.

The Government into whose hands prisoners of war have fallen is charged with their maintenance. In the absence of a special agreement between the belligerents, prisoners of war shall be treated as regards board, lodging, and clothing on the same footing as the troops of the Government who captured them.

Although conditions in the prisoner of war camps in Germany could be harsh, it was not always so. Private William Wadsworth, from York, was serving with the 1st Battalion, King's Own Yorkshire Light Infantry, when he was wounded and captured on 9 May 1915, during the Second Battle of Ypres.

I was lying down holding an artery, and a German private put his rifle up to shoot me, but desisted when I pointed out that I was wounded. He then threatened me with the butt, and I again told him I was wounded, when he dressed my wounds, gave me a drink of water and shook hands with me. After this, other German soldiers, who had passed me and been recalled by their officers, punched and kicked me as they returned. I was punched and kicked and spat upon by about six men.

(Post war returning prisoner interview)

Wadsworth received treatment to his leg wounds at a German field hospital and, after several days, was moved by train to a camp at Göttingen in Lower Saxony, where he was admitted to the camp hospital for further operations on his legs. He remained in hospital for several weeks.

> *So far as I personally was concerned, the food was excellent; my ordinary ration for the day was – two rolls of white bread and coffee for breakfast. Soup for dinner, coffee in the afternoon. Soup for supper; extras in the morning, a basin of milk; at 10 o'clock rice-pudding, two eggs; bouillon at 12 o'clock, custard or chocolate pudding, & c.; 3 o'clock, basin of milk and two glasses of wine, 5 o'clock potatoes and meat; 9 o'clock, two glasses of wine. I received extra rations for two or three months...... I received letters and parcels regularly; two or three times a week. The letters were opened by the Germans before I received them; the parcels were opened by an orderly in my presence. Matches and letters in the parcels were confiscated – these were prohibited in parcels. I was allowed to write one postcard a week and two letters a month.*

He continued to have problems with blood circulation and, at the end of June, it was necessary to amputate the toes on his right foot. He remained a prisoner until May 1916 when he was released and allowed to return to Britain in accordance with the rules for the repatriation of prisoners no longer posing a military threat. Food in the hospital was much better than that enjoyed by other prisoners. Often there would be nothing more than bread and soup, whereas the Hague Convention required men to be fed as well as German troops. The difficulties of getting adequate food worsened as the Allied naval blockade of Germany took effect. In March 1917, *The Times* reported that the ration consisted of a four-inch square of bread and acorn juice or chicory as a substitute for coffee in the morning; vegetable soup at midday, containing small quantities of potato and meat; and a small piece of cheese and coffee substitute in the evening.

Men became increasingly dependent on the parcels from home, as mentioned by William Wadsworth. In response the Central Prisoners of War Committee of the Red Cross started to send regular food parcels to all troops held in PoW camps. As well as parcels sent as part of its own programme, it co-ordinated parcels being prepared by many voluntary bodies across the country. By November 1916, the Stockport and District Comforts Committee was sending weekly parcels to seventy-four prisoners with local connections, including the three Cheshires mentioned earlier. The parcels always included two loaves of bread, a tin of jam and a tin of meat. The Committee was planning to send them a special Christmas parcel which would include a box of chocolate, one pair of socks, a tin of Nestle milk, another tin of veal and ham, a loaf, packet of tea, a pot of veal and ham paste, a 1lb tin of marmalade, biscuits and a Christmas pudding.

Stockport residents continued to be generous in their donations to the Comforts Committee and, by August 1917, it had been possible to increase the contents of the regular parcels to prisoners. The most recent had contained a tin each of steak and onion, steak pudding, potted meat, spaghetti, jam and cocoa together with a packet of Quaker Oats, one of biscuits and eight ounces of soap, fifty cigarettes, and two ounces of tobacco. A total of 6,522 parcels were sent in the previous year.

Corporal John Hammond was a regular soldier who had been at the Battle of Mons in August 1914 (see Chapter 1). He was captured at the beginning of 1915 and sent to work on a German farm. His experience of captivity was better than for many who were kept in the camps. In a much later interview, he recounted:

I had exactly the same food as the German people. I sat at the same table as them and the first meal I had was a big bowl of potatoes tipped out on the table, in their skins. I was watching the old grandfather and I did exactly the same as he did. He took the fork and, peeling the potato, stuck the fork in. Open them out and he would take three or four at the time like that. I followed him doing the same and all at once the housekeeper came in with a bowl about that size and about that deep [presumably indicating with his hands] *with bacon fat and all that, run down into it. So, you got a piece of potato on the fork, dipped it in the fat and you ate that. That was your evening meal.*

In July 1917, the Red Cross decided to change its arrangement for sending weekly parcels to officer prisoners and, in future, there would be a four week rotation of the contents:[96]

Week 1 – 1lb beef, ½ lb vegetables (cabbage, sprouts, turnips), 1 tin rations, ½ lb cheese, ¼ lb tea, ½ lb Nestle milk, ¾ lb sugar, ½ lb margarine, 1lb jam, 1lb biscuits, 1 tin sardines

Packing food parcels to be sent to prisoners of war.

Week 2 – 1 tin sausages, 1 tin herrings, 1 tin OXO cubes or Marmite, 1lb biscuits, ¼ tin cocoa, ½ lb cooked ham, ½ lb dripping, 1 tin baked beans, ½ lb Nestle milk, 1 tin syrup, pepper, salt, mustard, Knight's carbolic soap

Week 3 – 1 tin beef, 1 tin salmon, ½ lb ration biscuits, ½ lb tin milk, ¼ lb tea, ½ lb sugar, 1 tin fruit, 1 tin OXO cubes, ¼ lb Grape Nuts or Force, ¼ lb figs, chocolate or dates, 1 tin potted meat, small suet pudding, ½ lb margarine or dripping, 1 tablet soap

Week 4 – 1 tin beef or rations, ½ lb tin ham, 1 tin sardines, 1 tin baked beans, 3 soup squares, ¼ lb tea, ½ lb sugar, ½ lb Nestle milk, ½ lb brawn, ½ lb biscuits, ½ lb dripping, ½ lb currant biscuits, 1 tin marmalade

The Red Cross was able to maintain an office in the neutral Netherlands, keeping a store there of emergency parcels. This allowed them to despatch supplies quickly to prisoners if there had been 'unexpected' numbers captured. Its services would be badly needed in the spring of 1918. A major German offensive had been anticipated for some time but it was not known when or where it would be delivered. The answer came in the early hours of 21 March.

By early 1918, the British had developed a new system for defence. Rather than a continuous front line trench, an attacker would encounter a series of redoubts, each the responsibility of a single battalion. The troops would be deployed in and around the redoubt. Approximately two miles behind the redoubts was what was known as the 'battle zone', a more traditional set of trench defences, with a reserve line to the rear of that. The strategy was that the men in the redoubts would slow up the enemy advance, giving time for the stronger forces in the battle zone to prepare and, indeed, allowing time for reserves to be moved forward to support the battle zone.

The plan may have worked had it not been for the strength and ferocity of the German attack on the British positions around the town of St Quentin. The 2/4th Battalion, Oxfordshire & Buckinghamshire Light Infantry was manning Enghien Redoubt north of the town and near to the villages of Fayet and Gricourt.

> *The ground shook to a mighty bombardment. At Amiens windows rattled in their frames. Trench mortars of all calibres and field guns, brought to closest range in the mist and darkness, began to pound a pathway through our wire. Back in artillery dug-outs the light of matches showed the time; it was 4.50 a.m. The hour had struck. Our guns, whose programme in reply was the fruit of two months' preparation, made a peculiar echo as their shells crackled through the mist. Some 'silent' guns fired for the first time. On all headquarters, roads, redoubts, and observation posts the enemy's howitzer shells were falling with descending swoop, and battery positions were drenched with gas.* [97]

The bombardment continued for several hours, the smoke from which added to the thick mist that enveloped the battlefield that morning. The defenders could see little in front of them and the first indication that the infantry attack was underway was when they came under fire from grenades. The men in the outposts in front of the redoubt were quickly overrun, killed or taken prisoner.

> *At one corner of the redoubt some of the enemy broke in but were driven out by D Company with the bayonet. Outside Headquarters the first three men to put their heads over were killed by Germans, who had crept close along the sunken road which leads from Fayet to Selency Château. The rifles and machine guns of the garrison opened up and gained superiority. The defence, destined to last for many hours, of Enghien Redoubt proved an important check to the enemy's advance and helped to save many of our guns.*

PRISONERS OF WAR

Customers must be prepared for parcels taking, in exceptional cases, a very long time to arrive. The quickest time is three weeks, and ten days for a reply.

Bread having been found unsatisfactory, the Firm recommend a substantial fruit cake, called "Scotch Bun," which weighs some 2 lbs and costs 1/9 each cake. It is enclosed in a crust and keeps for several weeks.

Box No. I (Prisoners)

1 Tin Butter	1 Tin Sardines
1 Tin Ox Tail Soup	1 Tin Jam or Marmalade
1 Tin Cheddar Cheese	1 Tin Mixed Biscuits
1 Tin Pressed Beef	1 Tin Water Biscuits
1 Tin Sliced Ham	1 Cake Chocolate
1 Tin Tongue	1 Tin Cigarettes
1 Bot. Sliced Mango Chutnee	1 Tin Cocoa and Milk

Price £1 : 0 : 0.

R Box
Glass Potted Meat
Tin Water Biscuits
Piece Cheddar Cheese
Packet Chocolate
Packet Quaker Oats
Packet Tobacco
Price £0 : 4 : 6.

O Box
1 Tin Jam
1 Tin Marmalade
1 Packet Quaker Oats
1 Tin Potted Meat
1 Box Fruit Biscuits (8 lbs)
1 Packet Chocolate
Price £0 : 10 : 0.

Q Box
Jar Imperial Cheese
Tin large Water Biscuits
1b Chocolate
Cake
Bottle Cresca Figs
Glass Potted Meat
Tin Smoked Sardines
Price £0 : 10 : 0.

V Box
1 Tin Pressed Beef
2 Packets Plasmon Luncheon
1 Tin Jam
1 Tin Camp Pie
1 Box Turtle Tablets
1 Tablet Carbolic Soap
1 Box Cigarettes
1 Tin Large Water Biscuits
1 Tin Smoked Sardines
Price £0 : 10 : 6.

T Box
Khaki Handkerchief
Pair Socks
Box Cigarettes
Tin Tongue
Tablet Coal Tar Soap
Pair Bootlaces
Packet Plasmon Luncheon
Tin F & M's Marmalade
Stick Shaving Soap
Tooth Brush
Tin Tooth Powder
Price £0 : 10 : 6.

S Box
1 Tin Galantine Chicken and Ham
1 Tin Strawberry Jam
1 Koboko Cheese
1 Tin F & M's Sardines
1 F & M's Rich Fruit Cake
1 Packet Chocolate
1 Bottle Malted Milk Tablets
1 Packet China Tea
1 Bottle Saccharine
Price £0 : 15 : 0.

"Scotch Bun," 1/9 each Cake.

A page from the Fortnum & Mason war catalogue showing boxes particularly suitable for sending to prisoners.

Towards late afternoon the men in the redoubt found themselves surrounded and had no alternative but to surrender. The Battalion history suggests that only fifty men were able to escape capture. Not amongst this small number was Private John Cummings. Records suggest that he had originally served with the Regiment's 6th Battalion and had only transferred to the 2/4th Battalion in the February when his original unit was disbanded. In the 1970s, Cummings answered a call for information from Martin Middlebrooke, then writing his book on that day *The Kaiser's Battle*. His observation was that

When we were in a German prison camp, the verdict we passed on
the 21 March fighting was that it was all a proper balls-up.

Cummings was sent to a camp at Langensalza in Thuringia. Within a
month, he received a food parcel from the Regiment's War Prisoners'
Fund. It contained cocoa, sugar, milk, cheese, tinned meat and vegetables,
beans, oats, biscuits, rice, potted meat and a bar of soap.[98] He notes that
another parcel was received on 18 June which included tea, sugar, milk,
jam, dripping, soap, Quaker Oats, dates, beef, beans and 'smokes'.

In October 1918, Langensalza housed just over 27,000 men, of whom
French and Russians made up 21,000. As well as British prisoners, six
other nationalities were represented – Belgian, Serbian, Rumanian, Italian,
Portuguese and American. There were harsh conditions at the camp, with
many men being sent to work in nearby salt mines.

The significance of food parcels may best be summarised by Percy
Holden, a pre-war Territorial from Stockport, who was taken prisoner,
probably around the same time as John Cummings. On his return to Britain
after the Armistice, his letter to the *Stockport Advertiser* was published in
its edition of 27 December 1918.

May I express my sincere gratitude to Mr Hollingsworth and the
officials of the Stockport PoW Comforts Fund, also the public of
Stockport and districts who by their support made it possible to
send parcels to us in prison camps. Oh, those precious parcels
without which many of us would never have returned to Blighty. We
who have experienced the horrors of a prison camp know their true
worth.

There were, of course, German prisoners. They would be held in camps
in Britain, America and Canada and would, generally speaking, fare
reasonably well. One camp was developed on the outskirts of the North
Cheshire village of Handforth, at a former bleachworks. In 1916, it was
inspected by the then neutral American Embassy in London, which found
it to be well run. The kitchen was run by a Feldwebel, two under-officers,
and twenty-two men.

The daily ration may be, and is, increased by the purchases made
by the kitchen committee from the profits of the canteen fund. There
was nothing found to criticise in the kitchen arrangements.

German soldiers just disembarked from a train in Handforth, Cheshire, before marching off to the nearby prisoner of war camp.

However, by the following spring, food shortages were becoming common in Britain and it prompted an anonymous guard at the camp to write to the local newspaper:

> *Considering the potato shortage, is it not scandalous that German prisoners should still have them every day for dinner? Only last Monday, fifty sacks were delivered at the camp for consumption by the prisoners of war. They are issued at the rate of 2½ sacks per day, while the men of the Royal Defence Corps, who form the guard at the camp, have only had potatoes for dinner twice during the past fortnight. When there is a shortage such as this, I think it is only right that the German prisoners should be the first to suffer, not English troops and civilians.*
> (Stockport Advertiser, 30 March 1917)

Potatoes were alleged to have been the cause of a riot amongst the German civilians interned on the Isle of Man. The riot took place on 19 November 1914 and had resulted in deaths. It was a serious matter and the camp was inspected a few days later by Chandler Hale of the American Embassy, his report noting:

> *The riot started, it is alleged, as the result of bad potatoes. The authorities admit that one shipment proved worm-eaten and they*

Vegetable growing at the Handforth camp.

The YMCA room at the Handforth camp.

were rejected after a few days. On the 18th November, the men declared a hunger strike at dinner. The following day they ate their dinner without any complaint and immediately after the withdrawal of the guards from the rooms, the prisoners suddenly, and evidently by pre-arrangement, started to break up the tables, chairs, crockery and everything they could lay on. Upon the appearance of the guards, the rioters charged them armed with table legs and chairs. The guards fired one volley in the air, but it had no effect. Finally, and in self protection, they fired a second round which resulted in the death of four Germans and one Austrian and the wounding of nineteen others. [99]

Hale's enquiries led him to conclude that the responsibility for the deaths lay with the rioters themselves, the group including several 'agitators'.

*   *   *   *

Sergeant Robert Johnston went overseas in May 1915, serving in Belgium for several months with the 9th Battalion, Royal Scots (see Chapter 2). Later that year, he was transferred to the 1st Battalion and, by January 1916, was serving in the Salonika theatre of the war in northern Greece. A combined force of British and French troops landed at the port in October 1915, at the request of the Greek government, to aid it in its obligations towards Serbia, which had been attacked by the Bulgarians. However, by the time the troops had arrived and organised themselves, Serbia had been defeated.

In spite of doubts about there being any benefits of doing so, it was decided that the troops would remain. This was against the wishes of some elements of Greek society which favoured the Central Powers. Not least amongst the opponents was the Greek King, who was married to the sister of the German Kaiser. He considered, with much justification, that this breached Greece's position of neutrality.

After increasing the defences of the port area, the troops moved forward into Serbia but, forced into a withdrawal, set up a 'front line' a few miles north of the city. Over the coming months, both the British and French increased their forces and were supported by Serbian, Italian and Russian troops. There would be little action in 1916. The following year saw attacks by both sides, neither being able to break the stalemate and it was not until September 1918 that there was a decisive Allied advance,

British field bakery at Salonika. Photo: Australian War Memorial, H10073.

Baking facilities at Salonika. Photo: Illustrated War News.

which resulted in Bulgarian surrender. Conditions for the men were difficult with very hot summers and bitterly cold winters. Malaria was rife and it caused 162,000 casualties. It is indicative of the nature of the campaign that almost as many men died from natural causes as were killed in action – approximately 2,600 in each category.

Food was never over-plentiful and an issue of unsweetened lime juice had to be taken every day to prevent scurvy due to the absence of fresh vegetables from our diet. Some days, bread came up in the rations from the army bakery at Salonika but most days it was hard biscuits! (Sergeant Robert Johnston, 1st Battalion, Royal Scots)

*   *   *   *

The final theatre of the war to be discussed is Mesopotamia, where British and colonial troops fought against the Ottoman Empire. As in later conflicts, British Imperial interest was in the region's oil. Discoveries of large reserves of oil had been made in neighbouring Persia (Iran) in 1908, and there was a large refinery at Abadan, operated by the British owned Anglo-Persian Oil Company, which had only gone into full production in 1913. This co-incided with a decision of the Royal Navy to start using oil rather than coal to fuel its ships. Securing the refinery from possible capture by Turkish troops in Mesopotamia was now a vital strategic interest. The nearest troops of the British Empire were in India and, on 16 October 1914, 16 Indian Brigade, part of the 6th (Poona) Division, was despatched to Bahrain, in readiness for action. On 6 November, the day after war was declared between Britain and Turkey, the Brigade went into action at Fao, on the Mesopotamian side of the border. Over the following fortnight, the remainder of the Poona Division landed and the troops pressed forward, taking the town of Basra, forty miles away, on the 21st. This meant that there was now a secure area around the oil refinery and the entire objective of the campaign had been met.

However, the ease with which the 6th Division had advanced gave encouragement to the senior command of the Indian Army that further advances might be possible, even taking Baghdad, nearly three hundred miles to the north. The advance, up the River Tigris would take many weeks, with the troops sometimes advancing on foot along the banks and, at other times, in a fleet of some 500 small boats. Starting in late April, conditions were difficult. The weather varied from cold nights to very hot days. The troops were also ill-equipped with insufficient artillery, ammunition and other supplies. A series of battles were fought, all of which saw the Indian Division continue its advance. However, the 6th Division and the supporting 12th Division were gradually weakened by illness and disease, as well as battle casualties.

By late November 1915 the advance had reached Ctesiphon, a few miles south of Baghdad. The Turkish troops were well dug-in and the battle, between 22 and 24 November, was inconclusive. In fact, both sides felt they had suffered a defeat and both retreated. Realising that the Poona Division was withdrawing, the Turks turned round and started to pursue them. The retreat continued until the town of Kut-al-Amara was reached on 3 December. Major General Charles Townshend decided to stay in the defensive positions in the town, intent on fighting off the Turks until reinforcements could arrive from Basra. The Turks caught up with them on the 7th and promptly laid siege to the town.

Luckily there was lots of food. In addition to our full ration the men found in the village hundreds of chickens, lots of ghee and flour, and hundreds of tons of barley lying about. I have never seen men eat like it, but they had hardly had a decent meal since 21st November and had had the devil of a time in addition. Leckie, our wonderful quartermaster, had found two cases of stout (ownerless?!) on the town front and put them in a safe place, i.e. our Mess! We had also some brown sherry and best of all [they] *sent us four hams by mistake for bully beef: we ate them up and 'regretted the error'! We were all very cheery and pleased with ourselves and put Christmas or early January as the outside by which time a big force would arrive from India, we should join up and drive the enemy back up the river again.*
(Major Ernest Walker, Indian Medical Service, attached to 120th Rajputana Infantry)[100]

Townshend also considered there was plenty of food – sixty days supply for both British and Indian troops.[101] The general satisfaction with the situation was not to last long. Amongst the 10,000 troops now penned in the town was Major John Stafford Barker. Commissioned in 1898, as an officer in the Royal Engineers, he had undertaken official duties in connection with the Delhi durbar, following the coronation of George V, for which he was made a Commander of the Royal Victorian Order. He was currently serving as the 6th Division's Field Engineer. In January 1916, Barker started to write what would become a long letter[102] to his wife, not knowing when the siege might be lifted and, therefore, when he might be able to post it.

[31/1/16] – *We have been eating horse for a couple of days now – the flavour is alright. And also brown bread which is really not bad, but I don't care for it. Whisky is at a very low ebb and we only allow ourselves butter at breakfast and tea. Sugar is very scarce and we have no pudding sometimes and seldom one worth eating. Here is my idea of ideal food for one day:*

    Breakfast – 2 boiled eggs, toast and Oxford marmalade
    Tea – a little bread & butter and some nice sponge cake
    Dinner – soup, roast chicken, a quite babyish pudding and a savoury.

[6/2/16] – *We are being starved a bit now – meat we get a decent allowance of, but there is no sugar, so puddings are scarce – and we all want more than our bread ration. I foresee two months more siege and all our butter and tea used up and bread rations even less. We had a glorious pudding three nights ago, made by one of our Sergeants. It was a roly-poly with a little jam inside. The pudding for all of us was a foot long and 5" in diameter, yet we ate 2/3rd of it without any trouble or ill effect. The next night we had the balance fried. I am looking forward to another suet pudding.*

[13/2/16] – *Have been feeling a good deal better today and would be quite fit if only I was not being starved – a little porridge and a custard pudding of two eggs – no sugar besides half a dozen pieces of toast being my whole allowance for food today.*

[12/3/16 – digestive problems meant that the medical officer had advised him to avoid eating meat for some time prior] – *I shall try meat again as my tummy is pretty well and alright again. Our bread has been cut down and we each get a 10oz loaf, a little porridge and a ration of horse or mule per day. I have two eggs and a half pint of milk as I am allowed no meat. Fortunately our store cupboard still has a little jam and cheese.*

[6/4/16] – *Our bread has been cut down to a 6oz loaf and we have no sugar, jam or saccharine left, only a scrap of butter, no cheese.*

[21/4/16] – *There are four days rations left. The hunger feeling is awful.*

Although there had been several attempts to lift the siege, these had been unsuccessful and the situation was now hopeless. Townshend notes in his memoirs that twenty men a day were dying of starvation. Now reduced to approximately 8,000 men, the garrison surrendered on 29 April, going into captivity for the remainder of the war. A significant number of them would subsequently die in the very harsh conditions to which they were subjected. Barker survived Kastoumi Camp, in Anatolia, and returned to India after the war, where he worked as the civilian Chief Engineer for the city of Indore.

It was a humiliating defeat, made worse coming so soon after the disastrous landings at Gallipoli. Changes in the high command were made and the new senior officers spent the remainder of 1916 reorganising their forces. Significant improvements were made at the port of Basra and along the lines of communication, so that both men and materials could be got forward more easily. Reinforcements arrived and, in December 1916, 150,000 troops advanced along both banks of the Tigris. Over the following weeks there were a number of significant engagements, including the retaking of Kut-al-Amara on 24 February 1917, with the Turks retreating towards Baghdad. That city fell to the advancing British on 11 March. The advance stopped here, the officer in command, General Maude, considering his supply lines would not extend further and that the heat of summer would making fighting difficult.

There is very little news, except that Baghdad gets more liveable in day by day, having now six decent hotels and a full bazaar. I have been through the bazaar today with the Bridge Instructor who speaks French, Arabic and Russian. He is improving my French and it is awfully useful to go round the bazaar with him and see the prices he gets things at. In order that your mouths in England may water, I'll give you some standard prices out here:

Eggs – 6d a dozen
Chickens – 2s each
Potatoes – 1s 4d each (brought by caravan across Russia and Persia)
A lamb costs about 5s.
Oranges – very big and sweet, 1d each
On the contrary, for a 1 pound tin of peas, we pay 2s 6d and the same for other tinned vegetables

(Unknown officer, Royal Field Artillery, letter home published in the *Stockport Advertiser*, 25 May 1917)

The offensive restarted in the early spring of 1918 and there was some significant fighting in the early weeks. The summer was again quiet and, with the collapse of the Ottoman Empire elsewhere, an armistice was agreed on 30 October and the fighting ended a few days later.

*   *   *   *

Mutton Broth
Simple Cookery for the People, 10th Edition, circa 1916

1lb scrag end of neck of mutton
1 small carrot
1 small turnip
1 small onion
1 quart of water
2oz pearl barley
1 teaspoonful of salt
½ teaspoonful of parsley
Average cost 8d

Trim off some of the fat from the mutton and cut it into small pieces and put it in the saucepan with a quart of cold water and teaspoonful of salt. Boil for an hour then skim well. Add the prepared vegetables, previously cut into dice and pearl barley, which should be well washed and leave to simmer for another hour. Season with salt and pepper and add the chopped parsley before serving. If liked, the meat may be cooked whole in the soup and dished separately.

Lentil Cutlets
The Times, 7 March 1917

1 pint lentils
1½ pints water
4 small onions
2 teaspoonfuls cornflour
Grated rind of one lemon
2 teaspoonfuls mixed herbs
¼ pint breadcrumbs
Pepper and salt

Soak the lentils in the water for 24 hours; put lentils to cook in the water in which they have been soaked; add the chopped onion; cook for 1½ hours; mash lentils; mix cornflour to a paste with a little cold water and add this to the lentils together with the lemon rind, herbs and seasoning; boil for 5 minutes, stirring continuously; remove pan from heat and add breadcrumbs; turn the mixture on a dish; when it is cold, shape into cutlets, coat with milk or egg and breadcrumbs; fry in hot fat.

Apple Tart
Thrift for Troubled Times, 1917

¾ lb flour
Small teaspoonful of baking powder
2½ oz of lard
2½ oz of dripping
2 apples
1oz Demerara sugar
A little spice
Little water

Mix flour and baking powder together. Put into this the dripping and lard. Mix together with sufficient water to form a paste. Divide the paste, roll out and cover a greased plate completely. Sprinkle over this two apples (chopped), 1 ounce brown sugar and a little spice. Cover with the rest of the paste. Brush over with water and sprinkle with caster sugar. Bake for 30 to 40 minutes.

CHAPTER 6

Back Home

❖

For many soldiers returning home, their first night's sleep back in Britain would be in a hospital bed. It has been estimated that, for every man killed in action, four were wounded. On 1 July 1916 – the first day of the Battle of the Somme – the author's grandfather and great uncle, Tom and Robert Brough, went 'over the top' with the Pals of the 17th Battalion, Manchester Regiment. They came through the day unscathed but 108 of their comrades lay dead and approximately another 450 were wounded.

There was a well defined process for soldiers getting treatment. An infantryman would first be seen by his own medical officer, at an aid post just behind the front line, but this would be little more than a quick assessment and dressing the wounds. Assuming the casualty could not walk, he would be taken by stretcher to a Dressing Station further in the rear, staffed by a Field Ambulance of the Royal Army Medical Corps. In urgent cases, emergency surgery might be carried out to stabilise a patient before passing him on to a Casualty Clearing Station. The Stations were usually tented field hospitals, located about twenty miles to the rear of the front line and men would arrive by horse drawn wagon, motor ambulance or, in some locations, by light railway. They were well staffed and equipped to deal with the wide array of injuries that presented themselves and, in general, if a man reached a Station, then he was likely to survive his injuries. As soon as possible after treatment, a man might be further evacuated to a base hospital. For casualties on the Western Front, most of these were situated on the Channel coast. From there, a man might be evacuated back to Britain to continue his treatment or convalescence.

Throughout the UK, existing hospitals took in military patients and, as the numbers of injured grew, other buildings were converted into hospital

Greek Street Military Hospital, Stockport. A school converted for war use.

accommodation, often under the supervision of a large regional hospital. For example, in the Manchester area, 2nd Western General Hospital had its headquarters on Whitworth Street, in the city centre, but supervised at least twenty other locations in the region. In Stockport, at least a dozen buildings, mainly schools, were turned into hospitals, during the period of the war, including two which specialised in shellshock cases. Every effort was made to ensure that patients had a good diet, to aid their physical recovery and also to raise their morale. The official efforts were supplemented by the town's local voluntary fundraising activities for the 'Comforts for Wounded Soldiers Fund'. After Christmas 1915, Mrs Elsie Lingard wrote to the *Stockport Advertiser* thanking local people for their generous donations, which had amounted to over £16 (worth over £1,000 at current values). It had allowed the Fund to buy turkeys, Christmas cakes, fancy cakes, biscuits, tongue, tinned fruit and jellies for the patients at the five hospitals that were operating at the time.

Similar fundraising efforts took place the following year, giving the patients at the converted secondary school on Greek Street as good a Christmas Day as was possible.

In the morning, each soldier found by his bedside a parcel containing suitable presents. The big event of the day was, of course, dinner and the tables were loaded with good things. The fare included turkeys, hams, sausage, plum pudding, mince pies, jellies, fruits and other dainties and, needless to say, the men did full justice to their dinner.

A nationwide organised egg collection, to be sent to military hospitals, had started shortly after the declaration of war and continued into the following year. The local Cork newspapers reported that a local resident who had donated an egg, writing her name and address on it, received a letter from the injured recipient:

An interesting letter has been received by Mrs Fitzgerald, of Ballyanon, near Midleton, County Cork, wife of an agricultural labourer, from Melrose Malter, of the Lancashire Fusiliers, now in the Stepping Hill Military Hospital, near Stockport, wounded in action in Gallipoli. Mrs Fitzgerald was assisted in the movement for collecting eggs for wounded soldiers by sending donations of eggs to a local ladies committee. The names and addresses of the donors are written on the eggs, and in this Malter got one of the eggs from Mrs Fitzgerald in his rations. He addresses her a letter in which he said: 'These few lines are from an Australian bushman, who travelled 13,000 miles to do his duty to the Mother Country. After arriving here in February last I enlisted in the Lancashire Fusiliers and went to the Dardanelles, where we fought side by side with famous Irish regiments, Dublin and Munster Fusiliers. God bless them!

I as a soldier will never forget the bravery displayed by these dear boys. I was wounded in a bayonet charge on June 4 last, and that day I shall never forget, all the boys fighting for their lives. We had a splendid gain that day, and killed many Turks. After two operations I have two fingers and half a palm of my left hand removed. I was also hit in the breast, but luckily that was not serious. I have no regrets for my sacrifice. Many are worse off. I am only glad to be one of the Australians serving in an English regiment. I have no friends here in this part of the world, but my people are always thinking of me, and that is some satisfaction. I have secured your name and address off an egg, so excuse me writing you these few lines. I enjoyed the egg, and I thought it only right you should know about it.'

The soldier named in the above article was James Melrose Mailer, not Malter. Born in Victoria, Australia, in 1878, he had served in the Boer War with the 3rd Victorian Bushmen's Contingent. He was still on the Imperial Reserve and was recalled to the Colours, leaving Melbourne on 22 December 1914. After recovering from his wounds, he was discharged from the army and, in May 1917, married Rosa Brown at St Aidens, Bradford, Manchester. The following year, the couple had a child, Dorothy. In 1919, he moved back to the Melbourne area, with his new family. He died in 1954 in a road accident, when he was struck by a car.

*   *   *   *

Life was always grim in the workhouse. A British Medical Journal inquiry into the conditions of workhouses in 1894 found the inmates of the Stockport one, at Shaw Heath, to be 'packed like sardines in a tin'. The management of the hospital appeared to be 'completely without plan or method' and the female wards were 'comfortless and barnlike'.[103] But, even here, the food on Christmas Day, 1916, was a treat for the inmates. Breakfast consisted of bread and butter, honey and plain cake. Dinner was roast beef, parsnips and baked potatoes followed by plum pudding and sauce, mineral water, an apple and orange and tobacco for the men and a packet of tea for the women. As reported in the local newspaper, the sick inmates had chicken and ham for dinner, followed by blancmange, jellies and fruit. *Mr & Mrs Hankins (master and matron) were assiduous in their efforts to make the inmates happy and comfortable.*

Although not necessarily resulting in becoming an inmate at the workhouse, there was real poverty across Britain caused by the war. Whilst the wife of a serving soldier would receive a separation allowance of 12s 6d per week (and more if the couple had children), this was only one third of what the husband might have earned in civilian life. In a time before social security benefits, many families would quickly come to rely on charity. Within days of war being declared, the Prince of Wales had instituted a National Relief Fund and, as its Treasurer, appealed for donations. Within a day, over a quarter of a million pounds had been pledged, much of it coming from the prominent families of the time. The Royal Family itself pledged over £10,000 but the largest donation of £50,000 came from the industrialist George Coats. By the end of October 1914, payments were being made to families 'in distress' at the rate of eight shillings a week, with an additional shilling per child.

Direct donations of food were also coming from the overseas dominions. In Stockport, the local committee of the National Relief Fund took delivery of a large consignment from Canada during January 1915, comprising:

1000 bags of flour (90lbs per bag)
300 sacks of potatoes (90 lbs per sack) – from the people of New Brunswick
75 cases of tinned salmon (48lbs per case) – from the people of British Columbia
160 cheeses – from the people of Quebec.

The Stockport committee was already providing financial assistance to nearly 600 wives and other dependants. The committee was also co-ordinating local fund raising events, including an auction sale, organised by the Cheshire Milk Producers Association. The *Stockport Advertiser* reported, on 23 April 1915, that the event had been opened by the mayor, who said that the generosity of those who had donated items refuted the old saying that 'Nobody gives owt for nowt'. Mr Butler, of Peacock Farm, Handforth had given a fat calf, whilst Mr Whalley of Underbank Farm in Heaton Norris had donated fifty new laid eggs and several sacks of potatoes. The event raised nearly £200.

The London Chamber of Commerce maintained a ledger of foodstuffs arriving at the Port of London from the empire.[104] It included flour, sugar, jams, butter, fruit, frozen beef and other meats and preserved meat. Crates of frozen rabbits from Australia were a major item, in early 1915:

4 January	–	850 crates
13 January	–	454 crates
20 January	–	152 crates
25 February	–	3856 crates
17 June	–	2000 crates

The rabbits were distributed to hospitals throughout Britain and were also donated to charitable organisations such as the Belgian Refugee Fund and the National Food Fund. In October 1914, the British government estimated that 60,000 Belgians may arrive in Britain, fleeing the advancing Germans. *The Times* reported that, on 11 October, over 5,000 had arrived that day.

The majority of the passengers on the first three Ostend boats were Antwerp people of the middle class, well dressed, comfortably off and bringing a fair amount of luggage. However, the last boat of the day brought 999 passengers, every one of whom was destitute. Huddled together on the deck, grasping the bags and bundles which contained everything which was left to them in the world. It was only a matter of days before the Refugee Fund was formed to help find lodgings for the new arrivals, together with food and clothing. The rabbits would have been most welcome.

Fund raising was also taking place in Stockport for the Soldiers' Comforts Committee which had recently sent four gross of handkerchiefs to the Territorials of the 6th Cheshires. Writing to thank the Committee, Captain Frederick Leah suggested that, if the Committee was thinking of sending anything else, small tins of condensed milk would be *of the utmost value, as the use of fresh milk is prohibited.*

Advert in the Stockport Express, 14 January 1915.

In the spring of 1915, there was much public concern about the increase in the price of bread, which had risen from 5½d in August 1914 to 9d. There were accusations that the bakers and/or the flour millers were profiteering. There was some justification in the complaint. Spillers Ltd, a major flour milling company, with its headquarters in Cardiff, had seen its profits rise from £89,000 in the previous year to £368,000. However, there were definite rises in commodity prices with *The Times* reporting, on 26 April 1915, that at Peterborough Corn Exchange the price of wheat was at a twenty-five year high. Similar high prices were also recorded at Reading and Dorchester. In Stockport, it would seem that local bakers were making smaller loaves, rather than increasing prices. It caused the same disquiet as indicated by a letter published in the *Stockport Express* on 20 May.

The diminution of the size of our loaves of bread, compared with former times, is a matter which calls for attention and reform. If the system adopted by the bakers were observed by other tradesmen the result would be a state of chaos. For example, what would be thought of a coal merchant who sought to cover the increase in the market price by charging, say, ten per cent more per cwt and only delivering three-quarters cwt, instead of one cwt i.e. 25 per cent short weight.

....If the bakers' system is right, I would commend it to the careful consideration of the butchers, tea and butter dealers. If it is not right for the latter tradesmen, then it cannot be right for bakers. Unquestionably, it is not a right system for the consumer.

It was matters such as these which, no doubt, prompted Councillor F. Plant to propose to the Council

That in view of the unwarranted rise in the prices of foodstuffs, coal and the other necessities of life, this Municipal Council of the County Borough of Stockport calls on the government to take immediate steps to protect the people's food on national lines and to take over the control of freightage and transport.

As far as is known, Plant's colleagues did not support the proposal, although, as the reader will see later in this chapter, the government did, in due course, take a hand in controlling food prices and rationing.

The spring of 1915 saw widespread rioting across several British cities in the aftermath of the sinking of the Cunard liner *Lusitania*. On her voyage from New York, the ship was known to be carrying munitions and the Germans had warned that, as such, she could be regarded as a fair target by U-boats. The German embassy in America placed a notice in fifty leading newspapers advising potential passengers not to travel on the ship, which was leaving for Britain on 1 May. On 7 May, Lusitania was within a few hours of docking at Liverpool when she was struck by a single torpedo and sank. Although several hundred people survived, 1,195 drowned. It caused great anger in Britain and America. Within days, there was serious rioting in several British cities, directed at shops owned by Germans or, at least, people with foreign sounding names. Many of the families had lived in Britain for decades and would have had their young men serving in the British army, but that did nothing to stop the mobs, which were intent on

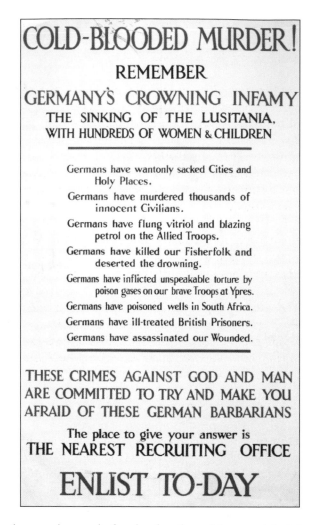

COLD-BLOODED MURDER!

REMEMBER

GERMANY'S CROWNING INFAMY

THE SINKING OF THE LUSITANIA,
WITH HUNDREDS OF WOMEN & CHILDREN

Germans have wantonly sacked Cities and
Holy Places.

Germans have murdered thousands of
innocent Civilians.

Germans have flung vitriol and blazing
petrol on the Allied Troops.

Germans have killed our Fisherfolk and
deserted the drowning.

Germans have inflicted unspeakable torture by
poison gases on our brave Troops at Ypres.

Germans have poisoned wells in South Africa.

Germans have ill-treated British Prisoners.

Germans have assassinated our Wounded.

THESE CRIMES AGAINST GOD AND MAN
ARE COMMITTED TO TRY AND MAKE YOU
AFRAID OF THESE GERMAN BARBARIANS

The place to give your answer is
THE NEAREST RECRUITING OFFICE

ENLIST TO-DAY

wrecking the premises and often looting them. Many pork butchers were of German descent and were often the most obvious targets.

> *A large pork shop at the corner of Smithdown Road and Arundel Avenue had been absolutely wrecked, all the windows had been smashed and the stock commandeered or thrown into the street. Women hurled strings of sausages at one another and one woman from a neighbouring street went down on her knees and scrubbed the pavement with a joint of pork. Other women went home with*

their aprons full of pork and bacon. After sacking the shops, the invaders went into the living room upstairs and spread destruction... (*Liverpool Echo*, 12 May 1915)

The Times reported that 200 shops in Liverpool had been gutted with, in many cases, the entire stock being looted. In Manchester, thirteen men and eight women appeared before the magistrates charged with disorderly conduct and wilful damage. Imposing what the newspaper described as 'small fines', the magistrate remarked that he realised the provocation people had had, but riotous conduct did not do any good. It also noted that the City's police were arresting all enemy alien shopkeepers to 'allay the angry feelings aroused'.

The Stimpfig family had a number of shops in south Manchester, where they carried on trade as pork butchers. Born in Germany, Johann Andreas Ernest Stimpfig had become a naturalised British citizen in 1908 and had Anglicised his forenames to John Andrew. By 1915 he was running two shops in the Levenshulme district. It is not known if these were attacked by the rioters but, in August 1915, John Stimpfig was sufficiently concerned about anti-German feelings that he changed his surname by deed poll to Simpson. After the war, he established a new company in Stockport which traded as Simpson's Sausages until it closed in 2000. His two brothers retained their original family name.

*   *   *   *

By the late spring of 1915, it had become clear that the war was not going to be over quickly and that the government must start to consider how food supplies might be maintained in the long term. By then it had been realised that voluntary recruitment to the army was not going to produce sufficient numbers and, whilst conscription was still some way off, the National Registration Act was passed in July. It required males aged between 15 and 65 to register giving details of their employment. This would provide the basis for the formal scheme which would be introduced the following year. It was assumed that agricultural workers would not be generally excluded from being conscripted. At about the same time, the Board of Agriculture formed a food production committee to consider what steps might need to be taken, including the possibility of new legislation.

One of the early decisions was to require county councils to establish similar committees. Cheshire formed its committee with the principal aims of organising the supply of agricultural labour and considering how food production could be maintained and improved. There was immediate work to be done as a letter from the editor of the *British Pig Breeder* magazine had just been published in local newspapers:

> *The agricultural returns show that on 4 June there were 3591 fewer pigs in Cheshire than on the corresponding date last year. It is imperatively necessary that the national food supply should be quickly increased and I beg to suggest that all who can keep pigs should do so. They would find it profitable for there is no other animal which provides such excellent, quickly produced and universally popular human food. I shall be pleased to send a copy of the British Pig Breeder, free of charge, to anyone in your county who wishes to take up pig breeding.*

A similar system was established in Scotland, where *The Times* reported the main committee had quickly concluded

> *No single factor will have a greater and more immediate effect in increasing home grown food supplies than artificial manure. Where practicable there should be an extension of land under wheat and oats, but the proposal that farmers should be induced to increase their cultivation of cereals by a guaranteed minimum price does not appear to the committee to be practicable. A greater number of calves should be reared and the keeping of pigs and poultry and the increase of egg production should be encouraged. The provision of more allotments, especially in the neighbourhood of towns and villages, is strongly advocated. In regard to farm labour, it should be represented to the military authorities that any attempt to increase, or even maintain, food production would be made impossible by a further withdrawal of experienced agricultural workers. It is urged that measures should be taken to kill off farm*

8th Battalion, King's Own Royal Lancaster Regiment in training at Romsey in spring 1915. Private John Palmer sits fifth from the left. Photo: David O'Mara.

pests. An appeal should be made to owners of deer forests and grouse moors to allow these to be used for grazing and the fullest possible use should be made for this purpose of golf courses. All artificial raising of game should be discouraged. In regard to a proposal that deer and other game should be killed and used as part of the national food supply, the committee do not feel they can usefully make suggestions, believing that the owners of forests and moors will no doubt act in the best interests of the nation.

County wide action to deal with farm pests was also considered at a joint meeting of the Ashton under Lyne and Stockport Agricultural Committees. The immediate problem was wood pigeons, which were destroying crops and it was agreed that farm landlords, tenants, together with 'shooting sportsmen', would be invited to an area-wide simultaneous shoot on 19 February 1917.

In May 1915, the Earl of Selborne joined the Government as President of the Board of Agriculture. He succeeded to the peerage in 1895 and, prior to that, had been a Liberal Member of Parliament. Over the following months he would lead the drive to encourage women to volunteer to undertake agricultural work, allowing more men to leave to join the army.

As reported by *The Times*, he addressed a meeting of agriculturists at Shrewsbury.

> He said to the farmers 'Use every shift you can for labour, for I warn you quite fairly and squarely that you are to lose many more of your men in the coming few months.' He had recently seen in Surrey what he believed nobody had ever seen in England before – a woman ploughing. It was no use saying it was perfectly impossible for women to plough because there were many women at the plough in Europe today.....Women of every class must assist – the squire's wife and the farmer's and the parson's wife and the wife and daughter of the labourer. Each in turn could make a contribution to agriculture, and so work for victory just as husband, son or brother in the Fleet or in the trenches. He would make a special appeal to the wives and daughters of men who were fighting, because they were well cared for by the nation. They had not been left, as the German women, in grinding poverty while the men were fighting the battles. It was not right that a woman in this country should live in greater luxury than she did before her husband or son went away to fight. She should do her part just as the men. She must go on to the land, if the farmer asked her, at a fair wage for a fair day's pay. (*The Times*, 4 October 1915)

Recruitment of women would become the responsibility of the county agricultural committees and it would be given an impetus by the formation of the Womens' National Land Service Corps. As might be anticipated with an organisation formed in Edwardian times, the organisers and supervisors would be drawn from the middle class, whilst the actual work on farms would be done by working class women. In North Cheshire, the principal organiser was Elizabeth Greg. Aged in her mid-50s, she was the daughter of Henry and Emily and lived at the family home, Lode Hall, in the village of Styal. The family were wealthy cotton spinners.

> Urgent appeals have appeared recently in all the newspapers for women to take up work on the land. Each month the need becomes more pressing as the men are rapidly being called up. In this crisis, with a very serious shortage of labour and when the produce of the land is of more vital importance than it has ever been before, the country is looking to women to help. Indeed, it can look in no other direction.

The assistance needed ranges from full time service on the farm (as replacing a man) to part-time work, as in milking or dairy work and seasonal work as potato picking, harvesting the crops, etc. The Board of Agriculture has made a strong appeal for the organisation of women for that purpose, recommending a general canvas throughout the whole of England, with the object of getting girls and women to register themselves for agricultural or horticultural work.

Cheshire is now organised along these lines. In this District, the registrars who will receive names and give information are as follows:

Handforth – Miss Cunliffe, Parsonage

Styal – Miss Crewdson, Spars

Wilmslow – Labour Exchange Branch or myself

(Elizabeth M Greg, letter published in the *Stockport Advertiser*, 17 March 1916)

The day after war was declared on 4 August 1914, the Aliens Registration Act was passed by Parliament. It allowed for the internment of foreigners from the enemy combatant nations who were of military age. Most ended up in large camps on the Isle of Man. As mentioned earlier, others of foreign heritage were detained in the aftermath of the Lusitania sinking and were also sent to the camps. By the spring of 1916, serious consideration was being given to the question of whether those interned might be used as agricultural labourers, replacing those who were now being conscripted into the forces. The Military Service Act was passed at the beginning of the year, introducing conscription and it was starting to impact on farm life.

The Cheshire Agricultural Committee met on 14 April and, whilst there was some appeal in employing internees, a Mr Hodgson voiced the worries of several members – '*I hope we are not going to turn spies loose in Cheshire.*' The Chairman, Colonel Dixon, replied '*They are aliens. I do not know whether they are spies.*' The Committee was also concerned that many Irish farm workers had returned to Ireland where there was no conscription. However, Colonel Dixon reported that his understanding of the Act was that Irish men working in England would not be subject to conscription. The Committee agreed to ask the Board of Agriculture to publicise this in Ireland in the hope it would persuade men to return.[105]

Men could apply for exemption from conscription on one of four grounds:

Stockport Express, 23 September 1915.

- that it was deemed in the national interest that he continue in his work
- if serious hardship would occur due to his exceptional circumstances
- ill health
- conscientious objection

Applications would be made, in the first instance, to a local tribunal. At the beginning of May 1916, one of the tribunals in North Cheshire considered the application for total exemption from a Rainow farmer. He had a farm of thirty-five acres, including fifteen cattle, six of which were milkers. He worked the farm entirely on his own and had no dependants. He said he had taken to farming on account of his health and '*had to get his own meals ready*'. He made butter from the milk and could '*make it as well as any woman*'. The application was dismissed, with Dr Murray describing him as a '*proper Robinson Crusoe*'. Perhaps unhelpfully, the Chairman, a Captain Rigby, added '*Perhaps you may get someone to carry on the farm.*'

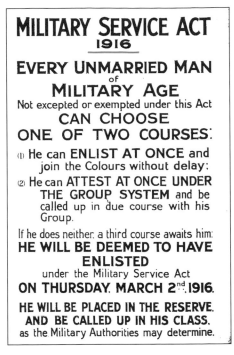

Three weeks later, Rigby chaired another tribunal hearing. In this case, a woman from Lower Withington was trying to get exemption for both her son and the cowman. The farm was sixty acres with nineteen milking cows and the applicant felt it needed two men. '*You cannot have both*', Rigby declared.

There was occasionally some humour in the process, as heard at the Stockport tribunal at the beginning of June. A farmer from Bucklow was trying to get exemption for his two workers. He had tried to get women but had not been able to do so. '*They will not go on the road*', he said.

The Chairman responded '*Oh yes, they will. I have seen them with brewers' drays.*'

Appellant '*But they will not bring manure.*'

At the end of the month, the nearby Bredbury tribunal appeared to have more sympathy with the plight of farmers. A man applied for exemption for his son, his other son having already been conscripted. The farm had over fifty-six acres and the hay and clover was nearly ready for cutting. The farm also had six milk cows, two horses, eleven acres of oats, four of potatoes and six of turnips. The Chairman responded

We don't want to interfere with the satisfactory result of farming. But I think farmers should avail themselves of the labour available. They could get it. I think, however, we shall consider this favourably.

By the early autumn of 1916, little had improved by way of the acceptance of women workers in agriculture. In North Cheshire notices had been issued inviting farmers to come forward and offer to train women in farm work, providing them with board and lodging for six weeks. The farmers would be paid 12s per week for the first two weeks and 10s thereafter.

Advert in The Times.

Farmers in the past do not generally seem to have taken very readily to the idea of women workers, outside their own family, but this should give them a fresh incentive.

The women who have offered their services in this direction are anxious to learn in order that they may 'do their bit' to assist the country in its present need. One cannot expect them to be as efficient as a male worker but we feel sure that their assistance at the ingathering of the harvest would be valuable and we have little doubt that there are farmers in the Cheadle Hulme district who will come forward to offer to train these women.

(*Stockport Advertiser*, 1 September 1916)

*   *   *   *

On 8 August 1914, Parliament had passed the Defence of the Realm Act (DORA). It was a brief piece of legislation, only a few sentences long. It empowered the Government to introduce such regulations as deemed necessary to prevent people communicating with the enemy. Over the course of the war, the Act was amended on several occasions, each widening the scope of the regulations that the Government might introduce. It would soon mean that DORA was significantly controlling the everyday lives of the population. Newspapers could be censored and it became an offence to spread rumours about military matters. The Government could, and did, take over factories, directing the company to undertake war work. Similarly, land could be commandeered for food production. Some of the measures introduced during the war became permanent – British Summer Time, for example, and the hours during which pubs could sell alcohol. By the end of 1916, regulations were being introduced which related to food supply. At the beginning of December, the latest regulation to be introduced prevented restaurants from serving more than three courses in a meal in the evening, or two courses at breakfast and lunch, as reported by the *Nottingham Evening News*:

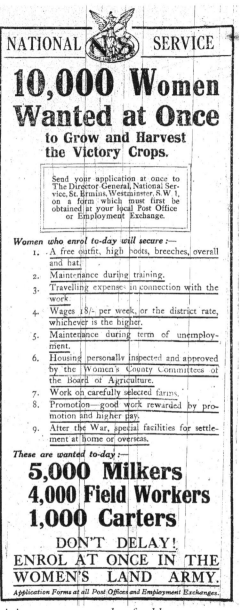

NATIONAL **N·S** SERVICE

10,000 Women Wanted at Once

to Grow and Harvest the Victory Crops.

Send your application at once to The Director-General, National Service, St. Ermins, Westminster, S.W.1, on a form which must first be obtained at your local Post Office or Employment Exchange.

Women who enrol to-day will secure :—

1. A free outfit, high boots, breeches, overall and hat.
2. Maintenance during training.
3. Travelling expenses in connection with the work.
4. Wages 18/- per week, or the district rate, whichever is the higher.
5. Maintenance during term of unemployment.
6. Housing personally inspected and approved by the Women's County Committees of the Board of Agriculture.
7. Work on carefully selected farms.
8. Promotion—good work rewarded by promotion and higher pay.
9. After the War, special facilities for settlement at home or overseas.

These are wanted to-day :—

5,000 Milkers
4,000 Field Workers
1,000 Carters

DON'T DELAY!
ENROL AT ONCE IN THE WOMEN'S LAND ARMY.

Application Forms at all Post Offices and Employment Exchanges.

Except with the express authority of the Board of Trade no articles of food shall be served or consumed in any Inn, Refreshment house, Mess, Hotel, Boarding house, Canteen, Restaurant, Club, Hall, or any place of public eating in the form of or as part of a meal consisting of more than three courses if the meal begins between 6 p.m. and 9.30 p.m., or of more than two courses if the meal begins at any other time. Plain cheese shall not be regarded as a course and hors d'oeuvres (not containing any preserved or freshly cooked fish, meat, poultry, or game), dessert (consisting only of raw and dried fruit), and soup prepared in the ordinary way which does

A wartime postcard.

not contain any meat, poultry, or game in a solid form, shall each be computed as half a course.

Any person eating in contravention of the above provision is guilty of a summary Offence against the Defence of the Realm Regulations. The order will apply to Great Britain and Ireland and will not come into force until December 18th 1916.

It is proposed shortly after to make a further order prohibiting both in places of public eating and in private houses, the consumption on certain days of meat, poultry, and game.
(*Nottingham Evening News*, 6 December 1916)

The Times reported on the first day of the coming into force of the new regulation and it noted customers were taking full advantage of the definitions of courses and half courses.

At the Piccadilly Grill Room, which was as crowded as usual, the table d'hôte luncheon list included vegetable hors d'oeuvres, clear soup, eggs, entrée, joint, sweets and cheese, but the choice from this menu was limited to the two nominal courses and the waiter took the complete order at the outset to avoid confusion. Three-fourths of the people who took the table d'hôte meal asked for hors d'oeuvres, soup, the entrée or joint with vegetables and cheese with biscuits or butter. For this the charge was 4s 6d to civilians and 3s 6d (the new maximum fixed by Major-General Sir Francis Lloyd) to soldiers.

The exclusion of fish or meat from the hors d'oeuvres did not prevent an appetizing variety being served. Eggs in sauce, potato salad, a salad of peas, beans, tomato and salad, and pickled red cabbage, all figured on the tray.

Another new Order would see Harold Holmes brought before the magistrates at Macclesfield in February 1917. He was charged with selling three loaves of bread and a quantity of biscuits in contravention of DORA. The regulations, which had been introduced just before Christmas, required shops to close at 7pm (later amended to 8pm). The intent was that, during the winter months, savings could be made in the need for lighting. The move had been welcomed by the Early Closing Association, which saw it as a benefit in reducing the working hours of shop workers. It was the first such case to come before the Macclesfield magistrates and the Chairman said that they would regard it as a technical infringement and only fined Holmes 2s 6d.

The Orders were published by the newly appointed Minister of Food Control, Lord Devonport. Announcing the creation of the new post in November 1916, Walter Runciman MP, the President of the Board of Trade, said that he would be 'the most essential man in the Empire'. Devonport, who would be generally known as the Food Controller, would have responsibility for all food issues and would be free to act as he thought best. In this he would have the power to make Orders '*in the interests of the public and for maintaining the supply of any article*'.

Although Devonport did not propose a formal scheme of rationing, he had suggested that there be voluntary restraint. It resulted in some panic buying. New Orders continued to be made regularly, as reported by *The Times* on 13 January 1917.

> *The order forbidding the use of sugar – whether icing sugar or not – or chocolate for the covering of cakes will mean the disappearance of éclairs from the teatable. The consumption in London restaurants alone reaches a total of many thousands every week. Now the éclair must give way to plain cake, biscuits and scones. The cream bun seems to have escaped attention for the moment.*

Sugar was one of the items Devonport had suggested be restricted by families – to ½ lb per week, together with restrictions on the consumption of bread and meat. Following soon after his curbs on éclairs, Devonport turned his attention to other cakes and scones in April 1917, with the publication of the Cake and Pastry Order:

> *The Cake and Pastry Order made by Lord Devonport under the Defence of the Realm Regulations and issued last night provides that, except under the Food Controller's authority, no person shall after April 21 make or attempt to make for sale, or after April 24 sell or offer to sell or have in his possession for sale:*
>
> *(a) Any crumpet, muffin, tea cake, or fancy bread, or any light or fancy pastry, or any other like article.*
>
> *(b) Any cake, bun, scone, or biscuit which does not conform to the requirements of the two following provisions of this Order.*
>
> *In the making of any cake, bun, scone, or biscuit, no edible substance shall be added to the exterior of the cake mixture or dough after it has been mixed, or to the article during the process of or after baking.*
> *CAKE. - No cake shall contain more than 15 per cent of sugar or more than 30 percent wheaten flour.*
> *BUN. - No bun shall contain more than 10 per cent of sugar or more than 50 per cent wheaten flour.*
> *SCONE. - No Scone shall contain any sugar or more than 50 per cent wheaten flour.*
> *BISCUIT. - No biscuit shall contain more than 15 per cent of sugar.*
> *(The Times, 19 April 1917).*

I CANNOT SEND YOU BANKNOTES,
    I CANNOT SEND YOU GOLD,
BUT THIS SUGAR AND POTATO
    ARE MORE THAN WEALTH UNTOLD.

A postcard from 1917.

By the following month, the restrictions on cakes were tightened, with outright bans on the manufacture of pikelets, crumpets, dropped scones, Eccles cakes and sausage rolls. It was also prohibited to make sandwich cakes, like a Victoria sponge, with fillings of jam, cream, marzipan, fruit or custard.

Most unusually, on 2 May, the King issued a Proclamation urging the population to *reduce the consumption of bread in their respective families to one-fourth of the quantity consumed in ordinary times, to abstain from the use of flour in pastry and, moreover, carefully to restrict or wherever possible to abandon the use thereof in all other articles than bread.* He urged all ministers of religion to read the Proclamation in the churches on the following four Sundays.

Although supplies of sugar were under some threat, the more immediate serious problem facing the country at the beginning of 1917 was a likely significant shortage of potatoes.

No doubt many of your readers experienced difficulty in getting a supply of potatoes on Saturday. The writer was sent on a voyage of discovery and received information that a certain shop in the Newbridge Lane district had a supply. Sure enough, on entering the shop, I saw a hamper partly filled with the vegetable. A man, presumably the shopkeeper, said 'What do you want, sir?' and, on asking for a few pounds of potatoes, said 'We've none to sell. Only for us own.'

To my mind, a case like this warrants the intervention of the Food Controller who should be given power, if he does not already have it, to compel shopkeepers having goods exposed for sale, to supply them at the ordinary price to any would-be purchaser and, thus, prevent any petty monopolists, like the individual on Saturday, from picking and choosing their customers.

(Letter to the editor, *Stockport Express*, 15 March 1917)

The scarcity of potatoes was not confined to north west England. *The Times*, in its edition of 5 March, reported that *In the suburbs of Cardiff, shops were besieged by women, and in some instances, queues 300 yards long waited from an early hour. The stocks soon exhausted and the crowds dispersed. At Penygraig, Rhondda Valley, women, on being informed that no potatoes were to be had, invaded the local shop. Women customers threatened the girl assistants at Tonypandy and the latter had to seek police protection. At Swansea market, the police kept back the crowds and ordered the sales at 1½d a lb. Stocks were quickly sold but no customer was allowed more than 2lb.*

The solution, encouraged by the Food Controller, was two-fold. First, there must be more land given over to agriculture and secondly, people must come forward to replace farm workers who were now in the army. When the conscription appeals tribunal met at Compstall, Cheshire in February 1917, the clerk had learned that the government had cancelled a previous calling-up of 38,000 agricultural workers. It encouraged the tribunal to conditionally exempt the son of a local farmer, noting that the farm had forty acres, of which six were down to potatoes. The man would have to re-appear before the tribunal at the end of April if he wished to apply to extend his exemption.

Many local authorities had already turned over recreational land to agricultural use. Manchester City Council had ploughed over some 450 acres of land for cultivation and, in the spring of 1917, was considering extending this to allow for the keeping of pigs and poultry. The labour would come from the Boy Scouts, which had 800 members in the city and consideration was being given to asking the War Office if German prisoners of war could work on the land. In due course, the War Office gave permission for the employment of the Germans and they were put to use across the country. *The Times* reported in its issue of 29 August 1918, that over 200 men from the camp in Handforth, Cheshire were being used daily.

Every day, 26 guards, armed only with their walking canes, take from the camp over 200 prisoners (last Saturday the number was 213) and distribute them at 96 different farms within a radius of three miles. The guards go each with six to 10 prisoners and drop them like postmen dropping letters, one at one farm, three at another and so on. If there are over three and up to six the guard (one man) remains with them; otherwise they are left on the farms all day without guards and the guards go the same route in the evening and pick them up again. If a farmer wishes to keep his prisoners later, he is allowed to do so provided he sees them back to camp and hands them over to the provost sergeant on duty.

It did not always work well, the same issue of *The Times* reporting that four prisoners engaged on farm work in Faringdon, Berkshire had been arrested and charged with criminally assaulting a sixteen-year-old girl. They would be dealt with by the military.

Similarly, Stockport Council prepared vacant land for cultivation and, by the beginning of February 1917, had received over 400 applications for allotments. Its efforts were boosted by the offer of thirty acres of land owned by Crossley Motors. The company, which had produced cars at its Heaton Chapel factory since 1906, had moved to production for the Royal Flying Corps at the outbreak of war. Since 1914, it had produced a vehicle which could operate as an ambulance or as a light tender. From 1917, the company also manufactured planes for the Corps at the site, producing around 400 DH9 bombers before the armistice.

The Cultivation of Lands Order, 1916, permitted local authorities to appropriate vacant land for cultivation but many landowners voluntarily turned over land to their council. Like Crossley Motors, the Sutton Bequest, a Bristol charity, donated 15 acres of land on which it had originally intended to build houses. It brought the total acreage under cultivation in the city to nearly 100 acres. By the end of 1917, 183,000 allotments had been created on land acquired in Britain under the Order.[106]

*   *   *   *

In February 1917, the Army's Labour Corps was founded. It was comprised of men conscripted into the army but whose health made them

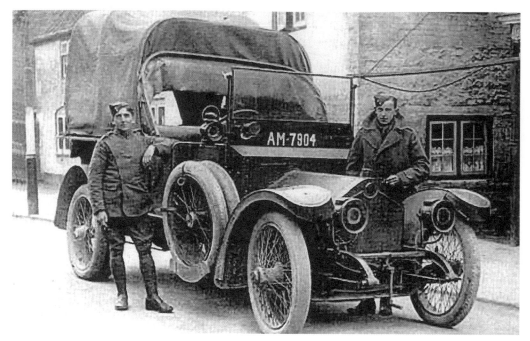

Crossley tender built for the Royal Flying Corps.

unsuitable for front line service in the trenches. Most of the Corps' companies undertook labouring duties behind the front line in the various theatres of war. However, a number of them were home service companies, including newly created agricultural companies. By the end of the war, over 75,000 men would be working on British farms, many of them without prior agricultural experience. It was a move welcomed by the Cheshire Chamber of Agriculture at its March meeting:

> *Mr James Sadler said that what was called an Agricultural Battalion would be released if farmers made their wants known to the authorities. They would be suitable men for land work. He suggested that a perfectly friendly raid should be made upon the big, strong, healthy boys of the schools for potato planting and manure spreading. Let them be employed in gangs and, if need be, their teachers might go with them. It was decided to appeal to the Education Authority and ask them to consider the question with a view to the older boys assisting in food production.*
> (*Stockport Advertiser*, 23 March 1917)

Labour Corps soldier on farm.

The creation of the new units was still in its early stages and there was a danger that insufficient manpower would lead to the ploughing season being a failure. In the middle of March, all skilled ploughmen serving in the army in Britain were ordered back to their depots and sent on agricultural furlough. It meant some 18,000 men were now back on the farms, albeit temporarily.[107]

Once the ploughing was over, the next major demand for manpower was, of course, at harvest time, in the late autumn.

> *Farmers who are experiencing difficulty in obtaining labour for potato lifting are urged to apply to the Agricultural Executive Committee which is in a position to supply labour of soldiers or of women. In most of the depots in the principal potato growing districts there are soldiers available who can be obtained at short notice.....It is of urgent importance that there should be no delay in lifting any potatoes still in the ground."*
> (*Stockport Advertiser*, 23 November 1917)

Labour Corps troops, Women's Land Army and local men all help out on the farm. Photo: Merchants House Trust.

In Cheshire, the troops would be supplied by 421st Agricultural Company, based at Orford Barracks, Warrington, the *Advertiser* noting that *The Company supplies soldiers with agricultural knowledge to farmers and any others who require labour for farm or agricultural work for long or short periods.* In fact, it was far more likely that the troops did not have previous experience or knowledge. There was also something of an irony that the troops were not in a high state of fitness or health, yet were being required to work in one of the most physically demanding of industries. Some men, like Private William Howells, did have farm experience. Originating from St David's in South Wales, he joined up in December 1915, leaving his job as a ploughman. Howells was posted back to the reserve and was not called up until January 1917. By the following year he had been transferred to 533rd Agricultural Company at Carmarthen. He died, from pneumonia, on 26 November 1918, no doubt as a result of catching Spanish 'Flu – a pandemic which killed millions worldwide in the latter part of the year.

Although the men were not exposed to the dangers or rigours of the trenches, farm work was not always easy, as a Private Herbert Killoch discovered in August 1918. With others he had been sent to work on a potato farm near Woking, owned by Henry Baldry. Soon after, Baldry accused Killoch of slacking and ordered him off the field. Killoch refused, at which point Baldry hit him on the head three times, knocking him down and then proceeded to kick him. The local magistrates fined Baldry £5.[108]

The other new organisation which would supply farm labour was the Women's Land Army, formed in February 1917, by the Board of Agriculture. It would expand on the work previously undertaken by the Womens' National Land Service Corps and, by the end of the war, it would employ 113,000 women. Recruitment got off to a brisk start, with the women being paid at least 18s a week, as well as receiving board and lodging at the farms. There was an urgent need for training facilities and, at the end of March, the Duchess of Teck officially opened an agricultural college for women at Upton House, near Chester. The property was owned by Dickson's Ltd, a plant nursery; training would be given by the nursery foremen.

In an undated diary, a Miss B. Bennett described her early days, as a trainee, working on a farm at Tonbridge, Kent.[109] The days mentioned are spread over a number of weeks:

Thursday (at a Land Army Hostel) – *Breakfast and prayers are at 7.15 am. We were on the farm by eight o'clock but could do nothing owing to the wet. We stacked potatoes all day and then sorted out the blighted ones. We carried them in a sack on our backs across a field and got up to our knees in mud. We came home to lunch at twelve o'clock and were back at 1. We milked a rubber cow full of water and got on fine.*

Monday – *I groomed Boxer and harnessed her in the cart and went down to the turnip field for a load. We emptied it in the cow shed, watered the Gee Gee and got another load. We ride down in the cart and walk back. After lunch we took the horses and went through the hop fields for cabbages. They had to be cut and pitched onto the cart and some we got were 12lbs. We led this lot back and went for another load.*

Women's Land Army 'girls' working in Buckinghamshire.

Wednesday – *I harnessed Boxer to the mud cart and got a load of cinders for the boss. I had to take them two miles and pave an old road through the woods. I drove back and got another load before lunch. After lunch Ross and I went for cabbages – two loads. It poured with rain all the time.*

Friday – *I was walking through the cowsheds with a doorstep of bread and cheese in one hand when the Governor told me I was to go to Penhurst for a cow. I fed and watered three new cows which arrived last night then caught the ten to eleven train. I had to walk two miles when I got out along muddy fields uphill. I got the animal and walked back seven miles, leading it. It was grand – the sun shone and it was quite hot.*

Wednesday – *Today I finish as a trainee. Tomorrow, I start earning my £1 a week.*

Sunday – *We did fine with our milking and went home for breakfast. We got in a load of turnips and then went down the town shopping in all our mud and glory. We got in a load of cabbages after lunch.*

Monday (about 2 weeks later) – *I am now head of our gang and after getting the girls to work, I went cutting hop vines in the orchard. These are used for litter for the calves. They are cut by machinery and my work was to feed the machine and keep it clear underneath. Although I was working without hat or coat and only sleeves rolled above my elbow, the perspiration rolled down my face. I shovelled and pushed and slung for 3½ hours without stopping and I am tired out.*

As might be expected in Edwardian society, the Women's Land Army was generally divided by social class. Organisers and supervisors tended to come from the middle classes, while the actual agricultural work was undertaken by young working class women. Miss Marguerite Russell-Ferguson was an exception. Originating from a successful Glasgow family, she wrote in her memoir that, when she first joined the Land Army, *I used to feel very strange among so many girls, all of them so very different from any I had hitherto met.*[110]

After training as a milker in the autumn of 1917, she was sent to a farm in Suffolk at the end of October. There were twenty-two other Land Army workers there. There were eight other milkers and, apart from two "head girls", the rest were carters.

We were in charge of 100 cows and a good number of calves. Being winter time, it was very dark when we turned out at 5 in the morning and also extremely cold.

Our first job was to tie up the cows. They slept in the yards at night but were not tied up. It was a fearful job to get hold of the right cow in the dark, as they all had their own places and had to be tied up there. As we milked each cow, we had to take the milk to the dairy where we weighed it and it was then entered in the dairy register by the girl in charge there.

Milking done, our next job was to feed our cows, giving each one a bushel and a half of artificial food followed by a double handful of cotton cake. Then we filled the racks and mangers with hay and tramped cheerily into breakfast.

Breakfast over, we go out again and drive the cows out to the pasture fields, some of which were a long way from the farm. This done, we start our various jobs, mine being to muck out the yards and cowsheds.

She wrote that the afternoon was often the busiest period when they made the 'artificial food'. This was mainly mangle-wurzels, ground up using a piece of machinery which shredded them.

Dinner then follows and we troop to the house, hot, dusty, dirty and famished and sit down to a meal which consists of glorified stew mainly consisting of gravy. There are occasional lumps of meat but they are few and far between – but this is the time of ration cards for everything and everyone knows what that means. However, we have a pudding of some sort, which helps to fill the gaps inside.

After dinner we usually have half an hour's recreation in which we read, chat or sleep and then the bell rings which turns us out again. Firstly we feed the calves, then the cows have to be fetched and tied up in their respective places. Then it's time to milk once more.

About nine o'clock, we start to get our supper. It took the form of a raid on the larder and seizing of every available eatable in sight – sometimes lumps of cold suet pudding, leftover from dinner or something equally tasty.

In March 1918, she was transferred to a farm in Leicestershire, where she

Working in all weathers.

was the first Land Army worker employed. At first she was picking potatoes and spreading manure.

I did this in company of one of the men who regarded me with a mixture of curiosity and scorn. He was evidently not used to women discarding feminine apparel for breeches and smock and coming to work in the fields.

At the beginning of July, the hay harvest commenced and our first job was to go round the fields turning the hay over first with a rake and, later, with a fork. Now as the hay had started and four four-acre fields were cut, the entire staff of the farm, including the master and various old men from the village, turned out. Every now and then, there was halt made and the men would produce large bottles of beer, supplied by the master, and proceed to gulp it down at an alarming rate, while we girls partook of cold tea, which we brought in bottles.......

........By this time, we were beginning to feel the strain of the long hours without sufficient food, as we never had a decent meal owing to the difficulty in getting it ready. Half an hour is not long enough to cook meat, with the result we generally just had an egg followed by milk pudding and then when we came home late at night, famished and often soaked through, to find no fire even, it was a bit hard – and we were far too tired to start and cook then, but just fell into bed and slept.

She remained in the Land Army after the Armistice, working at the Royal Dairy Farm at Windsor for several months of 1919, before returning to Glasgow.

Winifred Bennett came from a similar middle class background to Marguerite Russell-Ferguson. Born in 1879 in Penzance, her father was a wealthy surgeon. Although he had died by the time of the war, her mother could still afford to employ live-in servants and there was no need for Winifred or her sister to work. In her diary, she recorded her work as a WLA Group leader in West Cornwall:[111]

3 January 1918 – Visited Mrs Thomas, WLA Registrar at Germoe. She took me round the parish to farms. A farmer's wife became angry when asked if one of her daughters might join an emergency gang. They just manage to keep the farm going by hard work.

Inadvertently, she put me on the track of some idlers that I must try to get.

7 January 1918 – Walked to Trengwainton. Saw Farmer Piercy who wants three girls for sorting potatoes.

15 January 1918 - Saw Lady St Levan, district commissioner, who says we must be careful not to interfere with women already working on the land. So we must try to get up an emergency potato gang before long. Saw Mrs Penny who will get it up and told her to work along those lines.

24 January 1918 – Bicycled to see Mrs Launeuse. She said no female labour required beyond farmers own people. Soldiers preferred, about six in district. Farmers not inclined to put themselves out, she is not sure they are doing as much as government requires.

26 March 1918 – Took charge of gang of eight women at Park, dropping potatoes. Saw Mr Crewe in evening. He is very much interested in womens' agricultural work. He is going to employ a gang on the 50 acres of moorland he is ploughing for oats if accommodation can be managed.

27 March 1918 – With gang at Park potato dropping. Finished work – 12 acres.

16 June 1918 – To see Olive Bennetts at Polgoon, working with Iris picking up new potatoes. She has got three other girls ready to go to Mr Hitchens when he needs them. To see Mrs Jelbert who applied for girls to pick up potatoes. Saw them at work.

18 June 1918 – Early train to Gwinear Road and bike to Leedstown. Picked up potatoes with gang at Polglase Farm till dinner time, working over an hour in the rain. Stayed in, too wet to work in afternoon.

18 July 1918 – To Perranporth. Saw Miss Hugo who gave me a list of farmers to see and names of women who are willing to do field work. I called at thirteen farms. Two have Conscientious Objectors – one a boy. Only one seemed driven up for labour and that a woman whose husband has been sent away. At all but two places, the news of a gang being available was well received and several said they might apply.

In 1919 the Land Army was disbanded and there was a farewell ceremony on 27 November, attended by Princess Mary. She awarded fifty-five

Jean Battersby.

women with the Distinguished Service Bar – said at the time to be the Victoria Cross of the Land Army. And certainly there was bravery amongst the recipients. Jean Battersby, from Carnforth in Lancashire, had started work on a local farm in May 1917. Sometime later, she was at the Carnforth gas works yard when a horse overturned its cart and bolted. Reports of the time record that *At the risk of her own life, she succeeded in stopping the animal.*

Peggy Fisher was another medal winner. She tackled a bull which was goring a discharged soldier who was also working on the farm, kicking the animal's snout with her hob-nailed boots until it stopped and ran away. She was a winner in another respect as, in the late summer of 1919, she married Harold Morris, the man she had rescued.[112]

*   *   *   *

The problems with sugar supply continued through the spring of 1917, with *The Times* reporting, on 18 May, that there had been queues at London shops. The German submarine war was having a serious effect on imported goods. It drove retailers to try to impose conditions, contrary to regulations, on purchases by customers. At Stratford Police Court one defendant was alleged to have said to a customer that she should give him her regular weekly order but he contended he was within his rights in refusing to sell sugar to people who were not regular customers. The magistrate did not agree, fining him the very significant sum of £15.

The manager at James Pegram Ltd's shop on Stockport's Lower Hillgate was more fortunate, as reported in the local newspaper on 24 May. It was alleged that a Miss Stringer had asked for a pound of margarine and a bag of flour but had been told she had not bought enough to be sold sugar. She then bought additional items, totalling 3s 5d and was served with sugar. The manager had said that she could have brown sugar but she wanted white. The local newspaper reported *There was something of a scene*. The police were called and they interviewed the manager, who said no conditions had been imposed. Clearly not believing his story, the magistrates fined him but it was an almost nominal 10s. The Chairman of the Bench said he hoped that all shops would regard it as a warning.

As the year developed, more people would find themselves in front of their local magistrates for breaches of food control regulations. In June, an Order was introduced restricting the domestic purchase of sugar for making preserves, such as jam, to those who were also growing the fruit in their own garden. Mrs Ellen Wilde, from Stockport, was fined 5s when it was brought to the magistrates' attention that she had bought 56lbs of sugar but had no fruit trees in her garden.[113]

From the same town, grocer Tom Hobbs appeared before the Bench in September 1917. He had obtained fruit from an uncle in Worcestershire and had bought 196lbs of sugar to make jam to sell in the shop. In mitigation, he claimed that he could not have read the regulations carefully. The magistrate replied *The instructions are quite clear. It is a very serious offence*. Hobbs and the wholesaler who sold him the sugar were both fined £10.

Florence Horsbrugh.

It would only be a matter of weeks before sugar was subject to first a voluntary rationing scheme and then, in 1918, to one of compulsion.

Across the country, there were a number of schemes established to assist in providing nutritious food. In London, Conservative politician Florence Horsbrugh helped the YWCA to establish a war workers' restaurant, which operated from late May 1917.

It was intended for girls employed in the various government departments, but is regularly patronised by some of the male clerks. Sixty to seventy voluntary helpers assist daily for as many as 1800 lunches have been served in two hours on some days and these demand a large staff of waitresses. No meal costs more than 1s 3d. It includes soup, entrée or joint, sweets, biscuits and cheese. Tea or coffee, if served without sugar, costs a penny, with sugar a halfpenny more. The rule might well be carried out at all restaurants. (Stockport Advertiser, 3 August 1917)

The establishment of 'National Kitchens' was another successful government initiative. Opening the Borough's first one in July 1918, the Mayor of Stockport said that people would be able to buy *well cooked meals at low prices. Instead of spending the whole morning in preparing dinner for her family, the housewife will be able to send to the depot for so many portions of whatever she chooses to select from the menu and not only will her own time be saved but there will be considerable economy to her purse and there will be no waste.* The menu for the first day was:

Boiled cod in parsley sauce	5d
Potato pie with meat	4d
New potatoes and mint sauce	2½d
Rice pudding	2d
Stewed rhubarb and custard	2d

In the middle of 1917 Viscount Rhondda took over as Food Controller, replacing Lord Devonport. Until the general election of 1910 he had been MP for first Merthyr Tydfil and then Cardiff. He was an extremely wealthy man having inherited the family business, Cambrian Collieries Ltd, in the 1890s. Rhondda and his daughter, Margaret, were both survivors when the *Lusitania* was sunk in 1915. He would only be in office for a year before he died on 3 July 1918, but he presided over the Food Control Department in its most difficult period of the war. One of his first acts was to require local authorities to establish food control committees to which would be delegated many of the powers held by the Ministry, including the setting of maximum prices for particular foodstuffs. Although the Order required that each committee must include at least one woman and one representative of labour, there were complaints lodged almost immediately that the members of the committees were heavily drawn from food retailers and wholesalers. Responding to one such complaint from the Shettleston Co-operative Society in Glasgow, *The Times* reported that John Clynes MP, Rhondda's deputy, had responded that

> *No persons should be appointed to these committees to represent any trade or business in relation to food supply. The rights of consumers only should determine the constitution.*

In the event, many local committees, such as those in the Bermondsey and Fulham areas of London, did not appoint any members from the food industry. Elsewhere, it was felt that to exclude the industry totally would not be beneficial and a mix of representatives were appointed. For example, in the London borough of Lewisham, the committee comprised seven members of the council, one woman, one labour representative and three tradesman – a baker, butcher and corn chandler.

In North Cheshire, the Food Control Committee of the Cheadle & Gatley Urban District Council met at the end of October to agree a number of price increases. Amongst the decisions, roasting brisket would increase from 10d per pound to 1s 2d, breast of mutton from 11d to 1s 1d, although scrag neck of mutton would remain at 11d. Suet would go up from 1s to 1s 4d.

Suet would become increasingly scarce over the following weeks. The manufacturers of Atora, the leading brand then and now, announced in February 1918 that

> *Some difficulty may be found in purchasing Atora regularly and in sufficient quantity. The reason is the Food Controller has commandeered all fats which can be used for increasing the production of margarine. We can only supply our customers with a part of their orders until such time as we may succeed in our effort to obtain from the Food Controller a recognition of the public need for beef suet and permission to obtain our usual supplies. The present retail price is still 1/8 per pound.*

Captain J C Dunn, Medical Officer, 2nd Battalion, Royal Welsh Fusiliers was home on leave in the middle of November 1917. Returning to his unit on the 25th, he stopped off for an early dinner in the Belgian town of Poperinghe.

> *Dining at La Poupée, I contrasted the abundance of food in this part of "poor Belgium" with the meagreness and makeshift at home. Dinner cost 4s – a good soup, whiting, roast chicken and potato, cauliflower au gratin, coffee; bread, butter, sugar without limit – no margarine, saccharine or other substitutes as at home. London can't offer anything like it.*[114]

The contrast between what could be obtained in Belgium as opposed to the shortages in Britain was still in Dunn's mind when he sat down to his Christmas dinner.

Everything was bought locally. I don't suppose anything like the dinner could be got at home.

He was probably right. Dunn and his brother officers enjoyed hors d'oeuvres, clear oxtail soup, fresh whiting, dressed cutlet and celery, stuffed turkey and trimmings, plum pudding (made by Parry, the Mess cook), angels on horseback and a further dessert.

Foodstuffs were not the only products where there were now shortages. Steel was desperately needed for military use and, during the year, extensive experiments were carried out to find a replacement for the steel plate that was used for canning food. Several factors had contributed towards a shortage, including considerable industrial unrest in South Wales. The solution was a waxed spiral-wound cardboard container, of the sort still used today for products such as cocoa. It was so successful that, in 1918, the War Department purchased over 200 million containers for various ration products, saving at least 16,000 tons of steel plate.[115] The new product was also of interest to senior civil servants with responsibilities towards British prisoners of war being held in Germany. These soldiers were receiving regular food parcels from Britain which included canned products and the concern was that the Germans could recycle the metal cans. The Restriction of Enemy Supplies Department of the Ministry of Blockade was aware that the new containers could satisfactorily store semi-liquid products such as honey, jam and cream and hoped to also propose the use of the new containers for condensed milk, which had the consistency of cream. The new containers also came into civilian use, initially being used for syrup.

In January 1918, Stockport's mayor, Thomas Rowbotham, wrote to the local newspapers in his capacity as chairman of the food control committee.

A deputation of retail and wholesale butchers waited upon me last evening and demonstrated to my satisfaction that, under present regulations and prices, they cannot carry on business without actual loss, which they were not willing to bear. In view of the necessity for the purchase of livestock for this week's supply being made

Stockport Express, 31 January 1918

first thing this morning, I was faced with the alternative of an increase in retail prices or the town being without meat this weekend. Under the circumstances, I consented to the retail price of beef being advanced by 1½d per pound and mutton by 2d per pound for this one week, commencing today. (*Stockport Advertiser*, 18 January 1918)

It would not be long before local magistrates were hearing cases of butchers overcharging. Walter Taylor, of Buxton Road in Stockport, put up something of a novel defence when charged with pricing a piece of top rib of beef at 1s 8d a pound, when the local price was fixed at 1s 5d. He claimed that he had sold the Inspector the particular piece as frying steak. *It was not easy to determine when a particular cut ended and another began*, he said. This line of defence, from an experienced butcher, was not accepted and Taylor was fined 40s.[116]

The *Stockport Advertiser* suggested, in an editorial of 25 January 1918, that people needed to come to terms with the shortages and accept that the situation was not going to improve quickly:

We heard of one person going into a shop a few days ago and ordering a pound of bacon. The shopkeeper told him he had no bacon, whereupon the man said, in deep disgust, 'And are we to starve?' The shopkeeper pointed out that he had a good supply of other eatables which he could sell but the man left with an air of resentfulness, feeling apparently much hurt that he could not get his pound of bacon.

The person who will starve for a pound of bacon deserves to. People are going mad for things they find most difficult to get. People who never used to touch bacon are now feeling they cannot do without it. 'We must have bacon', they cry, 'or we shall starve.' A little common sense in using the commodities which are at hand would obviate many of the present difficulties.
(*Stockport Advertiser*, 25 January 1918)

Even by late 1917 the Food Controller was anticipating that the introduction of compulsory rationing might be avoided. However, on 4 December, he met a delegation from the Women's Party – recently founded by suffragettes Christabel and Emmeline Pankhurst. *The Times* reported that every member of the delegation was a housewife and all urged the

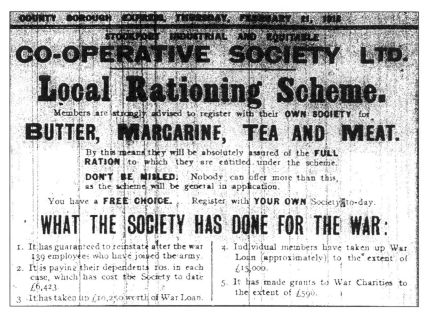

COUNTY BOROUGH BURY, THURSDAY, FEBRUARY 21, 1918

STOCKPORT INDUSTRIAL AND EQUITABLE

CO-OPERATIVE SOCIETY LTD.
Local Rationing Scheme.

Members are strongly advised to register with their OWN SOCIETY for

BUTTER, MARGARINE, TEA AND MEAT.

By this means they will be absolutely assured of the FULL RATION to which they are entitled under the scheme.

DON'T BE MISLED. Nobody can offer more than this, as the scheme will be general in application.

You have a FREE CHOICE.   Register with YOUR OWN Society to-day.

WHAT THE SOCIETY HAS DONE FOR THE WAR:

1. It has guaranteed to reinstate after the war 139 employees who have joined the army.
2. It is paying their dependents 10s. in each case, which has cost the Society to date £6,423.
3. It has taken up £10,250 worth of War Loan.

4. Individual members have taken up War Loan (approximately) to the extent of £15,000.
5. It has made grants to War Charities to the extent of £590.

Stockport Express, 21 February 1918.

introduction of compulsion. Mrs Williams, from Swansea, cited the long queues of women and children outside food shops. Some had had to stand for up to six hours for sugar and butter. Mrs Whittlestone, from Sheffield and a member of her local co-operative society, said there were never queues outside the society's shops, as every member of the society was rationed according to the number in the family.

For now, there was no option but to queue. Once served, Mrs Elizabeth Fernside, of Fulham, adopted a rudimentary disguise to get more. Writing to her son, then serving as a sergeant with Royal Artillery coastal defences on the Firth of Forth, she said *I got a quarter pound of butter last Saturday, then changed my hat and fur and ran back for another.*

Queues continued in the run-up to Christmas and so did the discontent. *The Times* noted, on 19 December, that there were

> *no queues for the well-to-do. A deposit account at the stores will secure all the food you want...Business men, whose wives are finding difficulty in getting their orders fulfilled in the suburbs, are resorting to the practice of sending out office boys to buy tea and*

butter in the City. These boys swell the queues and probably prevent poor people from getting supplies.

Scarcity also affected prisons, the *Stockport Advertiser* noting that inmates at Parkhurst had received *the usual roast beef but suet pudding and jam in lieu of Christmas plum pudding.*

Edwin Bennett was another to receive a letter from home in the winter of 1917/1918.[117] An office manager from Walthamstow, he joined the army at the end of 1915, leaving his wife, Edie, at home with their daughter, Ruby. After training and service in Ireland, he was posted to Mesopotamia, as a gunner with the Royal Artillery. As with many men serving in that theatre, Bennett fell ill and was twice hospitalised – first with malaria, then with dysentery. Edie wrote to him on 8 January 1918:

I think things are [getting] *much worse as we are being slowly starved out. We have had to line up for everything now and register for everything – tea, sugar, margarine. A joint of meat is the thing of past – last week, two and half hours lined up for meat and only a few had any. Hundreds had no joint or chop, only sausage meat or tinned stuff and the shops were raided for that. All the butchers were closed down Friday afternoon. What a life to think we should come to this, dearest, and our dear ones fighting so we should have*

Food queues in 1918.

it OK and we should have to line up in this bitter cold weather,
inches thick with snow. We wouldn't mind so much if we could see
any prospect of the end.

The Food Controller had, at last, recognised the problems that Edie and
thousands of others were experiencing and, at the beginning of January,
published a new Order permitting local authority food control committees
to start to take some action. His model scheme, suggested to councils,
included a requirement that customers must register with particular shops
for particular foodstuffs and would not be able to buy elsewhere. Food
control committees would ensure that supplies were divided
proportionately between retailers based on the number of registered
customers. For the present, margarine or butter would be limited to 4oz
per person weekly and tea to 1½ oz. Birmingham was one of the first areas
to institute the system of local rationing and, after its first week, *The Times*
reported that it was working reasonably well. Queues had diminished and
there was an equitable distribution of supplies.

A widespread scheme, covering London and the South East, was
introduced on 25 February and it was expected that, within two months,
there would be a full national scheme. A scheme in Manchester was
planned to come into effect in March and, in preparation, a warning was
given to shops selling tea. It had come to the notice of the Food Control
Committee that some retailers were 'unloading' their stocks on the
assumption that the Committee would give them fresh stocks. The result
was that most grocers had empty shelves. They were warned that they
must conserve stock and *if it should be found that they have been selling*
out their stocks too freely, they will be liable to have their registration
cancelled, their supplies stopped and their registered customers
transferred to other retailers.

The plan to introduce a rationing scheme in Stockport did not go well,
as reported by the *Stockport Advertiser* on 8 March. The scheme was
intended to include sugar, tea, margarine and butter.

The rationing scheme in Stockport did not come into operation
under favourable circumstances. The supplies of margarine and
butter were inadequate to go round, although, of course, that was
not the fault of the Food Control Committee.

The meat difficulty is more serious that than of tea and
margarine and it will be noticed that the national rationing scheme

which should have come into force on 25 March has now been postponed until 7 April. The Stockport butchers are adopting a scheme of their own until the national scheme comes into force. They have decided to allow each of their adult customers a ration equal to a shilling's worth and for children under ten sixpenny worth.

Mr A. Moore, a one-time Stockport resident now living in Sydney, Australia, wrote home to a friend.

We receive some very doleful letters from our friends in Stockport describing difficulties in getting supplies for food. One lady said she had to pay 3s 6d for a rabbit and that tea, sugar and butter are almost unobtainable. We don't realise what that means in 'Happy Australia' for we have an abundance of food. New laid eggs have been selling for 1d each, fish 3d a pound and people are grumbling about having to pay 9d for rabbit. We really have more food than we want. The proceeds of two years' harvests are lying at railway stations, much of it being wasted by the ravages of weevils and damp. There's millions of rabbits laid by in cold storage, all purchased by the British government and waiting to be sent to England. The explanation is that none of the Allies can spare ships to take it away.

There is no record of how the letter was received by Moore's friend but, it must be suspected, there may have been a feeling that he was 'rubbing it in', particularly at a time when economies were being urged. Newspapers carried recipes for economical dishes or for using leftovers such as this one, published in the *Stockport Express*, for 'Fish and Eggs':

Any remains of cooked fish may be used. Pound the fish, denuded of bones and skin and mix with a thickened sauce made with flour, butter, milk, salt and pepper and, if possible a spoonful of cream. The cream may, however, be left out. When the sauce is thick and smooth, mix it with the fish and form into round cakes. Slip a poached egg onto each cake and pour over thickened tomato sauce. These make excellent breakfast dishes.

Even though rationing was helping to even out the distribution of supplies, traders were still intent on breaking the law in the hope of making extra profits. Alfred Rickard, a wholesale butcher in Stockport, appeared before the magistrates charged with seventy-five counts of selling meat to retailers above the fixed maximum price. He had taken advantage of the shortages and obtained meat in Ireland. Giving evidence against him, a retail butcher at the town's market, James Normansell, said he knew he was being sold meat above the price but *we were glad to get it anywhere*. Rickard was fined £100 – approximately £4000 at current values.

Before you REGISTER make sure of getting

B R O O K E   B O N D'S
T E A

Call at the shop. Ask your dealer if he will continue to supply you with Brooke Bond's Tea under National Rationing. If he says "Yes," register with him and thus secure the best tea obtainable.

Rationing advert. The Times, 10 June 1918.

A few weeks later, Oliver Jepson, of Hill Top Farm, Woodford, also appeared before the Bench. He was well known to the magistrates and had appeared on several occasions charged with watering down milk. He had done it again. Jepson said that, if convicted *I will give up and will not fetch another pint to Stockport*. The magistrate quickly replied *You made a similar remark when you were last convicted.* He then fined him £15, plus costs.

A national system of ration books was introduced on 14 July 1918. Without a book, people could not buy meat, butter, margarine, lard or sugar. The food coupons in the book allowed for a weekly purchase of fresh meat to a value of 1s 9d, 8oz bacon or 12oz ham, 8oz sugar, 5oz butter or margarine, 2oz lard and, although not yet on formal ration, tea would be limited to 2oz per person each week. Within a few days, the meat ration was slightly reduced but bacon was removed from rationing.

Sitting in between the bureaucracies of the Ministry of Food in London and the local authority food control committees was a Divisional Commissioner and his staff. The Commissioner acted as an advisor to the local food control committees and would also exercise oversight on their work.

In north west England, the post was held by Edward Bohane, previously the Secretary of the Royal Lancashire Agricultural Society. The staff would come from a variety of backgrounds – mainly local authority staff and discharged army officers. A brief history of the work of the north west staff notes that one of the men joining in the early part of 1918 was

Lieutenant William Gibson, who had been discharged from the Loyal North Lancashire Regiment.[118]

> *Lieutenant Gibson was one of those unfortunate persons who were as much victims of the war as those who were killed in the trenches. The experiences he had undergone and the injuries he had received had produced a state of nervous depression or melancholia from which he never recovered, and, to the grief of his colleagues, he shot himself within two months of his joining us.*

With the approval of the regional office, local food control committees were able to trade directly in produce.

> *The Lancaster Food Control Committee bought and sold imported meat and tea, and manufactured jam, and made a profit on each of these transactions. The Committee was led to engage in the purchase and sale of meat in order to assist the butchers to obtain supplies, but they continued to do so long after the butchers should have assumed the responsibility themselves. Much the same state of affairs existed for a time at Barrow in Furness, where the butchers at first, for some reason or other, omitted or declined to form a local Committee and to appoint a buyer and distributor, so that the Food Control Committee had to undertake the duties of buying and distributing for them. When meat was rationed the total requirements of a district were calculated from the numbers of customers registered with the butchers, and were either bought alive in a market or obtained dead from wholesalers, or despatched in a frozen condition by importers. It was expected of the butchers that they would form an organization to order the authorized supplies, to pay for them and to distribute them, but in several cases they neglected to do so and the Food Control Committee did the work for them in order that the meat supply might be maintained. For the services they rendered to the trade they charged a small percentage, which was merely intended to cover any expenses they might incur, but in some cases this had amounted to a considerable sum when the control of meat came to an end.*
>
> *The Workington Food Control Committee traded in milk, margarine, tea, and sugar. In the shortage of tea the Ministry occasionally authorized supplies to be obtained from some*

wholesaler who was able to provide them, but as the wholesaler had probably had no previous transactions with the retailers of the district he would only consign the tea to the Food Control Committee. As it could not be obtained in any other way the Committee bought it and paid for it, and as there were nearly always a few incidental expenses in connection with the transaction which it was difficult to add to the cost, the venture, generally, as in the case of Workington, showed a slight loss.

When the margarine distribution scheme was first put forward the share of the work that was assigned to Committees was considerable. Certain modifications, however, were introduced at a very early stage, and the trade was allowed to take a larger part in it and to receive a remuneration for so doing. The Workington Committee, however, was not disposed to relinquish the position in the scheme which had originally been allotted to it, and continued to deal in margarine in spite of Ministerial protests and objections.

Food hoarding was an offence under an Order published in 1917, but its wording was vague, not properly defining what might be thought to be excess quantities being hoarded. It did not prevent the Divisional Commissioner, Edward Bohane, writing to local newspapers in October 1918.

I desire to secure, if possible, the co-operation of everyone in dealing more effectively with those who contravene the orders of the Food Controller.

I therefore hope that your readers will favour me by drawing my attention to any case of obvious or suspected profiteering or hoarding of food in the counties of Lancashire, Cheshire, Cumberland and Westmoreland. Such information will be treated as confidential and carefully investigated by my staff and, if necessary, effectively dealt with.

Local food control committees would continue with their work for many months after the cessation of hostilities in November 1918. They were wound up in 1920 and the following year the last of the wartime control orders was rescinded.

News that an armistice had been signed and would come into effect at

11am on 11 November was greeted with celebrations throughout the country. Winifred Bennett was still a group leader with the Women's Land Army and was with a work gang at Trenona Farm, north east of Falmouth, harvesting potatoes.

Heard that peace would be declared. Guns firing and hooters hooting at Falmouth. Finished at 4. Went for a walk in town with Ellen. Lights in street and shop windows again. String band on platform and crowds of people.

There will be more celebrations in the next chapter.

*   *   *   *

Italian Spaghetti Savoury
The Times, 12 February 1917

Recipe devised by the cookery staff of the Northern Polytechnic, London

3oz spaghetti
1oz grated cheese
Sippets of toasted bread

Sauce:
1oz margarine
1 scant oz flour
Seasoning
1 gill milk
1 gill water

Cook spaghetti in boiling salted water for about 10 minutes. Drain and place in a pie dish or fireproof dish. Melt margarine, add flour, and cook for a minute or two. Add liquid, stir till boiling and boil well. Season and pour over the spaghetti. Sprinkle grated cheese over and brown lightly under a gas griller. Garnish with sippets of crisp toast.

Haricot Bean Fritters
Eat Less Meat Book, 1917

½ lb haricot beans
¼ lb breadcrumbs
1 teaspoonful chopped parsley
1 teaspoonful mixed herbs
1 egg
Salt
Pepper
1 ½ pints water or stock

Wash the beans and soak them overnight. Put them into a saucepan with one and half pints of the water they were soaked in, or the same quantity of white vegetable or cereal stock. Bring to the boil and simmer gently till tender – about three hours. If they get too dry, add more stock. When soft, rub through a sieve, add the herbs and chopped parsley and seasoning. Beat up the yolk of an egg and mix all well together. Form into balls or shape like a cork, brush over with the slightly beaten white of the egg, roll in breadcrumbs and fry in hot fat.

Carrot Pudding
Stockport Advertiser, 29 March 1918

3 tablespoons cooked and mashed carrot
4oz ground rice
4oz cooked and mashed potato
1oz fat
1oz sugar
1 egg
¾ gill water from cooking carrots
1½ gill milk and water
½ teaspoon ground cinnamon
¼ teaspoon ground ginger
½ teaspoon baking powder

Cream fat and sugar, add egg, ground rice and liquids, then add carrot, potato, ginger, cinnamon and baking powder. Steam for 1½ hours.

CHAPTER 7

Better Times

One of the popular visions of the Great War is of men, or underage boys, spending their time in a front line trench, knee deep in mud, before they were ordered to 'go over the top' in yet another senseless attack on the enemy, only to be slaughtered by machine gun fire. Whilst elements of this were certainly part of army life between 1914 and 1918, the full story is very different.

Of course, the trenches were mainly occupied by the infantry. Many thousands of other soldiers served behind the front lines in the artillery or in the support units of the Royal Engineers, the Army Service Corps and the Labour Corps. The men of the Royal Flying Corps, later the Royal Air Force, were also based in the reserve areas.

Consider the life of a typical infantryman. He would start a tour of duty in the front line trench that would usually last three or four days. This would be a dangerous time. The trench would be the target of enemy artillery. And, from time to time, it could be the objective for a limited attack, or raid, by the enemy. Except at very quiet times, a tour of duty was likely to see men injured by shrapnel and, on many occasions, the injuries would be fatal. Unsurprisingly, the most dangerous time would be if there was going to be a British attack on the enemy. Then the soldiers had to leave the protection of the trench, get across No Man's Land, whilst being subjected to enemy artillery shelling and fire from machine guns and rifles. Then, more than likely, they would have to engage German soldiers in hand to hand fighting. Even when they captured the German line, they would have to hold it against determined counter-attacks.

After this tour of duty, he would spend a similar length of time in a second-line trench, acting as close support to the troops now in the front line and ready to go forward to support them if necessary. Then he would withdraw to the reserve area, well behind the trench system, for rest. This cycle would carry on for around six to eight weeks before his unit was further relieved to a rear area for training, working parties or, simply, rest.

Charles Carrington served as a junior officer with the 1/5th Battalion, Royal Warwickshire Regiment, later writing:[119]

> *I find that in the year 1916 I spent 65 days in the front line trenches, and 36 more in supporting positions close at hand: that is 101 days which may be described as under fire. In addition 120 days were spent in reserve positions near enough to the line to march up for the day when work or fighting demanded, and 73 days were spent out in rest. This leaves 72 days for various contingencies. Twenty-one days were spent in schools of instruction; 10 in hospital.....; 17 days on two short visits to England..; 9 days at the Base camp on my way to join the regiment; and the remaining 14 days in travelling from one of these places to another....*
>
> *The 101 days under fire contain twelve 'tours' in the trenches, varying in length from one to thirteen days.....we were in action four times during my twelve tours in the trenches. Once I took part in a direct attack, twice in bombing actions, and once we held the front line from which others advanced. I also took part in an unsuccessful trench-raid. On six other occasions I had to go up the line either for working parties or to reconnoitre. This must be a typical experience shared by many hundreds of thousands of infantrymen who spent a year continuously at the front during the middle period of the war.*

The author's grandfather, Tom Brough, served with the second of the Manchester Regiment's 'Pals Battalions'. He arrived in France on 8 November 1915 serving for 1,100 days before the Armistice on 11 November 1918. During that time, he took part in major attacks on German positions on only nine days. On a further nine days he was under attack and retreating from the German spring offensive of 1918. The remainder of his service was spent in the routine of tours of duty in the front line, followed by periods in the reserve, as described above. He was never seriously injured and, as far as is known, only spent a few days in a military hospital, believed to have been recovering from an illness, rather than injuries. His was typical service for the infantryman.

When men were relieved from their duties in the front and second line trenches, mail from home was most eagerly awaited. The Army Postal Service grew to be a mammoth operation over the course of the war. Starting with some 300 personnel at the beginning of the war, there were over 3,500 overseas by 1919. The Quartermaster General's report on the work of his Branch records that, even by March 1919, when some troops had started to return home, the Postal Service was processing eleven million letters a week being sent to troops on the Western Front, with a further nine million a week being sent home by soldiers.[120] All mail was sorted in Britain at a depot in London's Regent Park, operated by over 2,500 staff who, by the end of the war, were mainly women. Once overseas, mail would be finally distributed to units by the Field Post Office. The Quartermaster General described the FPOs as

For the most part, very makeshift. Sometimes, a regulation hut, but more often than not a ruined building, an abandoned dug-out, or even a few tarpaulins covering a structure of old biscuit boxes or petrol tins comprised the full accommodation. In fact, a Field Post Office may be described as a iron box under the care of a corporal and two sappers. The box held postal orders, stamps, cash, etc and could be lodged anywhere but, wherever it was placed, there was the Field Post Office.

Following close behind the need for news from home, soldiers would next seek out any parcels, which would also usually come with the mail. Unlike the officers' food hampers, which might have been commercially prepared, the parcels for the other ranks tended to be 'treats from home' of favourite foods sent by mothers or wives.

Received a couple of parcels from my dear wife, Elinor, containing my large black infantry kit bag, wrist watch which I had despatched to England for repair, box of Gold Flake cigarettes, box of Turkish Delight, box of chocolate, box of fruit drops, packet of tobacco, cake and a large pork pie. All of which gratefully delighted me and am more than grateful for them all. A new French/English dictionary was also included and a large mince pie. Bought some beef steak which I had for supper with fried chip potatoes at my billet. On duty at 9pm.
(Corporal Stapleton Eachus, Royal Engineers, attached to 4th Army Signal Office. Diary entry 5 February 1917)

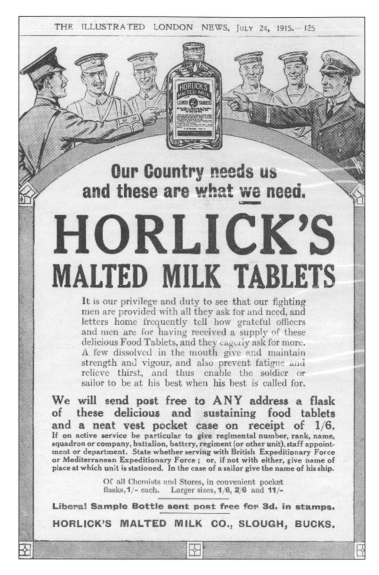

Larger parcels, weighing more than the usual Royal Mail parcel post, were not handled by the Army Postal Service but by the Military Forwarding Department, which spent most of the war under the supervision of the Railway Transport Directorate of the Royal Engineers. The need for the new department was identified within a few days of the British Expeditionary Force arriving in France. Its first commander was

Captain Eric Simpson. Simpson was not a military man and prior to the war had been the representative in Antwerp of the Lancashire & Yorkshire Railway Company. Awarded his commission and allocated just four clerks to assist him, he opened the first Forwarding Depot at Nantes on 22 September 1914.[121] The depot was soon transferred to Le Havre and, within weeks, Simpson had established depots at Boulogne and Rouen. On 19 December 1914 a special train was despatched from Le Havre, carrying an initial consignment of Christmas puddings towards the front. Further depots would open on the western front during the war and the Department would also take on new responsibilities, including the movement of 'comforts' for the troops, together with the free issue of newspapers. The Department would increase in size to eighteen officers and 515 other ranks and would handle a total of 3,379,936 packages up to December 1918.[122].

Depots were established in the other theatres of war, including Egypt, Italy and West Africa. In late 1916 or early 1917, Captain Simpson travelled to northern Greece to establish a Forwarding Department for the Salonika theatre of war. He returned to Britain on leave and, on 4 May 1917, was on his way back to Greece. He was aboard the troopship, *Transylvania*, which was being escorted across the Mediterranean by two Japanese destroyers. The ship was attacked by the German submarine U-63 and sunk. A few passengers were saved by one of the destroyers but most perished. Most bodies were never recovered but a number, including that of Simpson, were washed up, all along the northern coast of the Mediterranean. He is now buried in the communal cemetery at the French village of Gruissan.

In the August, the officer commanding the Forwarding Depot at Salonika was reported in *The Times* as saying that due to the time it took to ship parcels to Greece, it was almost inevitable that those containing puddings and cakes must become unfit for consumption. One of his colleagues in Britain also echoed the problem, particularly applying to Salonika, as reported in the *Stockport Express* on 23 August.

He thought more than half of the parcels sent to men must arrive spoilt as packages returned from overseas, as insufficiently addressed, were constantly found to contain articles such as eggs, butter, sausages, oranges and so on, the whole being in varying states of putrefaction.

There had always been a problem with sending parcels to the theatres of war far away from Britain, as noted by Private Edward Parry, 6th Battalion, Royal Welsh Fusiliers, writing home to his parents at Deiniolen, Caernarfonshire:

> *Don't send any more cakes. I cried to myself in some old hut in the ground here when I opened your parcel and saw the cakes were all mouldy. Cigarettes and matches are scarce here. I've reason to praise the Lord for being alive considering what's going on here. I hope to come home soon but it looks pretty grim for that at the moment.*
(Letter published in the local newspaper, *Herald Cymraeg*, 30 November 1915. Translated from the original Welsh)

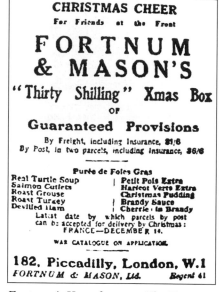

Fortnum's Xmas hamper. The Times, 23 November 1917.

The 6th Battalion was the local Caernarfonshire Territorial unit of the Fusiliers. They landed at Suvla Bay, Gallipoli on 9 August 1915, going into action the next day. Between then and 12 December, when the Battalion was evacuated from the Peninsula, they suffered eighty-four fatal casualties. Edward Parry was not among them and, as far as is known, he survived the war.

Colin Joss came from Bristol, where his father was a school headmaster. Joss followed him into the profession and, before the war, worked as a teacher at a boarding school in Warminster, Wiltshire. He received an officer's commission in the early weeks of the war and was posted to the 7th Battalion, King's Shropshire Light Infantry. Whilst the Battalion was still in training in Britain, he resigned his commission on 4 August 1915 and enlisted as a private, joining the Honourable Artillery Company. Going overseas on 10 November, he wrote home to his mother a few weeks later.

> *If anyone tells you they want to send me out something, tell them I like cigs or a cake or bulls eyes or chocolate. There! Isn't he greedy?*[123]

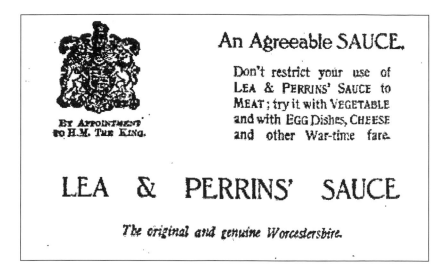

An Agreeable SAUCE.

Don't restrict your use of LEA & PERRINS' SAUCE to MEAT; try it with VEGETABLE and with EGG Dishes, CHEESE and other War-time fare.

BY APPOINTMENT to H.M. THE KING.

LEA   &   PERRINS'   SAUCE

The original and genuine Worcestershire.

His service file at the National Archives, records that he was wounded in the right leg on 20 November 1916. After treatment in Britain, Joss returned to his unit on 15 September 1917. Only a month later, he was wounded again in the same leg and it was more serious this time, necessitating amputation. In 1921, he married Emily McLean and the following year, they had a son, Derek. On the night of 1 October 1943, Derek Joss was piloting a Lancaster bomber on a mission to bomb the town of Hagen. The aircraft may well have been damaged by German flak as, on its return, it crashed in the Bristol Channel, killing him and all his crew.

As described in Chapter 4, Arthur Patrick Burke served with the 20th Battalion, Manchester Regiment – the fifth of its Pals' battalions. He went overseas on 9 November 1915 and a few weeks later, now in the trenches near the German held village of Fricourt, wrote home to his sister 'Tot'.

> *So Ma would like me to mention what I would specially like in my usual parcels – the Malt Wheat, butter and syrup are very tasty and go furthest but I often fancy some potted shrimp, Eccles Cakes, Garnett's (nr Cathedral) Genoa cake, Turner's caramel toffee, but these are only by the way. What I often long for is a nice piece of filleted fish but it's no use, they will all come again in good time.*

By the middle of February Burke had received his potted shrimps, as well as some lemon cheese and a cake, all of which he declared to be '*bon*'. To make sure he knew if a parcel had gone missing, the family had been numbering each package. Writing to his brother, Reg, he said

On Wednesday No 15 arrived - what joy - it was a grand parcel, those sweets were very comforting, to chew away the weary hours of sentry. The Choc, from Nel Bolton was delicious again - it's so kind of her, thank her very much. The Malt Wheat & syrup were our saviour as usual, they provide a good meal. Oh & the cakes, what a lovely dessert after stew. I took one to Roy whilst he was on sentry & his mouth did water - he did enjoy it, everything arrived in good order.

During the weeks of early spring, the 20th Manchesters spent much of their time undertaking fatigue parties in and near the front line.

Got over last night also, had a rotten job was out from 10.30 to 3.30 AM, working in the front line but things kept very quiet. Before setting off No 17 arrived - it was the goods, fortunately it was convenient to fry some of the Pig & it was grand, the remainder I got Alf Gortin (cook) to do for our breakfast this AM. We also had Tot's cakes so we had a good tuck in last night, & Tom had some eggs (hard boiled) with his parcel so we were landed. Have had a treat this morning - didn't get up until 11 AM breakfast in bed, but expect being out all night again.

It was not always a quiet or safe time for Burke. Writing to brother Reg on 18 April 1916.

Am rather shaken up to do much writing, but having the opportunity, & they are very scarce these days, am taking the advantage of same. We were doing our afternoon shift yesterday, seven of us working together when a rifle grenade fell amongst us. What a sight, two of the good chaps died in our arms whilst another chum & myself were doing all we could for them, but it was almost instantaneously. One of the boys you could have put your fist inside his head, the other had a similar wound over the heart & his nose blown off. A third of the party got his face, head, arm & leg severely wounded, no doubt he will be on his way to Blighty now, the fourth victim got a wound on the shoulder blade but was not detained. The remainder of us, 3, got off scott free, remarkable, the little fellow you read about in that account I sent home lay flat between one of the boys that were killed & the severely injured one - wonderful escape he was untouched.

Burke's two dead comrades were William Bottoms, from Hyde, and Frank Dodd, from the Levenshulme area of Manchester

As described in Chapter 4, Burke and his comrades attacked German positions on 1 July – the first day of the Battle of the Somme. When they came out of action, parcel 33 was waiting for him. *We celebrated the glorious victory, but there was many a face missed.* Although parcels continued to arrive on a regular basis, Burke rarely mentions the contents from this point on, although he clearly remains very appreciative of them. Writing to Reg on 3 March 1917, *Early in the hours of this morning, we arrived back from 36 hours in the line......No. 66 here waiting for me.....how grand when you return from such a hole.* Deaths were now so commonplace, that Burke cannot have felt the need to mention that three of his comrades had been killed during that brief tour of duty.

By April, he had become an officer's servant and, presumably, had access to the officer's supplies so was less in need of his own parcels. Writing to his sister, Tot, in June – *I received 81 parcel yesterday, many thanks for the goods but its a joke sending marmalade - it's like sending*

Spoof advert in the satirical trench newspaper, the BEF Times, 25 December 1917.

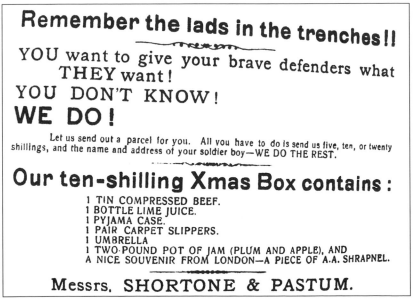

coals to Newcastle. Everything was top hole, the butter gets very oily these days - kindly take note when packing & dont put tin stuff over same for it sets like a jelly. Lemon cheese had been regularly included in his parcels since he had first gone to France, but in September, he wrote home asking his mother not to send any more – *Have got fed up with it.* Paddy Burke was killed in action on 9 November. He concluded his last letter home with the words *Have received all your many letters and parcels – thanks everybody for your subscriptions.*

Frank Haylett was another man writing home in 1917 to tell his family not to send food.[124]

> *Don't think me ungrateful but there is no need to send me out any tinned food or fruits, such as pineapple. We can get any amount of these. Also sardines. Of course, we pay for these extras but everything here is really very good and the meals excellent. An occasional ¼ lb of coffee would be welcome and also a pot of lemon curd. Don't send any jam – we get plenty and of the very best. Chocolate I can get any amount by paying for it but don't forget a cake – the stuff here would disgrace a dog biscuit.*

His letter, on 29 July, was to his wife and daughter, Lena and Gladys, at their home in Islington. Born in about 1875, he had been working as a manager for an oil wholesaler. Haylett was now serving with 42nd Kite Balloon Section, Royal Flying Corps. The Sections had five or six officers and up to 200 other ranks. They operated large hydrogen filled balloons, from which a passenger carrying basket was suspended. The basket would support a crew of two and the balloon would lift them to around 3,000 feet, where they had excellent observation over the battlefield. The main job of the balloon units was to act as spotters for the artillery. It was a dangerous job, particularly as developments in the manufacture of fighter aircraft meant they became easy targets. Haylett was not an officer, so he is likely to have been ground crew, maintaining the balloons and ensuring they remained secured to the ground when aloft.

Another letter home in August 1917 indicates he was still welcoming parcels from Lena.

> *The box of cake, lemon curd and coffee came duly to hand and we all had a very special Sunday tea with it.*

Around the same time, Private Leslie Moore was writing home to his mother in Poplar, London to thank her for a parcel.[125] He was serving in Salonika with the 2/15th Battalion, London Regiment, a Territorial unit, commonly known as the Civil Service Rifles:

> *I shall never be able to thank you good people enough for the way you look after me but I'll do my best when the war is over and I am once more safely at home. The socks were excellent. And the cake – well, you require a course of army biscuits to fully appreciate a cake like that...Will you please send me out half a dozen Gillette razor blades, two or three hankerchiefs, a tin of condensed milk and some tea and cocoa. An ounce or two of Chairman tobacco will also be a change from rations tobacco.*

Moore would never return home. On 20 June 1917, the day after writing his letter, the Civil Service Rifles moved to Egypt. The Battalion took part in a major attack on Turkish positions at Beersheba, in Palestine, on 31 October and in the capture of Jerusalem at the beginning of December. The men spent Christmas Day in support positions on the outskirts of the city. It had poured with rain and Christmas dinner had been nothing more than 3oz of bully beef and two biscuits. *Half starved and shivering with cold* was the observation of one man.

On the 27th of the month, the Turks launched a determined attack on the British held positions on two small hills where Moore and his comrades were supporting two other London battalions holding the front line. The Rifles were ordered forward as re-inforcements.

> *Between midnight and 0800 there were no fewer than eight assaults on Tel el Ful. Lieutenant T.H.E. Clark and two platoons of D Company went up and fought alongside the Westminsters. It was a grim struggle, ending with a sharp bayonet fight. The two CSR platoons suffered fifty per cent casualties. Just before dawn the situation was now critical. Two more platoons were ordered to 'eject the Turk with the bayonet'. This final counter attack, made under severe shell fire, finally pushed the Turks off the hill. But the two platoons became surrounded and cut off with disastrous results.[126]*

Leslie Moore was one of sixteen men to be killed during the night. He is now buried at Jerusalem War Cemetery. He was aged 20.

News of a death would take some time to reach family in Britain and, in the meantime, parcels would continue to arrive. They would be shared out amongst a man's close comrades. Before the war, Arthur Stuart Dolden was an articled clerk employed by a solicitor. By the autumn of 1915, the twenty-one-year-old was a private, serving with the 14th Battalion, London Regiment – the London Scottish. He arrived in France on 4 July. His first major action was on the opening day of the Battle of Loos – 25 September 1915. The Londons were designated as a support battalion who would go forward to bolster the initial attack. The leading troops had 'gone over the top' in the early morning and Dolden and his comrades were not ordered forward until nearly noon. As they advanced they came up against the German barbed wire, which remained uncut by the British artillery bombardment, and were hit by heavy rifle and machine gun fire at close range. Casualties were heavy – the dead, missing and wounded numbering about 25 per cent of the Battalion's full strength. Further re-inforcements were brought forward and these allowed the advance in this sector to continue, with the London

Scottish taking 400 prisoners. The Battalion remained in the forward area for several days. The British offensive was resumed on 13 October with the 14th Londons taking further casualties.

The Battalion parcel post had been kept back while we had been in action, but this was now served out and amounted to seventy mail bags. I received thirteen parcels and, for days, I hardly touched any rations. A new draft from Rouen was in the billet when we arrived from the trenches and, as they had been on short rations, the rest of us made a dump of unopened parcels on the floor and told the newcomers to sail into them. They thought we were the kindest fellows in the world, and never was a reputation so easily gained.[127]
(Private Arthur Stuart Dolden, 14th Battalion, London Regiment)

Like Frank Haylett, Jim McDonough was also aware that food was becoming scarcer as the war went on. Writing home to his wife, Nellie, in June 1918, he said:[128]

> *I received your parcel quite safely on Monday here and everything quite safe inside and not a bit crushed. The jam tart was a 'sweet' surprise and very nice too, also the cake which we had for supper last night. But you must not send them so often, dear, or you will spend all of your pocket money.*
>
> *You should see our larder – sardines, tinned French beans in tomato, tea and sugar, jams, bully beef, Maconochie meat and vegetable rations, besides biscuits and bread. So you can see we are well stocked. I'm telling you all this so you don't worry at all about me as regards food.*

McDonough served as a private in the Army Service Corps. In October 1918, he was awarded the Military Medal for a now unknown act of bravery. He died in 1937.

Tom Tomlinson lived all his eighteen years in Stockport until he joined the army in 1915. After training, he was posted to the 11th Battalion, Cheshire Regiment in the autumn of 1916. Not long after arriving in France, he wrote home to his brother, Laurence.

> *Some of the lads have had parcels and it's kind of set me longing so I hope you will do your best to let me have one, if not some cigs.*

Back home, communities had been raising money to send Christmas parcels to their local men. In the Heaton Mersey suburb of Stockport, the fund raising committee sent off a number of parcels in mid-November, to be sure they would get there in time. They included thirteen sent to Salonika, eight to Mesopotamia, three to India, two to Malta and three to men serving in the Navy. Many more would be sent to the Western Front, nearer the festive season. Each parcel contained one pound of Crawford biscuits, a half pound tin of Danish butter, a tin each of sardines, Christmas pudding, coffee and OXO cubes, a box of trench ointment and a khaki handkerchief.

In the middle of January 1918, a concert was held in Manchester to raise money for the Prisoners of War Comforts Fund. The stars of the show were the Minnehaha Minstrels, a long established local amateur troupe.

Other fundraising took place; most notably, the auctioning of a live goose raised £35. But this was not the end of it. The winner promptly offered it as a raffle prize, which raised a further £72. The winner was George Smith, of Heywood, who hoped to auction it again to raise funds for the Red Cross Hospital at Heywood. Mr Smith said he hoped the bird would then be pensioned off for life. The goose had originally been donated by William Britten, who farmed in North Cheshire at Handforth Hall.

Tom Tomlinson wrote another letter home on 25 January 1917:

> *In your letter you asked me if I had received the parcels alright the first one was traybon but the second I am sorry to say was smashed to bits. The only thing I could do anything with was the cigs. The dates & everything else were mixed up together.*
>
> *I only received it last week but never mind I have been very lucky. You can send me another one as soon as you like as I feel as hungry as a hunter & the rations wont allow anything to eat well. Its this way if I eat it now I'll have to starve tomorrow.*

A month later he was killed in action, aged 20, reportedly shot by a sniper. He is buried at Tancrez Farm Cemetery in Belgium and is commemorated on the Stockport War Memorial.

With parcels making such a major contribution towards the good morale of the soldiers, many men of the 16th Battalion, West Yorkshire Regiment must have been angry that two of their mates had been caught stealing them. Sergeant George Airton noted the matter in his diary, which is now held by the Liddle Collection, University of Leeds. The entry, for 19 January 1916, names the offenders as Private George Howland and a Private Smith. The details of their offence are not known but the commanding officer regarded it as sufficiently serious to award both men fourteen days Field Punishment No. 1. The less serious punishment, No. 2, gave the man extra fatigues 'as if he was undergoing imprisonment with hard labour' and may have involved him being kept in irons. Howland and Smith's penalty involved these but would also have seen them shackled to a fixed object, such as a fence post or a wagon wheel, for up to two hours each day. The extra penalty was intended to be a very public shaming.

George Howland survived the war. George Airton did not. He was killed leading his section into action on 1 July 1916, at the opening of the Battle of the Somme. The 16th Battalion was in close support of the Leeds

Pals of the 15th Battalion, in the north of the battlefield. Across No Man's Land was the German held village of Serre. In the five minutes before 'zero hour' of 7.30am, the Germans turned their fire on to the Pals' assembly trenches. By then the men were already climbing the ladders to get over the top of their trench when they were hit by heavy fire. Company Sergeant Major Cussins later wrote

> *A lot of men never got off the ladder but fell back; and many fell back from the parapet in getting over... On getting out of the trenches to take up our position in front, we lost heavily, through the line of shrapnel, machine gun and rapid rifle fire; by the time we attained our position....most of the officers, N.C.O.s* [Non-Commissioned Officers], *and many men were knocked out.*

The attack, in the north of the battlefield was a failure. George Airton was one of 140 Bradford Pals killed in the attack. As with many of his comrades, he has no known grave and is commemorated on the Thiepval Memorial to the Missing.

Before the war, Julius Jacobs is believed to have lived in the Higher Broughton area of Salford, where his father, Hyman, was a wealthy shipping merchant, able to afford to employ four live-in servants. As with many young middle class men, Jacobs joined one of the so-called Public Schools Battalions of the Royal Fusiliers at the outbreak of war. He served with the 20th Battalion, the third of these units, going overseas on 14 November 1915. On 22 December, he wrote home to his mother to thank for her for a parcel.[129]

> *I received your parcel yesterday. Thank you very much for it. The sausage had just a touch of mould on the outside but was quite good inside and I enjoyed it very much.*
>
> *I was at a dinner yesterday – a Christmas dinner supposedly but held earlier because we did not know when we might move. It was given by my old platoon and I was there as a guest of the officers and NCOs. We had a topping meal. Sixty of us at an estaminet in this village – and they had had the forethought to provide two of us of the faith with roast chicken in place of the main dish roast pork. Very decent, wasn't it? I can't say I enquired the name of the Shochet. Drinks we paid for ourselves and the champagne flowed freely.*

Two years later, Jacobs was commissioned as a second lieutenant and is believed to have continued to serve with the Fusiliers until he returned to civilian life. His medal entitlement records suggest that he emigrated to Palestine after the war and, in the 1920s, was living in Jerusalem.

*   *   *   *

Christmas would always be a special time, even in the trenches. Men who would be in the front line over Christmas would have their festive dinner before the tour of duty. The situation over the 1915 festive season would be very different from the previous year when there had been a truce and men from both sides met in No Man's Land to exchange food and gifts. Senior commanders on both sides issued orders that there was to be no repetition of the truce. In truth, there was little appetite for one. Men who had been on active service in 1914 had seen many comrades killed and wounded over the year and the increase in the size of the armies meant it was no longer a war between like minded professional soldiers.

> We spent Christmas Eve in the line. The men stood in the mud and sang Christmas carols that were drowned by the enemy machine guns. On Christmas Day, we lost a man in No. 3 platoon by a flanking shot through the head. Immediately after, the English attempted a friendly overture and put up a Christmas tree on their parapet. But our fellows were so embittered that they fired and knocked it over. And this in turn was answered with rifle grenades. In this miserable fashion we celebrated Christmas Day.
> (Ernst Junger, 73rd Hanoverian Fusilier Regiment[130])

In spite of the orders forbidding fraternisation and requiring troops to maintain combat readiness, the Western Front was generally all quiet on Christmas Day 1915, although fifty-three British soldiers were killed in action. The mood was relatively jovial in the front line with festive greetings being shouted across No Man's Land and, in one or two instances, there were brief attempts at fraternisation, before the men were ordered back to their trenches by the officers.

By Christmas 1916, British troops had spent many weeks fighting the Battle of the Somme and all thoughts of truces were completely behind them.

*On Christmas morning, Gerry bumped our quarters at Hardecourt
for nearly an hour, killing two horses and wounding three more
before we got them away – and we had Maconochie for dinner.
On Boxing Day, things got worse and we had bully beef and, by
way of a treat, the small biscuits instead of the usual dog variety.
My first Christmas in France, I was wet, miserable, muddy and
broke to the wide, having lost every sou a night or so before at
pontoon.*
(Sapper Jim Reynolds, 55th Field Company, Royal Engineers[131])

Samuel Chandley spent Christmas morning 1916 in the forward area near
Laventie, just behind the front line. The 5th Cheshires were their
Division's pioneer battalion and the men were, no doubt, taking
advantage of the quiet time to improve the trenchworks.

*We were working till 12 in the reserve trench and then came back
to a good dinner. Rabbits, potatoes, carrots, turnips, beans, sauce,
plum pudding, fruit and custard, oranges, etc. Captain Hartley said
a few words and the CO.*

Private John L. Smith arrived in France on 18 January 1915, serving as a
private with the Army Service Corps. His unit was one of the four
companies which made up the Divisional Train for 28th Division. These
were the main supply units with each of the companies delivering supplies
to one of the Division's infantry brigades (see Chapter 3 for further details
of the supply chain). 28th Division had been hurriedly brought together
from regular army troops returning to Britain from duty in the Empire and
had been sent to France as desperately needed reinforcements. As far as is
known, Smith was not a regular soldier and had had only very brief army
training before leaving for the Western Front. He would not have needed
anything like the amount of training that an infantryman would receive,
as he would not generally have to carry a weapon which would, otherwise,
interfere with his duties, most probably connected with the loading and
unloading of supplies. Later, Smith's unit was transferred to 33rd Division
and, by Christmas 1916, he was working at the Division's Ammunition
Sub-Park. Essentially, this was an ammunition dump or store to which the
Sub-Park's lorries would bring ammunition from the railhead, before it
was moved nearer to the front by other units. Smith kept a diary during
this time and it is now held by the Imperial War Museum. With the diary

is a set of accounts for the Ammunition Sub-Park's 1916 Christmas dinner so he was, presumably, involved in the planning for the festivities.

They spent 867 French francs, of which 500F had come by way of a grant from the divisional canteen. The remainder was raised by contributions from the men. There would have been around 340 men to feed. Purchases included onions, potatoes and sixty cabbages, along with the following items, itemised in the accounts:

10 geese	148F
9 turkeys	253F
50lbs pork	75F
150 oranges	15F
225 apples	12F

There was also expenditure of 130F on beer. Although quantities purchased are not known, presumably John Smith and his mates enjoyed a good Christmas.

The Royal Garrison Artillery fired the most powerful guns in the British Army. Their targets would be the enemy artillery positions as well as long range firing at German strongpoints, store areas, etc. 38th Heavy Battery arrived in France in March 1916 and is believed to have been equipped with six 60 pounder guns. These were physically large weapons, weighing over four tons and needing eight horses to tow them (by the end of the war, they were towed by motorised tractors). They could fire their shells over 10,000 metres. One of the Battery's wireless operators was Private J L Lewis.

Arose at 8am, proceeded forthwith to get breakfast. We actually had bacon issued with a quarter of a loaf. Late last night, we sallied forth to do our Christmas shopping having to tramp about 5km to a village named Louez. We managed to procure a tin of peaches, box of Quaker Oats, two tins of milk and two eggs. Thoroughly enjoying it all.

At 1.30pm, we adjourned for dinner. The menu being duck, roast beef, carrots, turnips, swedes and potatoes. I was unfortunate in being in the last three for this momentous feast, consequently my portion of dinner was microscopic, having to do with the potatoes. I succeeded in finding the duck underneath a piece of swede. It was small but choice. After demolishing this lovely dinner, we had our

John Jones, 38ᵗʰ Heavy Battery, will have also enjoyed his Christmas dinner near Louez.

60 pounder guns as operated by 38ᵗʰ Heavy Battery. They could fire their shells well over 10,000 metres.

half pound of Christmas pudding. Our weight must have suffered
like our money because my "half pound" weighed out 2½ ounces.
(Private J L Lewis, diary entry, 25 December 1916[132])

Louez, mentioned by Lewis, is to the north west of the French city of Arras
and the Battery was still in the same general area in the spring of 1917.
On 9 April, British and Canadian troops launched an attack on German
positions, on a broad front between Vimy and Bullecourt. The fighting
continued into May and, sometime during this period, Lewis was badly
wounded by shrapnel. It is not known when this happened but the records
of the Commonwealth War Graves Commission note that seven men from
the 38th Heavy Battery were killed between 3 and 10 May and Lewis'
injury was probably during this time. His injuries were so bad that it was
necessary to amputate his right leg.

The British Fourth Army fought the Battle of the Somme throughout
the summer and autumn of 1916. By Christmas, the Battle was over. A
million men, from both sides, had become casualties – dead, wounded or
missing. If there had been a winning side, then it was the British, who had
gained ground and inflicted heavy casualties on the Germans, which they
would find hard to replace. In February 1917, the Germans started to
retreat to prepared positions, some miles to the rear, known to the British
as the Hindenberg Line.

Stapleton Eachus was still working in the signals office of Fourth Army
Headquarters, well behind the front line near the town of Amiens.

Spent the afternoon divided between my new place at Querrieu and
my old at Pont-Noyelle. Only bully beef for dinner so that until 6pm
when we gather together to take part in the Christmas dinner which
is being got ready at the L'ecole de garcons, we must make
ourselves believe we are not hungry. When we entered, the tables
were decked out with spotlessly clean washable material and the
room was gay with bunting. The first course consisted of turkey,
ham and vegetable which was followed by roast beef and
vegetables. Afterwards some plum pudding with sauce. The drinks
consisted of beer, grenadine and vin rouge, all of which there was
an abundant supply. Nuts, apples, oranges washed down with divers
waters, also cigars and cigarettes were freely distributed among
the men.

Another signaller enjoying his Christmas meal was Sapper Frank Allcroft. Aged about 21, he had worked as a telegraphist for the Post Office before the war and was now doing similar work for the Signals Company of the British II Corps, near the Channel coast at Crecy en Ponthieu. Some effort had gone into making the meal, including the production of a menu (now held by the Liddle Collection, University of Leeds). As often the case with these unit menus, they are often written in French – some with better command of the language than others. Allcroft and his comrades enjoyed:

Soup
Poultry oie roti
Joint – porc roti
Pommes de terre frite
Haricot blanc
Choux fleur
Pudding Noel
Vin blanc et rouge
Whisky, cognac
Bière
Café
Cigarettes and cigars

Christmas dinner in a shell hole near Beaumont Hamel. Note the grave marker at the back. Photo: Australian War Memorial, H08544.

The officers of the 2nd Battalion, Royal Welsh Fusiliers enjoyed a good Christmas dinner in 1916, in the luxury of a hutted camp near the Somme village of Bray. They feasted on pâté de foie gras, curried prawns, roast goose, potato and cauliflower, plum pudding, anchovy on toast, dessert, Veuve Cliquot, port, cognac, Benedictine and coffee. They had moved to new quarters by the New Year where, at Pont Remy, they had haggis for lunch. The Medical Officer, Captain Dunn, recorded in his memoirs that they had an 'uncommonly good dinner' with vermouth as an aperitif. The food was hors d'oeuvres, clear soup, sole 'and a perfect sauce', roast turkey and sausage, celery, plum pudding: savoury – 'enigmatic but delicious'. They did not go short of alcohol with Veuve Cliquot, Benedictine and port all available.

Much more restrained was the 1917 Christmas dinner enjoyed by 24 Squadron, Royal Flying Corps. It was limited to just four courses – soup, cold salmon, turkey and plum pudding. December had been a quiet month for the Squadron. During the month they received brand new aircraft, the SE5, replacing the Airco DH5, which had not been a success as a fighter plane. It would allow them to resume offensive operations, with confidence. Over the course of the war they would destroy more than 200 enemy aircraft, creating thirty-three flying aces as they did so. Aces were usually men credited with more than five aerial victories. One was Ian MacDonald who, by the time of his Christmas meal, had only shot down one aircraft but went on to claim another nineteen victories before the Armistice the following year. Alfred McKay, a Canadian with ten victories to his name, celebrated his 25th birthday on 27 December. He was killed the next day, when his plane was shot down.

When Christmas 1917 came around, Stapleton Eachus and his comrades in the signals office were now near the town of Béthune, some 130 kilometres to the north east of where they had enjoyed the previous year's festive meal.

The day is less cold and started well with an egg, piece of fatty ham, bread and butter, plate of Bergoo and a bowl of coffee for breakfast. Dinner included roast beef, chicken, boiled ham, potatoes, Brussels sprouts, plum pudding, fruit, nuts, crackers, jellies, cigarettes and lemonade. Tea as usual. Spent the evening at my new cafe at Ruitz, where I had my own plum pudding, which was boiled by the kind lady and she and her daughter shared it with me. It was delicious.

Captain Alfred McKay, 24 Squadron.

The Bergoo mentioned by Eachus was nineteenth-century navy slang for porridge, made simply from coarse oatmeal and water.

The Stockport Territorials of the 6th Cheshires had been on active service since the autumn of 1914 and, as described in Chapter 1, had taken part in the Christmas truce of that year, when they killed and ate a pig in No Man's Land, sharing their feast with the Germans. Christmas 1916 was spent in the support trenches along the canal bank near the Belgian town of Ypres – they had gone into the line in the early hours of Christmas Day. As the previous year, there appears to have been no celebration. Christmas 1917 would be a much pleasanter time. The Battalion had been withdrawn to reserve billets at the village of Le Waast on 10 December.

> *This year we were billeted at Christmas in one of the most hospitable villages I have ever come across. The Commanding Officer and his officers set themselves out to give the boys a great time, and they had it. As a preliminary they managed to purchase the biggest pig in the village, and this was marched down in state to the village green and despatched with all the necessary rites and ceremonies in the presence of a vast mouth-watering multitude. Companies tossed up for choice of cuts, and then they set out among themselves to purchase the village turkeys and poultry. The people lent us their rooms and pots and pans, and also the bakehouses, where the meat and poultry were cooked and prepared in an admirable manner. We even had stuffing – what it was made of goodness knows, but it was real good; and apple sauce too! Breakfast was bacon and tomato sauce, and tea, bully, cold meat and cakes from home. We have been very generously treated by the good people at home, who supply comforts for the troops, and have had a good supply sent to us. In fact, for the first time for a long time one could see bread and cake left over from tea for supper – which, considering the enormous appetites of the lads, is really a sight for the gods. Christmas pudding was also very good and plentiful, and much appreciated, and it was really astonishing the amount that was put away.* (Battalion history)

In accordance with usual custom, the dinner was served to the men by the warrant officers and sergeants, one of them later writing:

> *Then we had our meal at a little estaminet which we have been using as a mess. We had turkey and a nice piece of pork, and a goodly supply of pudding and cakes. The band—which is now second to none—played Christmas hymns all the previous night at the different billets, and the Battalion paraded on Christmas morning for a further half-hour's service and more hymns, which went ripping. At eleven o'clock the band played for dancing on the village green, and as the snow had settled firmly it was good as being on the Armoury floor.*

Jim Reynolds, serving with 55th Field Company, Royal Engineers, did not get to eat his Christmas dinner until 7 January 1918. The men had been in the forward zone over the festive period and moved back to a rest area at Bronfay Farm, some three kilometres north east of the village of Bray sur Somme.

We celebrated our Christmas here in a big army canteen hut, having a jolly good spread which included real beer. By that, I mean English instead of the usual French tack.

*   *   *   *

The 3rd Highland Field Ambulance had its major celebration of the 1917 festive season on New Year's Eve. The Territorial unit was raised in Dundee and it would be no surprise that the men would want to celebrate Hogmanay. In the evening they sat down to eat Scotch broth, roast beef, potatoes, Brussels sprouts, plum pudding and custard, oranges and figs. They drank beer and coffee and afterwards a piano was borrowed from the Scottish Churches tent and a concert was held.[133]

Their Aberdeen comrades in the 2nd Highland Field Ambulance had a great time on 25 January 1918, celebrating Burns Night. They also started dinner with Scotch broth, before moving on to steak pie, potatoes, sprouts and peas. Dessert was tapioca blancmange, followed by fruit. They had borrowed the YMCA canteen hut and, like the Dundee men, held a concert. Privates Purves, Reid and Rennie opened the show with a selection of tunes on the violin, followed by singers both from the Field Ambulance and their comrades in the Royal Scots. Private Euman, of the Royal Scots, showed his skill as a bagpipe player and as a soloist, giving a rendition of Burns' 'Gae Bring to Me a Pint of Wine'.[134]

Of course, there were other opportunities for something of a celebration. On New Years Day 1918, the officers of 40 Squadron, Royal Flying Corps, held a dinner as a 'leaving do' for Captain Edward 'Mick' Mannock and Lieutenant William MacLanachan – known to his comrades as 'McScotch'. Mannock was leaving the Squadron, being posted back to Britain to a training role, whilst it is thought MacLanachan was going on leave. The two men had been good friends since MacLanachan had joined the Squadron in May 1917. Mannock was already one of Britain's most successful fighter pilots – by the time of the dinner, he had shot down twenty-one enemy planes, the latest being only earlier that morning, when he had fired on a two-man German reconnaissance aircraft, killing the pilot, Fritz Korbacher and the observer, Leutnant Wilhelm Klein. It was a good dinner – Captain Gwilyn Lewis kept a copy of the menu, which is now held by the Liddle Collection, University of Leeds:

> Huitres native
> Potage de Fampoux
> Carrelets Fritz
> Boeuf roti au rations
> Asperges en branches
> Fruits de Bruay
> Bonbouche des heraldes
> Dessert
> Cafe

Mannock returned to active duty in March 1918 and was posted to 74 Squadron. He would at least treble his aerial victories before he was shot down and killed on 26 July 1918. Much later, another flyer, Donald Inglis from New Zealand, described what happened after Inglis had shot down his first German plane:

Falling in behind Mick again we made a couple of circles around the burning wreck and then made for home. I saw Mick start to kick his rudder, then I saw a flame come out of his machine; it grew bigger and bigger. Mick was no longer kicking his rudder. His nose dropped slightly and he went into a slow right-hand turn, and hit the ground in a burst of flame. I circled at about twenty feet but could not see him, and as things were getting hot, made for home and managed to reach our outposts with a punctured fuel tank. Poor Mick...the bloody bastards had shot my Major down in flames.

Edward 'Mick' Mannock.

By the time of his death, Mannock had been promoted to major and had been awarded the Distinguished Service Order on three occasions, together with the Military Cross on two occasions. After much lobbying by old comrades, he was awarded a posthumous Victoria Cross in 1919, making him one of the most decorated of Britain's flyers.

There would be another 'leaving do' towards the end of April 1918. Second Lieutenant John Wallwork had been born in Radcliffe, to the north of Manchester, in 1898, where his father worked as an Assistant Overseer of the Poor. He maintained a connection with North Manchester as indicated in the dinner menu, which was nowhere near as extensive as the earlier New Year celebration meal for Mannock and MacLanachan:

> Skilly
> Cheval camouflage
> Manchester tramlines
> Sweets of Cheetham Hill
> Ammunition dishwater.

It is thought that Wallwork was leaving the service due to medical reasons. He died on 17 December 1922, aged 23, and is buried at St Mary's Church, Radcliffe.

In October 1915, Tom Heald received notification that he had been promoted to lieutenant, with the 5th Cheshires. The promotion was backdated to the previous March. By way of celebration, he treated three other officers to dinner.

> *Not bad for the trenches. We held it in the largest dugout and it was a huge success. Our batman turned up trumps and everything was very good and went smoothly.*[135]

The menu for the night was:-

> Hors d'oeuvres
> Consommé Argentine
> Lobster Mayonnaise
> Pate
> Canard rôti au 'George'
> Petit pois. Sauce des pommes
> Pomme de terre brouille
> Fruits, gateau
> 'Un petit piece de moutarde'
> Liqueurs. Cafe. Music

If possible, the 2nd Battalion, Royal Welsh Fusiliers, would try to celebrate on St David's Day – 1 March. It was a rough and ready affair for the officers in 1917 but leeks had been bought for the battalion to wear in their caps. As Captain Dunn noted in his memoir,

> There was *soup, lobster mayonnaise, stew, steam-pudding – the sauce was the thing, Scotch woodcock, dessert; whisky, port, champagne cup and coffee.......We had a jolly night. None of the traditional ritual was wanting and there were many to eat the leek.*

The following year, it was necessary to borrow crockery and cutlery from a nearby estaminet, as the officers' mess kit had been packed away prior to a move. This time the menu had something of a French style to it:

Consommé of gallos
Merlan Duglers
Escallops de veau Vilanairese
Gigot de mouton roti
Pommes rissoles
Choux Bruxelles
Pudding au chocolat
Scotch woodcock
Dessert
Cafe

Dunn notes that of thirty-one dining, twenty-three ate the leek (presumably raw) and that *After the Brigadier and CO had gone the younger members of the Mess resumed and made merry until near daylight.* No doubt the copious quantities of Veuve Cliquot, Benedictine and Kummel helped the proceedings along.

On 13 November 1917, the men of the 1/5th Battalion, Seaforth Highlanders, sat down to eat a meal celebrating their attack at Beaumont Hamel the year before, during the final days of the Battle of the Somme. Of course, it was also a meal during which they remembered many of their comrades who had died that day.

> *At 5.45am the signal, the exploding of a mine, was given, our artillery opened a terrific barrage fire on the German front line, and over went the infantry, not doubling, not even walking, but wading knee-deep and sometimes waist-deep through the morass of sticky mud and water and neck-deep shell holes which*

constituted no-man's land. The 5th Seaforths had the honour of leading the attack on one sector of the village, with their left flank on the Auchonvillers-Beaumont-Hamel road, their final objective being a German trench line 200 yards east of the village. The enemy's machine-gun fire and uncut wire in the centre held up the advance for a time so that the barrage went too far ahead, while owing to the dense fog, direction was lost and the attack split up into small parties yet, in spite of these difficulties, the first German line was easily carried, except for one or two isolated points where the enemy put up a good fight.

Dropping into the trench, sentries were posted at the dug-out doors while a few bombs were sent down as a gentle reminder of our presence. The first wave held this trench and arranged the disposal of prisoners, etc, while the second, third and fourth waves passed on to the succeeding trenches. The second line was also soon captured but, for the third line, the fighting was more stubborn, a machine-gun post and some snipers effectively sweeping the ground of our advance. Two bombing parties were hurriedly formed who advanced along the trenches, killed the machine gunners and captured their guns. To get these and the snipers, a party had to enter and pass through a dug-out and climb a stair into a concrete aperture little fort, the holders of which were thoroughly surprised at their secret entrance having been discovered.

(*War Diary of the Fifth Seaforth Highlanders*, Captain D Sutherland, 1920)

More humour from the BEF Times, *15 August 1917*

By 4pm, the troops had gained their objectives. Over 1,700 prisoners had been taken in this sector, of whom the 5th Seaforths had captured 500. But it had been at a terrible cost. The Seaforths lost many men – dead, wounded and missing and, by the end of the day, numbered only ninety.

The Seaforths were in action on several occasions during 1917 and, on 31 October, were relieved to billets at 'Y Huts' on the road between the town of Arras and St Pol. The War Diary comments about how pleasant was the countryside which, until recent weeks, had been behind the German lines.

> *Being a good country for fruit, each village had splendid orchards growing apples, pears, plums, etc. The dirty Boche before he left must have employed thousands of men cutting down these trees and now all that remains are the rows of stumps with the fallen trees lying alongside.*

On 13 November, the general commanding 51st Divison ordered that the day be regarded as a holiday. There were football matches and other sports and the rations were supplemented. It allowed the Seaforths to sit down to a dinner, as follows:

MENU

Soup – Barrage de tomato
Fish – First wave whiting with White City sauce
Joint – Roast beef de Dunvegan with sprouts de Mailly Maillet
Sweets – 2nd Avenue pudding
Salvo de Donald Dinnies
Savoury – Oeufs de Forceville
Biscuits de daily Mailly
Fromage de Beach Thomas
Cafe de L'Objectif
Counter attacks
Au de vie Georges Murray
Sherry a la brownline
SOS Port

*   *   *   *

When not in the front line, men were able to relax and, as mentioned, the place to which they often headed was the canteen. These were generally run by the army, as Expeditionary Force Canteens (EFC) or the Young Men's Christian Association and varied from small huts not far behind the front line, where men might buy snacks or a hot drink, to larger buildings offering meals and recreation facilities.

Among the Auxiliary Army Services, none can show a greater record of usefulness to officers and other ranks than the Expeditionary Force Canteens. This organisation was formed early in 1915 to provide canteen facilities for the troops in the field. Originally starting in France, its operations were extended later to all theatres of war and, through its agency, officers and other ranks could buy a variety of articles numbering more than two hundred, representing practically every necessity or luxury, the prices paid being exactly the same whether in France, Italy, Salonika, Mesopotamia, Gallipoli or Egypt.

To initiate the undertaking a loan of £27,000 was allocated by the Army Council from South African Garrison Funds, but the rapid growth of the business called for increased capital and further sums of £250,000 (guaranteed by Honorary Officials) and a £720,000 Treasury Loan provided by instalments were taken up. These sums, together with the whole of the subsequent trading capital and the necessary reserves for insurance, outstanding and unascertained liabilities were repaid from profits. It is easy to realise how this became possible, for no less than 577 Retail Canteens were opened in France alone.

(Report on the work of the Quartermaster-General's Branch)

From the small beginning of a single small hut at Le Havre, the Expeditionary Force Canteens would grow to become a very large trading organisation, as indicated by the sums of money taken in payments, recorded on the Quartermaster-General's postwar report:

1915	21,491,069 francs
1916	152,917,531 francs
1917	341,849,925 francs
1918	447,179,302 francs

The 1918 figure converts to approximately £16,562,000 – some £629 million at current prices, based on the rise of the retail price index.

On arrival from England at one of the French ports, a soldier's first refreshment might well be at a canteen operated by the army or a charity, such as the YMCA. A letter to *The Times*, on 2 December 1915, noted that the first 'British Soldiers Buffet' had opened at Boulogne on 14 November 1914 and had been in operation ever since, seemingly twenty four hours a day, serving up to 4,000 sandwiches and 1,500 eggs a day. The Buffet was run by Lady Angela Forbes, who had been in Boulogne early in the war. She had seen trainloads of wounded soldiers arrive for evacuation back to Britain with the men being left on the quay for hours without food or drink. She returned immediately to London and spent £8 on provisions at Fortnum and Mason, which enabled her to set up the Buffet at Boulogne's railway station. A second buffet at Étaples quickly followed and, with the increase in the number of troops in France for the Somme offensive, the Buffets were very busy. Lady Forbes later recounted that, one night, she was on duty and, between 4am and 7am, fried 800 eggs, assisted only by an orderly stoking the fires and a French girl making sandwiches of the eggs.

Much later in the war, complaints were made about the Buffets and questions were asked in the House of Commons. It would seem that the details of the complaints were not made public but they were sufficient

for the Commander in Chief, Field Marshal Haig, to recommend to the Army Council that the Buffets should be closed. Lady Forbes wrote to *The Times* on 24 January 1918, stating she had been given no opportunity to refute the complaints. In a postwar article, the *New York Times* suggested that there was some rivalry between the Buffets, the YMCA canteens and the army-run Expeditionary Force Canteens. It further alleged that the sole complaints were against Lady Forbes in person and that they amounted to nothing more than that a clergyman had once heard her say "Damn" and that she had once washed her hair in the canteen.

The difficulties with officialdom started in
1915 as Angela Forbes describes in her
autobiography:[136]

Lady Angela Forbes.

> *Colonel Wilberforce, who succeeded Colonel Asser as Commandant, did not, I fear, share his predecessor's views as to our usefulness, or rather, he wanted the EFC [Expeditionary Force Canteens] to supersede us and at one time our feeding of the leave men was seriously threatened. I was rather curtly informed that in future the men would go straight to the Central Station where*

the EFC had established a canteen. To prevent the men straying into the Buffet, we were ordered to close down when the men were embarking and disembarking. This was tantamount to telling me I was not wanted but the very day the order came through the leave boats were detained owing to submarines in the Channel and about 1,200 men who were already on board were clamouring for food. The EFC were closed so the poor British Soldiers Buffets were appealed to – and not in vain!

Stapleton Eachus (see earlier chapters) first went overseas in 1915, as a member of the Warwickshire Yeomanry. He transferred to the Royal Engineers in 1916, after further training, returning to France on 5 June:

Had some lunch at the YMCA. They have nothing whatsoever to eat and therefore had to satisfy myself with tea and cakes for all meals at the YMCA. They have no bread in stock.

He was still critical of the canteens a year later when he wrote in his diary that they were mainly catering for officers.

The local BEF canteen caters practically exclusively for these non-entities. This too in such a time of shortage of food when the ordinary Tommy finds it hard to exist at all.

Throughout the spring of 1916, the letters page of *The Times* was full of discussion over allegations that there was excessive profiteering by those running regimental canteens at home. It was a matter that would soon be raised in Parliament with the MP for Nottingham South, Lord Henry Cavendish-Bentinck, taking up the Duke of Bedford's allegations that contractors running canteens were charging up to 25 per cent more for fruit and vegetables than was being charged in local shops. This was refuted by Sir Charles Nicholson, the MP for Doncaster, who was also chairman of the Board of Control supervising the canteens. The arguments rumbled on for several weeks, resulting in the Board of Control being abolished and replaced with the Army Canteen Committee, which included senior army officers, members of the Quartermaster-General's department, together with several businessmen. The new Committee quickly took over almost all of the privately operated facilities

Frank Haylett, serving with 42 Kite Balloon Section, was admitted to hospital suffering from pneumonia but was at a convalescent camp at the beginning of July 1917.

> *I am absolutely stony broke and have to content myself with looking at chocolate and toffee which I see peacefully reposing behind the canteen counter.*

The YMCA canteens were often quite large recreational buildings, with books, games and gramophones. At the main base camps near the Channel coast, there would be facilities for sports such as cricket and football. A newspaper reporter described a typical YMCA hut at Boulogne.

> *The main room was some 50 feet long, with a canteen at one end. The body of the room was filled with tables and benches at which men were sitting eating, smoking or playing games. At the far end was a "quiet" room, where men can read or write undisturbed, while off one wall ran an annexe which housed, on one side, a billiard room with three tables and, on the other, a bathroom in which hot baths are now being installed.*
> (*The Times*, 21 September 1915).

Many of the huts near the Channel were run by middle class women, able to travel to France at their own expense.

> *Lady workers who are prepared to pay their own expenses are required for the YMCA huts at the base camps in France. Ladies whose husbands are on active service in that country need not apply. Unmarried ladies below the age of 30 or above the age of 48 are not eligible. Precedence is given to ladies whose husbands have fallen on the field of honour.* (*The Times*, 6 December 1916)

Writing home from the YMCA canteen at Romescamps, Captain Arthur Gibbs, Welsh Guards, had this to say about the facility.

> *We investigated dinner at the canteen and found it excellent. Stewed rabbit and sausage, Christmas pudding and splendid hot coffee. They provided us with an excellent breakfast this morning, likewise the lunch. And very reasonable.*

The
Y.M.C.A.

A Dug-out
in France

The YMCA also ran canteen huts well away from the safety of the Channel coast.

> *The Y.M.C.A. have got a canteen up here in the trench about 1,000 yards, or rather less, behind the front line. They supply free cocoa (hot) and a packet of biscuits for all the men every night. We have only to send down a note, asking them for cocoa and biscuits for 130 men, and we get it. I really do think the Y.M.C.A. people are wonderful. The men can't say enough for the hot cocoa in the middle of the night.*
> (Captain Arthur Gibbs, Welsh Guards, diary entry 15 January 1918)

The History of the Welsh Guards also has something to say about the YMCA canteen which had been established in a sunken road near Humid Trench.

> *The man who runs the shanty is a Scot of about fifty years of age – round, red face, scrubby moustache and round tummy. He is fired up here all alone and exists and runs his place entirely on charity – that is to say, he has to beg for parties to carry up what he wants, chop his wood and lend a hand generally. He sells cigarettes, chocolate, writing paper, odds and ends, but gives away tea and cocoa to all who want it.*

Of course, running a canteen near the front line could be dangerous and a particularly dangerous time was during the German offensive in the spring of 1918. They attacked the British lines with overwhelming force on a number of occasions, driving the troops back many miles.

> *The canteen work of the Expeditionary Force Canteens was carried on everywhere as usual until rendered impossible by the military position. Troops were served in many cases under heavy shellfire and stores were evacuated to other positions to replace the sixty-two canteens destroyed. The discipline of the EFC personnel in these circumstances was excellent and considering the huge quantities of supplies involved, very little fell into German hands.* (Quartermaster General's report)

Canteens were also run at unit level. Gunner F R Jolley, serving with the 31st Divisional Ammunition Column, Royal Field Artillery, was posted to set one up under the direction of the padre. He started on 17 December 1917:

> *Like this new job immensely. We do very well for grub as we draw our rations from the QM and cook them ourselves and, being a small party, get plenty to eat. Bread every day with bacon, cheese,*

A divisional canteen. Photo: The Sphere, 27 January 1917.

Enjoying the offerings of their canteen – men of the 132nd Heavy Battery, Royal Garrison Artillery. In the first photograph, Bombardier Percival Mogg is seated on the right. He was later taken prisoner and died of his wounds on 18 July 1918. Photo: Mogg family

German canteen at Hartsmannsweillerkopf in the Vosges Mountains of Alsace. Photo: Gwyneth M Roberts.

jam & butter and fresh meat. This is a welcome change from bully beef and biscuits

Very busy in here during the evening and also started a dry canteen where we sold biscuits, chocolate, toothpaste, cigarettes, etc which we obtained from the Expeditionary Force Canteen which were a sort of wholesale warehouse formed to supply canteens like ours.

(Diary entries, 19 & 24 September 1917[137])

Jolley was also able to make sure he ate well on Christmas Day 1917. Breakfast was porridge, bacon, tomatoes, bread and tea. This was followed by lunch at 1pm where, no doubt with the other members of the Column, he ate roast pork, apple sauce, potatoes and cabbage, followed by Christmas pudding with rum sauce. Tea was at 5pm and included ham, bread, butter and tea. And finally, no doubt back in the canteen tent, he finished the day with jelly, custard and cake.

The padre came over and gave us 2/3rds of a bottle of Vermouth, which we did not care for at all.

American troops started to arrive in France from June 1917 and were generally welcomed as reinforcements, although they would not start to deploy into the front line until early 1918. They were not, however, universally welcomed by the British troops, who by then had been fighting for three-and-half-years. There was particular resentment at the significantly higher rates of pay in the American Expeditionary Force.

It happened to be pay day in our section and our Captain was using our tent to pay out the men. Up came these Yankees without taking any notice of our Captain and, finding our tent was the canteen, interrupted the 'paying' by enquiring 'Say guy, have ye got any eats? Have ye got any crackers or charcalate?' Mansell & I resented their insolent manner and refused to serve them but our Captain ordered us to. We happened to have a small stock of chocolate which they had the cheek to ask us to sell by the boxful as they were well stocked with money, while our chaps could only afford to buy one or two pennyworth at a time. They did not like it when we restricted their buying to reasonable amounts. We

afterwards found that they would not serve our fellows in their canteen which only shows what rotters they were.
(Gunner F R Jolley, 31st Divisional Ammunition Column, diary entry 15 May 1918)

Whilst the main business of the Expeditionary Force Canteens remained the running of canteens and the supply of goods to unit canteens, it diversified over the course of the war into other profitable enterprises. These included rest houses for officers (equivalent to the canteens for the 'other ranks'), cinemas, laundries, facilities producing sausages, brawn and pickled tongue, mineral water factories and bakeries, together with construction units, maintaining the huts and an upholstery service for furniture. It was a peculiar situation. Here were men, nominally soldiers serving in the Army Service Corps, but who were running profitable official businesses. When the British Soldiers Buffets were thrown out of France, in 1917, the EFC was quick to take their place, perhaps prompting the view that the complaints against the Buffet had been manufactured to achieve this aim. Their canteens became known as 'leave billets'. The EFC was responsible for feeding men at the ports who were going on or returning from leave, together with the feeding of newly arrived re-inforcements – British, Dominion and American alike. In 1919, with men being de-mobilised, the kitchen at Le Havre served as many as 22,000 meals a day and could serve just over 7,000 in an hour. In 1918, the port 'leave billets' sold over twelve million francs worth of food and other goods.

The Expeditionary Force Canteens would also operate their outlets in the other theatres of war, reportedly opening its first canteen in Italy only four days after the fighting troops arrived in the autumn of 1917. In Salonika, thirty-five canteens were opened with foods being imported from its depot in Bombay to satisfy the needs of the Indian troops fighting there. In Mesopotamia, a mobile canteen was set up on a steamboat on the River Tigris. It was reported to be tied up and ready for business within an hour of the capture of Kut al Amara, from the Turks, in early 1917.

*   *   *   *

There were other opportunities for soldiers to relax and find a meal that was not army food. There were the pre-war estaminets in villages – cafes

American troops in an estaminet.

which also served food. There were also less formal arrangements, where a nearby farm might provide snacks and meals to troops.

Charles Jones went overseas on 27 October 1915. He had left his job as an abstractor at the Board of Trade, joining many of his colleagues in the 1/15th Battalion, London Regiment. A pre-war Territorial battalion, it was generally known as the Civil Service Rifles. The battalion left Britain in the March and it is probable that Jones had been too young to join them until the autumn.

> *Estaminets are open from 11am to 1pm and then 6pm to 8pm and*
> *the best ones supply cutlets, beef steaks and chips for 1F 50C. Also*
> *a huge variety of drinks, cafe au lait, cafe noir.*
> (Private Charles Jones, 1/15th London Regiment[138])

On the night of 14 September 1916, Jones and his comrades went into the front line in preparation for an attack the next day. The Battle of Flers-Courcelette would be part of the Battle of the Somme, which had been raging since the beginning of July. They were packed into the assembly trenches. Their objective was High Wood – which the Germans held strongly with machine gun posts and many snipers, as well as their main defensive lines of trenches. There had been previous attempts to dislodge the enemy and all had been unsuccessful. The attack started at 5.30 am and, immediately, the Londons came under heavy fire. Within minutes they were pinned down in No Man's Land. The day would see tanks used for the first time and four had been assigned to the High Wood attack. Three of them quickly became stuck in the mud and the fourth, whilst reaching the German trenches, then burst into flames. Jones and his comrades in the Battalion's A Company fared better than the other three companies. They captured their objectives – the first two lines of German trenches, engaging in fierce hand to hand fighting and taking several prisoners. They moved forward through the German trench system, throwing grenades in front of them to clear the way, until realising they were not supported by the rest of the Battalion. By late morning, a heavy barrage from British artillery and the supporting Trench Mortar Battery (which fired 750 rounds in just 15 minutes) allowed the three companies, and other pinned down battalions, to move forward and, finally, capture the Wood. There had been devastating numbers of casualties – killed, missing and wounded. Later records showed that 137 men from the 15th Londons had been killed. Among them was 20-year-old Charles Jones. His body was never identified.

In mid-December 1917, Gunner F.R. Jolley, 31st Divisional Ammunition Column, was based near the village of Therouanne, about halfway between Calais and Arras. On the 14th of the month, he walked into the village where he bought his supper at an estaminet. He had egg and chips and coffee to drink. He later recalled that it was a *'popular feed with the Tommies'* as it reminded the men of home.

Egg and chips was also on the menu for Shallett Raggett (see Chapter 2), 22nd Battalion, Royal Fusiliers. Towards the end of March 1916, the Battalion moved by train and route march to the village of Ourton, to the south west of Béthune. Raggett said they had a pleasant time resting there until 17 April, when they went back into the line.

We had a good billet and, across the road, found a French woman who was always ready to supply us with fried eggs, chipped potatoes and coffee. Needless to say, we were pretty often in there.

Percy Jones' encounters with army food were also mentioned in Chapter 2. He went overseas with the 16th Londons on 1 November 1914. After a lengthy tour of duty in the trenches, the Battalion was relieved by the 1st West Yorkshires during the afternoon of 5 December. It was a very welcome opportunity to bathe, get clean clothes and enjoy a proper night's sleep. On the 7th, Jones and some comrades walked into Armentières in search of a dinner that was not army food:

> *I spotted a cafe restaurant. Monsieur came to attend to us in person in his private room where, by candle light, we had a supper of soup, roast beef, fried potatoes and cabbage with sweets, pastries and white wine. Total cost 1F 50C. After a fortnight's bully beef, I was delighted with the fare and the low prices charged and swore eternal friendship with Monsieur in broken French, assuring him that he had 'le plus bon cafe de tout France'.*

Jones was captured on 1 July 1916 (the first day of the Battle of the Somme) during his Battalion's attack on German positions at Gommecourt, remaining in captivity until after the Armistice. He is understood to have died in a drowning accident, at Festiniog, in 1919.

Within days of returning to France with the Royal Engineers, Stapleton Eachus (see Chapter 2) had found a nice little cafe nearby in the village of Epagne-Epagnette.

> *I conversed in French with Monsieur et Madame and their daughter. I remained with them until 10 pm, partaking supper at their table, which consisted of steak, sausages and beans, together with beer, followed by a couple of eggs especially fried for myself and two cups of tea. The whole only costing 1F 50C.*

A Manchester Regiment man did not have the same good experience. In November 1915, Second Lieutenant Thomas Nash was serving with the Regiment's 16th Battalion – the first of the city's Pals units. They had only been in France for a few days when they billeted overnight at a small village called Villers Bocage. He and three other officers found themselves staying at *the one very dirty cafe the village possessed.*

> *The girl brought us some coffee, a little bread which reminded me vaguely of cider and some butter that was frankly rancid. Ten minutes later, she produced a tin of sardines and after another long pause some beans simply swimming in grease. We begged for some meat; we were hungry and would pay anything she liked but we wanted some food. In response to our entreaty she brought us a mottled slab of meat with a thick layer of solid grease on top. This*

she called galantine of pork. Fletcher was Medical Officer to the Battalion and after a rapid post mortem examination he said it resembled nature's rejection of the chosen meal of a foul-feeding dog. This completed our uneaten, untouched dinner. By this time, we were uproarious with laughter.[139]

Before the war, Ernest May worked as a clerk in one of Stockport's several hat making factories and had previously worked in the same capacity for Kent & Swarbrick Ltd. That company were tripe dressers, with several shops in the town. On 16 November 1914, he enlisted into the army, travelling into Manchester to join the fifth of the Pals Battalions of the Manchester Regiment – officially known as the 20th (Service) Battalion. Whilst still in training, Ernie May was promoted first to corporal and then to lance sergeant. The Pals went overseas on 9 November 1915 and, within a few days, he wrote home from the training billets at Mouflers.

Our own billet adjoins a farm and we were soon on good terms with Madame. Our conversationalist efforts and "dumb show" would send you into hysterics. From her, we augment our army rations with a few small purchases of what few luxuries were available. Since arriving here, we have had a few short parades and one or two route marches. We have just dined at the farm by special request with the following on the menu – soup, rôti poulet des pommes de terre, frites, salads, vin rouge, pudding macaroni. Who wouldn't be in the army!
(*Stockport Express*, 17 December 1915)

On 1 April 1916, May was promoted to sergeant and, a few days later, he undertook an act of bravery for which he was awarded the Distinguished Conduct Medal, then second only to the Victoria Cross. The official citation, published in the London Gazette records:

For conspicuous gallantry and resource. He carried out a daring reconnaissance within five yards of the enemy's lines and, though snipers were active and there was brilliant moon light, he completed his work and rendered a valuable report. He received a further promotion, to second lieutenant, on 30 June 1916 and, the following day led his men into the attack on the opening day of the Battle of the Somme.

On 26 August, Ernie led his men back towards the trenches for what would be his last tour of duty. They left their billets at Dernancourt and relieved the 12th Battalion, King's Liverpool Regiment, in the trenches opposite Ginchy, ready to take part in an attack the following day. The unpublished history of the Battalion, held by the Regimental Archives, takes up the story:

During the move up in the dark, "B" Company and the Headquarters Company had thirty men killed owing to an enemy 5.9 shell dropping on a stack of Mills bombs, stored in a dump by the roadside. The place became a shambles as, owing to the Hun fire, lights could not be used and searchers had to grope in the dark and this was not the end of their troubles, owing to counter orders from a higher authority, only one company got into the line, the remainder being scattered and the Battalion was not really collected together again until the following day. And then, owing to bad weather, the attack on Ginchy had to be postponed. During the night of 26/27th and all day on the 27th the enemy heavily bombarded the line and the trenches which were poor to begin with were soon almost unrecognisable. New trenches were dug during the nights 27 – 29th but the enemy bombardment was almost continuous and the Battalion suffered many casualties...

Ernest May, Manchester Regiment.

Ernie was one of these many casualties. The Battalion's Commander, Colonel Smalley, wrote to Mr and Mrs May explaining what had happened.

He was killed just before dawn on August 29th by shrapnel shells bursting just in front of him, while out on the dangerous work of withdrawing some advanced posts we had put out in front of our lines close up to the Germans. We buried him that morning close to our front trenches. Your son was killed instantly. I want to tell you how much we miss him. He was loved by the whole battalion and we all felt very proud of the splendid work he has done for this

Battalion since we came out to France and am sorry he has not lived longer to enjoy the honours he has so well won. May was a fine soldier, always cheerful and willing and no trace of fear when doing his duties as a scout officer and I shall miss him personally very much. He was a general favourite with the other officers and we were delighted when he got his commission.

Ernest May was 25. He was buried near to where he was killed at Ginchy but, in 1920, his body was exhumed and moved to the nearby Delville Wood Cemetery, Longueval, Somme.

*   *   *   *

The greatest reason for celebration during the war was, of course, its end, with an Armistice signed and coming into effect on 11 November 1918. There were great celebrations in London and Britain's other cities, which were mirrored in the cities of the various Allied nations. *The Times* reported that many people were unable to properly express how they felt but

with comparative soberness made the streets merry. Human nature is tongue-tied at its greatest moments and London with a great moment to celebrate abandoned the hope of suitable words and made festival by the ringing of handbells, the hooting of motors, the screaming of whistles, the rattling of tin trays and the banging of anything that could be banged.

Fighting continued right up until 11am, when the terms of the agreement said that hostilities would end. For the British, there might have been a sense of 'déjà vu'. Some of them found themselves back at Mons, where they had first gone into action against the Germans in August 1914. The first and last British casualties of the war, Privates John Parr and George Ellison are now buried opposite each other at St Symphorien Cemetery, Mons. A Canadian private, George Price, is generally regarded as the last man killed during the war. Almost inexplicably, only minutes before 11am, a patrol of the Canadian 28th Battalion was sent across a canal at the village of Ville-sur-Heine. Once across, they started to search the houses. Price was warned by occupants that the Germans were close by. Moments later, he was shot through the heart by a sniper. He died at 10.58 am and is also buried at St Symphorien.

Armistice cartoon. Toronto Telegram, 11 November 1918.

There seems to have been little celebration in the trenches. Of course, no one in the front line could be sure that the peace would hold and men were very cautious. Official war diaries suggest that news was received with quiet relief that it was probably over. Everywhere, men commented about how quiet it was.

There had been so much talk of an armistice that a Brigade message in the morning telling us of its having been signed at 8 o'clock, and that hostilities were to cease at 11, fell somewhat flat. The event was anticlimax relieved by some spasmodic cheering when the news got about, by a general atmosphere of 'slacking off for the day' and by the notes of a lively band in the late afternoon. .....The local civilians were overjoyed. They were hospitable with their poor means. They brewed an awful decoction of baked and ground oats in place of coffee which had been unobtainable for a long time. To me, the most remarkable feature of the day and night was the uncanny silence that prevailed. No rumbling of guns, no staccato of machine guns, nor did the roar

Armistice celebrations, London.

*of exploding dumps break into the night as it had so often done.
The war was over.*
(Captain James Dunn, Royal Army Medical Corps, attached to 2nd
Battalion, Royal Welsh Fusiliers)

The Stockport Territorials of the 6th Cheshires were in action until the end
of October and, on 11 November, were on a route march to new billets at
Fourquepire when they received news that hostilities were to cease. The
news was *received with acclamation by the troops and inhabitants, and
everywhere along the route the troops received a magnificent reception
from the liberated villagers.*

Walter Williamson had been with the Cheshires since 1916.[140] He recounted that there had been something of a party the night before in the village where they had been billeted. At the end of the day's march on the 11th, the cooks were ordered to serve dinner as soon as possible. It was not a successful meal and Williamson reckoned that the cooks must have been suffering from hangovers from the previous night's excesses. He was later billeted in a small house with his mate, Bill. They started to make some supper from the last bits of their rations when the old man who owned the house produced a jug of milk, a slab of cheese and some butter – and would take no payment.

An armistice signed but troops overseas would still want their Christmas parcels.

The New Zealand Rifle Brigade was in training on 11 November. The Brigade's History records that

The great news was received with extraordinary calmness by all ranks; there was no excitement whatever, and training went on without interruption. After parade hours the terms of the armistice and the prospects of an early and certain peace were quietly discussed by little knots of men, who left unspoken their deeper thoughts of thankfulness.

The Brigade was assigned to the Army of Occupation in Germany and had planned to have a double celebration on Christmas Day. However, due to supply difficulties, dinner was postponed until New Year's Eve, when 'absent friends' were remembered, as well as a celebration of the coming year which would see the men return home. Sapper Frank Allcorft and his comrades with 2nd Corps Signal Corps, Royal Engineers, did get to celebrate Christmas Day in Germany. Then based at Cologne, they dined on roast beef, chicken and ham.

The officers of the 5th Battalion, Cheshire Regiment celebrated the Armistice at their Christmas dinner, their menu reflecting their passage through the war:

Hors d'oeuvres des Allies
Potage Quatorze Fevrier
Tomate Neuve Eglise
Dinde roti a la mode d'Ypres
Farce a la Gommecourt
Sauce Arras
Pommes a la Somme
Petits choux de Lavantie
Pouding de Noel de Cambrai
Oeufs Armistice
Cafe feenish la guerre
Desserts.

MENU.

———

POTAGES.
Consommé a la Royale
Potage Anglais

ENTRÉE.
Curried Salmon.

POULTRY.
Roast Turkey. seasoning.

JOINTS.
Roast Beef, Yorkshire Pudding.

VEGETABLES.
Potatoes. Baked and Boiled.
Cabbage. Carrots. Turnips.

SWEETS.
Xmas Pudding. Cognac Sauce.
Apple Pie. Custard.
Compote Figs.

SAVOURY.
Cheese Straws.

New Year's Eve, 1918. Dinner for the New Zealand Rifle Brigade.

Shortly after Christmas 1918, soldiers started to return home in large numbers to be demobilised but it would not be until 12 September 1919, that the final cadre of the 6th Cheshires returned to Stockport. Headed by their band, they marched along Wellington Road and paraded outside the Town Hall. The Battalion history notes that they were formally welcomed home by the Mayor.

In the evening the event was celebrated by a dinner at the Armoury, and a joyous re-union took place, tempered by thoughts of the gallant lads who had marched away never to return.

The menu for the dinner is not recorded but surely the men will have been relieved that it was not bully beef and biscuits.

*   *   *   *

Brown Fricassee
Thrift for Troubled Times, 1915

1lb fish
1oz flour
1oz butter or fat
Pepper, salt

Bunch of sweet herbs
Blade of mace
1 teaspoonful lemon juice
1 onion
Half pint of fish stock or water

Cut up the fish and roll each piece in a little flour and fry it a nice brown. Fry 1 ounce flour in 1 ounce butter or fat and stir in a little pepper, ground mace, one onion, chopped up, a small bunch of herbs and a little salt. When this has all fried a good brown, add ½ pint of fish stock or water and stir together till the flour thickens and is cooked; then strain it, add a teaspoonful of lemon juice or vinegar. Put the pieces of fish into this sauce, make all hot together, and serve.

Gipsy Pudding
Housekeeping on twenty five shillings a week
National Food Economy League, 1915

1 rabbit
1 onion
2 oz grated cheese
2 tablespoonfuls breadcrumbs
1 teacupful rabbit stock
And a little margarine

Stew the rabbit slowly until tender, remove all bones and cut meat into small pieces. Mix in grated cheese, onion (either fried or par-boiled and chopped), liquid and seasonings. Turn into pie-dish, sprinkle some breadcrumbs over and put the margarine on top. Bake in a moderate oven for 1 hour.

Christmas Pudding
Simple Cookery for the People, 10th edition, circa 1916

¼ lb flour
¼ lb breadcrumbs
½ lb chopped suet
4 oz currants
½ lb sultanas or raisins (stoned)

6 oz mixed peel (shredded)
¼ lb caster sugar
1 lemon, rind and juice
3 eggs
Milk to mix

Average cost 1s 6d to 1s 8d

Mix all the dry ingredients. Stir in the beaten eggs and sufficient milk to make the mixture rather moist. Fill in well-greased pudding basin, cover it well and boil for about 4 hours.

Notes

1. National Archives, WO95/78
2. Cyril Helm rose to the temporary rank of Lieutenant Colonel during the war, commanding 42nd Field Ambulance. He was awarded the Military Cross and the Distinguished Service Order. He left the army in 1921, but served again during World War II. Extracts are taken from his personal account, published on the website of the Western Front Association, and used with the permission of Toby Helm.
3. Extract from transcript of interview held by the Liddle Collection, University of Leeds. Born in Alderney in about 1894, Hammond worked as a bottle washer in his father's wine and spirit business, before joining the army in 1912.
4. Chambers' diary is held by the Liddle Collection, University of Leeds.
5. William Meredith's diary is held by the Liddle Collection, University of Leeds.
6. Biographical detail taken from the 'RAMC in the Great War' website (http://www.ramc-ww1.com/index.html)
7. 'Battles & Bivouacs, a French soldier's notebook', Jacques Roujon (translated by Fred Rothwell), 1916
8. 'I Remain Your Son Jack', Morten, 1993
9. National Archives, WO95/78
10. www.greatwardifferent.com
11. 'Food Prices as affected by the War', Department of Labor, May 1915
12. Sheldon's account of his service with the Battalion is held by the Manchester Regiment Archives.
13. Duncan was killed in action on 3 May 1917, when the dugout in which he was sleeping received a direct hit from an enemy shell.
14. *Stockport Advertiser*, 4/12/14
15. As quoted in 'Christmas Truce', Malcolm Brown and Shirley Seaton

16. 'Stockport Lads Together', David Kelsall

17. Boardman's diary is included as an appendix to the War History of the 6th Battalion, Cheshire Regiment

18. Percy Jones' diary is held by the Department of Documents, Imperial War Museum.

19. Brennan's diary is held by the Department of Documents, Imperial War Museum, London. Further information from the Brennan family is acknowledged.

20. 'Diary of an Unprofessional Soldier', Nash, 1991

21. Higson's memoir is held by the Manchester Regiment Archives

22. William Taplin's memoir of his war service is held by the Liddle Collection, University of Leeds

23. 'Statistics of the military effort of the British Empire during the Great War', HMSO, 1922

24. National Archives, WO 95/2859/1

25. Foster's notebook is held by the Department of Documents, Imperial War Museum

26. A transcript of Binks' diary is held by the Liddle Collection, University of Leeds

27. Raggett's memoir of his war service is held by the Department of Documents, Imperial War Museum

28 Now held by the Liddle Collection, University of Leeds. Hargreaves returned to civilian life in March 1919 and died two years later.

29. Held by the Department of Documents, Imperial War Museum, London

30. 'Mammoth Book of How it Happened: World War 1'

31. 'The Sherwood Foresters in the Great War'. Captain W.C.C. Weetman, 1920

32. Hounsom's letters are held by the Department of Documents, Imperial War Museum

33. 'A Yankee in the Trenches', Robert Derby Holmes, 1918

34. Basil Miles' letters are held by the Liddle Collection, University of Leeds

35. Imperial War Museum

36. *The Times*, 17 August 1916

37. Clark's poem is held by the Liddle Collection, University of Leeds

38. 'Battles and bivouacs, a French soldier's notebook', Jacques Roujean (translated by Fred Rothwell), 1916

39. Braund's letters are held by the Imperial War Museum

40. Ridsdale's diary is held by the Liddle Collection, University of Leeds
41. Extract courtesy of J. Wickett
42. Extract courtesy of E. Davies
43. Chandley's diary is held by the Imperial War Museum
44. Report on the work of the Quartermaster General's Branch [QGB], National Archives, WO107/69
45. 'Statistics of the military effort of the British Empire during the Great War, 1914 – 1920', HMSO, 1922
46. Ibid
47. National Archives, WO95/4467
48. QGB, National Archives, WO107/69
49. National Archives, WO95/4738
50. National Archives, WO95/4943
51. QGB, National Archives, WO107/69
52. www.1914-1918.net
53. QGB, National Archives, WO107/69
54. Charles Lovell's papers are held by the Imperial War Museum.
55. QGB, National Archives, WO107/63
56. 'Statistics of the military effort of the British Empire during the Great War', HMSO, 1922
57. QGB, National Archives, WO107/63
58. Commonwealth War Graves Commission
59. QGB, National Archives, WO107/63
60. Ibid
61. 'Campaign Reminiscences', R.T. Peel & A.H. MacDonald
62. Quoted in 'Defeat at Gallipoli', Nigel Steel & Peter Hart, 1994
63. Rowland Luther's memoir is held by the Imperial War Museum
64. Extracts used with permission of Peter Carter.
65. Hansard, House of Lords, 4 March 1914
66. 'Social History of Edwardian Britain', James Bishop, 1977
67. *The Times*, 22 January 1914 and 11 February 1914
68. Potts' letters are held by the Liddle Collection, University of Leeds
69. Quoted in 'Tommy', Richard Holmes, 2004
70. 'Poor Bloody Infantry', B.D. Martin, 1987
71. 'Wearing Spurs', J. Reith, 1966
72. 'Diary of an Unprofessional Soldier', Nash, 1991
73. 'The Burgoyne Diaries', Gerald Achilles Burgoyne, 1985
74. Quoted in 'Tommy', Richard Holmes, 2004
75. Ibid

76. Quoted in 'Subalterns of the Foot'. Anne Woolf, 1992

77. Burke's papers are held by the Imperial War Museum and extracts are used with the permission of the family

78. Nevill's papers are held by the Imperial War Museum

79. Lawrence's diary is held by the Imperial War Museum

80. 'History of the Welsh Guards', C.H. Dudley Ward, 1920

81. Gibbs' papers are held by the Imperial War Museum

82. http://wwi.lib.byu.edu/

83. Phillips' diary is held by the Imperial War Museum

84. 'I Remain Your Son Jack', Morten, 1993

85. Quoted in 'Defeat at Gallipoli', Nigel Steel & Peter Hart, 1994

86. 'The Fifth Battalion Highland Light Infantry in the War 1914-1918', F L Morrison, 1921

87. Transcript of interview held by the Liddle Collection, University of Leeds

88. Quoted in 'Defeat at Gallipoli', Nigel Steel & Peter Hart, 1994

89. Oxtoby's papers are held by the Imperial War Museum

90. Bowden's letters are held by the Imperial War Museum

91. Book of Remembrance, 5th Battalion (Prince Albert's) Somerset Light Infantry, The Great War, 1914-1918

92. Milsom's account of his service is held by the Imperial War Museum

93. Quoted in 'The Remains of Company D', James Carl Nelson, 2009

94. Ibid

95. Prisoners of the Great War. Authoritative Statement of Conditions in the Prison Camps of Germany, Carl P. Dennett, 1919

96. *The Times*, 21 July 1917

97. 'The Story of the 2/4th Oxfordshire and Buckinghamshire Light Infantry', G K Rose, 1920

98. The Liddle Collection, University of Leeds, holds correspondence relating to John Cummings

99. Quoted in 'Barbed Wire Disease', John Yarnall, 2011

100. Quoted in 'The Great War' , Peter Hart, 2013

101. 'My Campaign (Kut)', Sir C.V.F. Townshend

102. Barker's letter is held by the Imperial War Museum

103. www.workhouses.org.uk.

104. Held by the Imperial War Museum

105. *Stockport Advertiser,* 21 April 1916

106. *The Times,* 10 December 1917

107. 'No Labour, No Battle', John Starling & Ivor Lee, 2009

108. *The Times*, 2 September 1918

109. Bennett's diary is held by the Imperial War Museum.

110. Held by the Liddle Collection, University of Leeds

111. Winifred Bennett's diary is held by the Imperial War Museum

112. *Evening Post*, New Zealand, 27 November 1919

113. *Stockport Express*, 24 May 1917

114. 'The War the Infantry Knew', Dunn, 1938

115. 'Statistics of the military effort of the British Empire during the Great War', HMSO, 1922

116. Ibid, 24 January 1918

117. Edwin Bennett's letters are held by the Imperial War Museum

118. 'Food Control in the North West Division', H.W. Clemesha, 1922

119. 'A Subaltern's War', Charles Carrington (writing under the name of Charles Edmonds), 1923

120. National Archives, WO107/69

121. 'British Railways and the Great War', Edwin A. Pratt, 1921

122. Quartermaster General's report on the work of the Branch, National Archives, WO107/69

123. Joss' papers are held by the Liddle Collection, University of Leeds.

124. Haylett's papers are held by the Imperial War Museum

125. Moore's papers are held by the Imperial War Museum

126. 'The Civil Service Rifles in the Great War', Jill Knight, 2004

127. 'Cannon Fodder', A.S. Dolden, 1988

128. McDonough's papers are held by the Imperial War Museum

129. Jacobs' papers are held by the Liddle Collection, University of Leeds.

130. 'Storm of Steel', Ernest Junger, 1920

131. Reynolds' papers are held by the Imperial War Museum

132. Lewis' diary is held by the Imperial War Museum

133. National Archives, WO95/2859

134. National Archives, WO95/2858

135. Quoted in 'Subalterns of the Foot', Anne Wolff, 1992

136. 'Memories and base details', Lady Angela Forbes, 1923

137. Jolley's diary is held by the Imperial War Museum

138. Jones' papers are held by the Imperial War Museum

139. 'Diary of an Unprofessional Soldier', Nash, 1991

140. 'A Tommy at Ypres', 2011

Index

224, 226, 228–9, 242, 246, 253, 277, 292, 296, 303, 316, 319
Jam manufacturers, 58, 93–4, 177
Jewish troops, 227, 321–32
Joffre, Joseph, 21, 175
Johnston, Sgt Robert, 95, 176, 249, 251
Jolley, Gnr F.R., 343, 345–6, 348
Jones, Pte Charles, 347–8
Jones, Pte Percy, 47, 115
Joss, Pte Colin, 312–13
Junger, Ernst, 322

Kampite trench cooker, 78–9
Kantara, 140, 229
Keeling, Pte George, 175
Kelly, Cpl A.R., 223
    Kut-al-Amara, 252, 254, 346
Kenya, 128
Kerr, Lt Cmdr Charles, 189
Khartoum, 27
Killoch, Pte Herbert, 282
King's African Rifles, 206–207
King's Liverpool Regiment, 1st Bn, 18
King's Own Royal Lancashire Regiment:
    1st Bn, 65
    1/5th Bn, 87
King's Own Yorkshire Light Infantry:
    1st Bn, 240
    2nd Bn, 12, 16, 19, 21–2

La Gorgue, 62
Labour Corps, 118, 155, 279–82
Landrecies, 12
Lawrence, Pte Walter, 185–6
Le Cateau, 13, 15, 19

Le Havre, 11–13, 23, 119, 122, 126, 148, 311, 337, 346
Lee, Pte Thomas, 127
Lembet, 141
Les Mezieres, 18
Lewis, Capt Gwilyn, 332
Lewis, Pte J.L., 324–6
Liebig's Extract of Meat Co., 86–7
Lincolnshire Regiment, 1st Bn, 18
Lingard, Mrs Elsie, 258
Liver, 26, 28, 58, 190
Liverpool, food prices, 35
London Regiment:
    2/1st Bn, 218–19
    2/4th Bn, 160
    14th Bn, 186–7, 318
    1/15th Bn, 347–8
    2/15th Bn, 317
    16th Bn, 45, 77, 115, 348
    19th Bn, 128
    2/20th Bn, 73
    22nd Bn, 85
    28th Bn, 55
Long, CSM Thomas, 51
Looting, 20, 22, 234, 264–5
Louez, 324, 326
Lovell, Drvr Charles, 147–8
Lune Valley Engineering Ltd, 54
Luther, Drvr Rowland, 160–1

MacArdle, Lt Kenneth, 90–1
MacDonald, 2nd Lt Ian, 328
MacLanachan, Lt William, 331, 333
Maclean, Capt Joseph, 170
Maconochie Brothers Ltd, 38, 73–4
Maconochie, rations, 38, 62, 75, 79, 82, 88, 96, 103, 106, 108,